123 → Canonnier(?)

92 Jean Lemard

Sortie

Photocopie ? gauche

Blu Montindustriell
Blv

Blu Moralme

Jean Lemard

Blu Bureau

30 à droite

Jean Lemard

2e Sortie canillac

E-COMMERCE LOGISTICS AND FULFILLMENT
Delivering the Goods

Deborah L. Bayles

Prentice Hall PTR
Upper Saddle River, NJ 07458
www.phptr.com

ISBN 0-13-030328-3

9 780130 303288

Library of Congress Cataloging-in-Publication Data

CIP data available

Editorial/production supervision: *Patti Guerrieri*
Acquisitions editor: *Mary Franz*
Marketing manager: *Dan DePasquale*
Manufacturing manager: *Maura Zaldivar*
Editorial assistant: *Noreen Regina*
Cover design director: *Jerry Votta*
Cover designer: *Nina Scuderi*
Cover image: *Robin Jareaux/Artville LLC*

© 2001 by Prentice Hall PTR
Prentice-Hall, Inc.
Upper Saddle River, NJ 07458

Prentice Hall books are widely used by corporations and government agencies
for training, marketing, and resale.
The publisher offers discounts on this book when ordered in bulk quantities.
For more information, contact: Corporate Sales Department, Phone: 800-382-3419;
Fax: 201-236-7141; E-mail: corpsales@prenhall.com; or write: Prentice Hall PTR,
Corp. Sales Dept., One Lake Street, Upper Saddle River, NJ 07458.

Printed in the United States of America

10 9 8 7 6 5 4 3 2

ISBN   0-13-030328-3

Prentice-Hall International (UK) Limited, *London*
Prentice-Hall of Australia Pty. Limited, *Sydney*
Prentice-Hall Canada Inc., *Toronto*
Prentice-Hall Hispanoamericana, S.A., *Mexico*
Prentice-Hall of India Private Limited, *New Delhi*
Prentice-Hall of Japan, Inc., *Tokyo*
Pearson Education Asia Pte. Ltd.
Editora Prentice-Hall do Brasil, Ltda., *Rio de Janeiro*

To Jerry, for his love, patience, and unfailing support.

CONTENTS

Payment Processing, Fraud, and Other Taxing Issues   93

Customer Service   125

Send It Back! The Role of Reverse Logistics 257

Outsourcing the Whole Thing 301

FOREWORD

The Internet represents a new frontier for commerce. Hundreds of authors have expounded on the promise of the e-commerce frontier: vast open areas, untapped markets, and an unlimited number of potential customers just waiting for you to arrive and stake your claim. However, like the American West frontier of the 1800s, e-commerce is filled with both promise and peril. The road can be rough, the weather unpredictable, and the natives are not always friendly. Ventures must prepare for the hazards ahead.

Over the past year, several e-commerce ventures have failed in spectacular fashion. However, their failures should be taken as lessons to be learned rather than as a sign that the frontier is unassailable. Consider how many wagon trains failed to make it to California in 1846-48—the difficulty of that trek did not lessen the value of their destination. Learn from the mistakes and successes of those who have already blazed a trail, partner with others when there is mutual benefit, hire experienced guides to help you through parts unknown, and never assume that the road ahead is just like the road behind.

Perhaps the hardest thing about a venture on the Internet is coming to grips with what you do not know. In order to succeed, it is necessary for you to know your own business, but it is also necessary to know who you need to partner with to make your business work. In order to make money, you must understand your expenses before establishing your prices, and the most flexible among the expenses is the charges of your partners for advertising, banking, shipping, software development, Internet hosting, etc. Just like any business partner relationships, success will be obtained by making sure that you are earning money, making sure that your partners are earning your business, and making sure that your partners are earning money from your business. The last part is frequently overlooked, but when storms arrive and the road becomes difficult, partners without mutual benefit will focus their efforts elsewhere.

Learning. Understanding. Being prepared for the venture ahead. That is what this book is all about. Deborah L. Bayles has analyzed the challenges of the e-commerce frontier and authored a guide that will help ventures prepare for the road ahead. Lessons learned from previous e-commerce ventures are recorded here, along with pointers for obtaining experienced guides and understanding the types of partners you will need to support the money-making portion of your new business: logistics and fulfillment. Altogether, this book forms an indispensable reference for those who wish to succeed in the new frontier.

Roy T. Fielding, Ph.D.
Chief Scientist, eBuilt, Inc.
www.eBuilt.com
November 2000

PREFACE

Introduction

Almost 40 percent of the cost of selling online takes place *after* the customer presses the Buy button. At that moment—when the visitor has just become a customer—the most crucial part of the relationship just begins. Payment processing, order fulfillment, product delivery, and product returns handling are the largest gaps in electronic commerce today. These important but unglamorous, messy, and often expensive functions are *not* optional in true e-business. They can make or break your customer relationships, profitability, and future business.

Identifying and managing these functions, termed *e-commerce logistics* and *e-fulfillment,* is the subject of this book.

Until now, most merchants thought electronic commerce was achieved by hooking an online catalog to one of the many electronic shopping cart packages, then waiting for orders to be emailed to them. Not one key electronic commerce vendor mentions that the real work for the merchant actually starts when the order is received. This book demystifies a process that is sure to be new for most B2B and B2C online merchants today.

Here are other features that distinguish this book.

- Forrester Research says that half of all business will be online by 2002. Business-to-business e-commerce will grow to $1.3 trillion by 2003, from $43 billion in 1998—yet until now there hasn't been a single book that addresses the unique challenges of e-logistics and e-fulfillment in the context of electronic commerce. This is the first book to do so.
- This book provides practical, proven techniques to assure your customers receive the products that they order from your Internet site in a timely, efficient, traceable way.
- You also find out the ins and outs of reverse logistics (handling product returns)—or how to outsource these functions cost-effectively.
- Useful tools such as planning templates, checklists, and spreadsheets are included throughout the book and on a Web site.

Audience

This book is aimed at technically savvy executives, information technology professionals, and other enterprise leaders who are faced with the challenge of delivering the goods their organizations sell online. Whether the reader is an electronic commerce or logistics practitioner or provider, this book will be an extremely useful addition to the "How To" books of his or her library.

The Organization of This Book

The first three chapters of the book describe the issues and tasks surrounding setting up and costing an electronic commerce infrastructure to handle e-logistics and fulfillment.

Important FTC rules and regulations, defining your business processes, and calculating potential return on investment are among the many topics discussed. An infrastructure planning template and an ROI calculation spreadsheet are provided to give you a running start.

Chapters 4 through 7 tackle the challenges that take place after the Buy button is clicked. The topics of order processing, taxes, online fraud, order fulfillment, shipping, and customer service are presented and a number of checklists are provided, including a useful chart to help you determine what is taxable.

Chapters 8 through 10 cover the convergence of e-commerce and logistics on a global scale, including taxation of international e-commerce transactions, emerging data exchange standards, and reverse logistics—a field unto itself.

The final two chapters of the book wrap things up by addressing whether or not to outsource the entire e-commerce logistics and e-fulfillment processes, and offers two user perspectives by pioneers in the field.

Contact Information

Although I have frequent opportunities to teach and speak throughout the world, I'm not an academician or researcher— I'm out in the trenches full-time, just as you are. I always appreciate your real-world suggestions, comments, and other feedback to continue to improve the book's usefulness. You can reach me by email at *deborah@bayles.com,* or stop by the Web site I've set up, *http://www.bayles.com,* to check out the book-specific tools I've posted there and to contribute your experiences and advice. Enjoy!

ACKNOWLEDGMENTS

I thought that after publishing my first book, *Extranets: Building the Business-to-Business Web*, the second book would be much easier. I was definitely mistaken! This book, like the first one, involved a tremendous amount of help and support from many talented people (some of whom were still recovering from my first book project!). So, with an extra dose of humility, I'd like to extend my gratitude to the following friends and colleagues.

First, thanks go to reviewers David P. Martin, II, C.P.L. and John Reber, who provided very valuable insight and feedback throughout the process. Guy Abramo, Fran and David Barnes, Bridget Belden, Hamir Bhatia, Tom Burke, Harvey Karlovac, Wendy Kennedy, and Julie Hoffman Walsh provided case studies, suggestions, resources, and encouragement, and are much appreciated.

Editor extraordinaire, Mary Franz of Prentice Hall, once again provided unfailing encouragement and motivation, and Patti Guerrieri yet again performed her magic in the production department. Carol J. Lallier and Michelle Zinkevicz also worked tirelessly during the copyediting and permissions phases of the book.

I would like to thank Angela Jeantet of the University of California, Irvine, and Julie Lim of the Singapore Institute of Management for providing me with the opportunity to teach e-commerce classes. I would also like to thank my students, who have supplied all manner of war stories, suggestions, and support over the past few years.

Finally, many thanks go to logistics professionals, such as Bill Martindale of Pacific States Logistics Management, who have dedicated their lives to furthering the profession. The melding of the sciences of logistics and electronic commerce will provide some of the most exciting opportunities to come. Let's enjoy the future together!

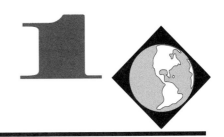

1

THE NEXT BIG CHALLENGE IN ELECTRONIC COMMERCE

While many online gurus pontificate about creating "sticki-ness"—how to hook customers into Web sites—or gush about how to increase the number of "eyeballs"—Web visitors—there is a quiet crisis building behind the scenes in electronic commerce today. That crisis is associated with all of the events that take place *after* the Buy button is clicked. Most online businesses are doomed to fail because they won't be able to fulfill orders or ship their products adequately to their custom-ers as sales grow.

E-commerce logistics and e-fulfillment represent the myriad activities that are needed to ensure the customer gets what the customer wants when the customer wants it. They are the least glamorous but most critical functions in electronic commerce. They can also be the most expensive. All too often, newcomers to the electronic commerce world, or those undercapitalized, fail to recognize that almost 40 percent of their cost of goods sold is buried in fulfillment and back-end logistics. Now add the fact that most online merchants don't even *know* what their total costs are, and it becomes apparent that many e-commerce businesses will slowly bleed to death without knowing why.

The E-Logistics Landscape

Electronic commerce has revolutionized not only the way goods are sold, but how they are delivered. The tenets of one-to-one marketing that online firms are adopting must be carried over to their fulfillment operations, and this is creating mass-scale chaos. Customers demand customized products delivered at very high speed with complete order flexibility and convenience. Gone are the days when a merchant could simply state "Allow 6 to 8 weeks for delivery." Today's online customers want to be able to track their orders instantly, from the moment they click the Buy button until the moment the package arrives on their doorstep. They want to be able to reroute packages, determine delivery costs and time-in-transit, and break up their orders for multiple ship-to addresses. The shift of power from the seller to the buyer has created a new era of expectations, and buyers—whether they are consumers or businesses—won't tolerate experiences such as partial shipments of goods on an "installment" basis, poor product return policies, or surprise back orders.

The most common form of logistics has traditionally been based on moving large shipments of items in bulk to select strategic customers in a few geographic locations. Shipments have also traditionally been tracked by container, pallet, or other unit of bulk measurement, not by individual item or parcel. Manufacturers have backed up their trucks to loading docks at retail stores or distribution facilities, relying on those entities to deliver the goods through the final links of the supply chain to the individual customer. Often the various links of the supply chain have had limited visibility into the operations of one another. The capability for end-to-end visibility of a package from manufacturer to customer has been virtually nonexistent in a traditional logistics environment.

With the advent of electronic commerce, however, traditional logistics is being radically transformed. Electronic commerce demands an agile, high-velocity, granular approach to logistics. The typical electronic commerce customer is an unknown entity who orders products on an individual basis, according to impulse, seasonal demand, price, and convenience. A manufacturer or online merchant must be able to customize an individual order; ship it directly to the buyer anywhere in the world; track the whereabouts of the item at any given time along the supply chain; handle customer inquiries; handle product returns; and even offer gift wrapping—all at ten times the speed and at a fraction of the cost of traditional shipping and fulfillment.

Forrester Research sums up the vastly differing characteristics between commerce site logistics and traditional logistics in Figure 1-1.

	Traditional Logistics	Commerce Site Logistics
Shipment Type	Bulk	Parcel
Customer	Strategic	Unknown
Demand Style	Push	Pull
Inventory/order flow	Unidirectional	Bidirectional
Average order amount	More than $1,000	Less than $100
Destinations	Concentrated	Highly dispersed
Demand	Stable, consistent	Highly seasonal, fragmented
Accountability	One link	Through the entire supply chain

FIGURE 1–1   Commerce Site Logistics Differ from Traditional Logistics
Source: Forrester Research, Inc.

These fundamental differences in traditional logistics versus commerce site logistics are the foundation of the complete shift we are seeing in the e-logistics landscape. Opportunities are arising all along the e-logistics continuum to better service customers, whether the customer is another business or a consumer.

Forrester Research calls it *end-to-end logistics,* and essentially, it is defined as order visibility and service continuity from the Buy button to the final destination—and back, in the case of product returns. The goal of this book is to explore the whys and hows of these unglamorous but essential elements of a well-run e-commerce logistics and e-fulfillment operation. First, however, you have to decide, at the top level, where you want your business to play.

Where Will You Play?

The real challenge for any organization that wants to compete in electronic commerce is to choose the best strategy for success. Cisco Systems has developed an Internet Value Matrix that summarizes where today's electronic commerce players are operating. You can see the matrix at *http://www.cisco. com/warp/public/750/icorporation,* but it may be easier just to imagine a graph that is broken into four major quadrants.

The vertical axis expresses the degree of business criticality, with the lowest level on the bottom and the highest on top. The horizontal axis describes the amount of newness, running from a very low degree of innovation on the left side of the graph to a high degree of newness on the right.

Firms that subscribe to the New Fundamentals philosophy populate the lower left quadrant, where business criticality is low and newness is at a minimum. These firms are taking the low-risk road in order to build experience in e-commerce. They are focused on the Internet as a new channel for doing old things—using the Internet mainly to improve productivity, streamline some operations, and achieve cost savings.

Catalog companies are best positioned to make the shift to the New Fundamentals quadrant. Their lines of business are already defined around brand identities, and their product categories lend themselves to intuitive online searches. They generally employ sophisticated data-mining techniques that enable them to constantly update their offerings, and they already have the product fulfillment and customer service infrastructures in place. Land's End and Victoria's Secret are two catalog retailers that have transitioned to the Internet very successfully.

The main danger for product suppliers and physical retailers residing in this quadrant is in refusing to think of e-commerce as a business in its own right. Instead of pursuing e-commerce single-mindedly, they try to protect their traditional model. The key to success here is to realize, and even encourage, the new business to cannibalize the old

E-commerce players that inject new organizational practices into areas that are not business-critical fall into the lower right quadrant Cisco defines as Rational Experimentation. These firms are focused on organizational learning and how the Internet can be leveraged inside the organization. By making some medium- to high-risk experiments in new market segments, new sources of revenue, and shifts in business models, these firms are hoping to boost their hit rate for investment successes. Hopefully, these Internet experiments lead to the overall operational excellence or breakthrough strategies described in the other quadrants.

The gamblers of the Internet are those firms that occupy the upper right, Breakthrough Strategies, quadrant. They are e-commerce players that hope to achieve the early mover advantage by boldly venturing into new markets, new channels, and new products. These firms are focused on business-critical processes and competitive advantage. They are not afraid to take high risks in business-critical areas in order to create new markets and are not content simply to dominate old ones. Amazon.com is the example that most people think of as the leader in Breakthrough Strategies.

The upper left, or Operational Excellence, quadrant—the area where a low degree of newness intersects a high degree of business criticality—is the prime area in which e-logistics players can achieve success. The expected area of return in this quadrant is in achieving frictionless execution and value innovation. Internet initiatives in these companies are focused on critical process and practices. The orientation is toward external applications and how the Internet can transform mission-critical processes and product features and create new forms of customer value.

Companies that strive for frictionless execution ask themselves questions such as

- What percentage of our orders are 'clean'?
- Are we reducing returns and credits from customers?
- What percentage of customer problems are resolved on first contact?
- How much of our customer information can be viewed on one screen?
- Are we increasing inventory visibility across our entire supply chain?

Value innovation can be measured through assessing such factors as increases in market share and gross margins, lowered customer acquisition costs, increases in new customer acquisition, and better retention of existing customers.

Operational excellence in e-commerce logistics and e-fulfillment is key to the overall survival of any online organization. The first step in achieving operational excellence is to define your businesses processes, starting with defining exactly what business you're in.

What Business Are You In?

One of the first questions to answer when defining your business processes is *What business am I in?* Then determine the complete range of products that you plan to stock and to offer online. If you already have a brick-and-mortar presence or are a catalog retailer, then you might want to start out with the top 20 percent of the products that represent 80 percent of your business. Are all of your offerings physical goods, or will you be selling digital goods, such as service contracts, insurance policies, or software? Digital goods distribution is very different from physical goods distribution, especially online. Electronic Software Distribution (ESD) is actually quite a bit easier because you can offer immediate downloads through the Internet—no packaging, no shipping, and product return hassles are negligible.

You also need to figure out how many unique products, including variations in size, color, fabric, texture, and other features, you want to offer, and develop a Stock Keeping Unit (SKU) system for your product line. Will you be selling a product mix that will change frequently (e.g., seasonally) or technical products with constantly updating versions and data? Are any products hazardous in any way? Are there any special packaging requirements? Are any products perishable? What are the care requirements? Do any products require assembly?

Product descriptions, promotional verbiage, care instructions, sizing charts, and a whole host of other documentation needs to be written and assembled so that your online product catalog can be comprehensive and your customer service staff can be fully informed.

You should also weigh each product and measure its dimensions (both packaged and unpackaged) so that you will have that data for shipping purposes as well as for customer reference online.

How Much Will Your Products Cost?

On the Internet, you can store your entire product pricing, including price variations based on the buyer, in a database. When a buyer logs in, you can present a screen tailored just to them, with the pages assembled on the fly from the database.

This means that you can offer dynamic pricing based on the customer relationship. If the buyer is a distributor, you can show them one set of prices, whereas a new end user might get full retail pricing.

You will need to determine if different groups of customers will see different pricing on the same items, whether you'll offer special promotional pricing, whether you'll have seasonal sales or other forms of temporary price reductions, and whether you'll offer volume discounts, "club" pricing, online coupons, manufacturers' rebates, Buy One Get One Free (BOGO), or any other pricing variations.

This also brings up the touchy subject of channel conflict. As the Internet is disintermediating increasing numbers of middlemen, former standard distribution channels are becoming increasingly wary. Make sure you address how your pricing strategies will affect your offline distribution channels, so that you don't unwittingly undercut them with an online venture.

Do You Want Fries with That?

Many successful sites offer automated suggestions for accessories, add-ons, or other compatible products throughout the product selection process. Some sites not only cross-sell and up-sell, but know when a product is out of stock and offer substitutions (be aware of Federal Trade Commission (FTC) rules, however—you need to offer the substitution *before* the customer places the order). You'll need to develop a set of contingencies if products are out of stock, and map suitable accessories to each product, where applicable. Even if you don't have it all online, your customer service staff should have that information readily available during a customer call. The FTC's major rules and regulations regarding shipping and fulfillment are covered in Chapter 2.

Navigation

One of the most important features customers remember is whether or not they can easily navigate through your site to find what they are looking for. Put yourself in their place and try to figure out the terms they would use for search engines, for categorizing products, for price ranges, for brands, for specific features, or for other criteria when looking for a product.

The more fun and engaging you can make this process, the more often a customer is likely to return. The Land's End apparel site, for example, has an online, three-dimensional model that you create with your characteristics. You can drag and drop clothes onto your model, and Land's End also suggests outfits that would suit your particular body type. This kind of ingenuity allows shoppers to more easily visualize how clothes might look on them, and it creates a memorable site experience.

Custom Configurations

Many sites, particularly those for computer products, have online product configurators. These programs walk the buyer through building a custom computer configuration. The program asks questions and automatically chooses those components that will work properly together. Dell Computer's online configurator is so accurate that there are fewer product returns from customers who have used the configurator than from those who used Dell customer representatives to configure their orders! If you have a site that lends itself to custom orders, you may want to consider having a developer create an online product configurator for your site.

Online Diagnoses

Another popular site feature is to offer solutions. You can build online questionnaires that will recommend products based upon profiles of the customer's needs or upon a particular problem that needs to be solved, such as a home improvement project. These recommender sites are often found in vertical portal (vortal) situations, where a customer will go to a portal that specializes in construction, for example, and the portal may offer a variety of products from their portal participants that will solve a problem. In addition, they may offer online product comparisons based on price, features, models, or other attributes. You should decide how much information you want to provide to customers in order for them to make decisions. Too much data may confuse a buyer, and too little may cause the buyer to leave your site to look elsewhere.

Customer Dialogs

When you open an e-business site, you will be open for business 24 hours a day, 365 days a year. The opportunities for answering questions and assisting customers will never stop. Before the deluge begins, you must determine how you will respond to questions and conduct customer dialogs throughout the sales cycle.

Who will answer emails? Will you accept phone calls, faxes, and snail mail from customers asking questions or placing orders? What scripts will you use for the most frequently asked questions? Do you have written policies and procedures for handling customer inquiries? Many sites offer live chat, online videoconferencing through NetMeeting or other software, and 24-hour toll-free customer service. What kind of response times will you offer? The challenges of customer service are covered in Chapter 5.

Order Processing

There are many issues surrounding online order processing. First, if you're selling to consumers, you'll have to provide an electronic shopping cart or other electronic "bucket" in which customers can collect a number of items before "checking out." Many sites actually use the shopping cart analogy. Others, such as garden sites, use wheelbarrow icons as their online "shopping carts."

If you are selling high-ticket items, buyers may not want to put the hefty sum on their credit cards. In this case, you'll have to decide if you want to offer terms, take purchase orders or credit applications, and set up a billing infrastructure.

If your customers typically reorder the same items each time, you need to build the database functionality so that repeat buyers can log on and see their past order history or be offered a permanent shopping list that they can use to quickly reorder their favorite items. Business-to-business sites often provide automatic replenishment options that their registered customers can take advantage of. In this case, when a customer's supply drops to a certain level, or when a preset time period has passed, an automatic event trigger signals the reorder.

Tax and Shipping Calculations

If you want to compete effectively online, you simply must set up your site to automatically calculate all taxes and shipping expenses and add them to the total cost—prior to the customer placing the order. No one will put up with calculating their own taxes and shipping, and besides, since you will be pre-authorizing payments (you will offer real-time credit card authorization, won't you?), you must calculate tax and shipping in advance.

I'll cover the delightful topic of taxes more in depth in Chapter 4, but be aware that there are software and services such as those offered by Vertex and Taxware that can provide the tax calculations for your site. You should be familiar with the states in which tax is applicable to your sales and which items you'll be selling that are taxable.

Shipping

Shipping will be explored in Chapter 6—a chapter dedicated to that topic—but here are a few things to consider.

First, consider which products are small enough to ship with the United States Postal Service, United Parcel Service, Federal Express, or other small-parcel carriers. For larger products, you may be dealing with a variety of shipping methods, such as by truckload, Less Than Truckload (LTL), train, ocean carrier, and so on.

Also, it's important to note that some U.S. carriers do not ship or deliver on New Year's Day, Martin Luther King, Jr. Day, Presidents' Day, Memorial Day, Independence Day, Labor Day, Columbus Day, Veterans' Day, Thanksgiving Day, and Christmas Day. You'll need to make provisions in your infrastructure and on the site to deal with possible scheduling conflicts.

International E-Commerce

Chapter 8 is devoted to global logistics, but here are some top-level considerations if you decide to sell goods to international buyers.

First, make sure that your site covers all of the expected e-commerce conventions for the United States. In other words, you should include privacy and customer service policies; contact methods (English only or other languages?); participation in industry groups (Better Business Bureau, etc.); seal programs (Verisign, Truste, etc.); and clear product guarantee policies. Also include any information about restrictions, limitations, or conditions on purchases; instructions for proper use of products, including safety and health care warnings; cancellation or refund policies; gift-wrapping and special handling; and ongoing customer service.

Next, decide if you will handle all sales in U.S. dollars only or if you will also handle other currencies, and how many ways you will post prices on the site. Determine how long will it take an order to be delivered to various worldwide locations and if any unexpected taxes or duties may be added to the cost. In addition, check if any of your products may be subject to export restrictions.

Your goal is to offer the customer a full, itemized list of costs involved in each sale, with a clear designation of the currency involved, terms of delivery or performance, and terms, conditions, and methods of payment.

Finally, think about whether you will localize the site for different countries. Localization is more than language translation; it is transforming the site according to local customs and idioms so that a native buyer will feel comfortable. Investigate any laws about providing foreign languages; for example, if you will be selling into France you must, by law, provide the site in French.

Paper or Plastic?

There are several ways of taking payments from customers, and you will have to decide which ones you will implement. For example, if you are selling to consumers, you will probably offer several types of credit card payment options (Visa, American Express, etc.). Check out the rates and policies for each. Some sites are set up to take debit cards and micropayments and to invoice customers on private accounts. If your site will be a business-to-business site, determine if you will be handling purchase orders, if you will actually tie in your customers' back-end systems to handle automatic replenishment or order management, if you need to utilize EDI (electronic data interchange), or if you will be required to handle special messaging requirements (e.g., RosettaNet). Emerging data standards, such as RosettaNet, will be addressed in Chapter 9.

Fraud Checking, Validation, and Transaction Clearing

Since most online fraud is against the merchant, not the customer, I highly recommend that you employ some type of electronic fraud checking. Firms such as CyberSource *(http://www.cybersource.com)* offer ways to "frisk" a customer electronically by running anti-fraud algorithms against a customer's credit card, in addition to other kinds of authentication. As the merchant, you determine what level of risk you want to accept, and that threshold score will determine which transactions will be rejected. CyberSource also checks the customer's card number against a database of known invalid and stolen numbers; in addition, the cardholder's bank performs an address verification service (AVS). Ideally, you'll want to authorize cards and transaction amounts with the cardholder's bank and reserve the funds before issuing order numbers.

Integrating with Inventory and Fulfillment

An amazing number of e-businesses have yet to integrate their on-line order capture process with their order entry, inventory, and fulfillment systems. They literally receive orders as emails generated by their shopping cart software and then manually reenter them into their other systems. The possibility of errors skyrockets each time an order is manually reentered. The necessity for integrating an e-commerce site with a business's inventory and fulfillment systems is critical.

Product Availability

When you first launch your site, I strongly suggest that you offer only those products that are in your immediate inventory. Later on, especially if you have a vast product catalog, you can build customer expectations correctly for those items that will not be in immediate inventory or will be drop-shipped from the manufacturer. If customers come to the site for the first time and their selections are not available, chances are they'll never return.

Back Orders, Substitutions, Custom Orders

As was discussed previously, there will be times when items will be out of stock and you'll have to notify the customer that an item can be back ordered, or you may decide to offer a substitution. Keeping in mind the FTC 30-day Rule (covered in Chapter 2), you'll need to develop policies for all of the possible options, along with corresponding customer messages. The best situation is to have real-time order management and inventory control so you can prevent surprises, and if a product is out of stock, the customer can be notified before the order is placed.

You'll also have to figure out policies for when you want to stop offering an item for sale—when inventory count is at a minimum or when there are none left in inventory. Also, chart whether the same policy should be applied to all products or should differ by product.

Processing Orders

Some very successful sites offer the ability for a customer to place an order by 5:00 p.m. for overnight delivery and have the order leave the dock that same day. Other sites batch up their orders and only process them at the end of each day. The timing and techniques of how you'll conduct order processing is of paramount concern, and setting customer expectations for what you can deliver can be very challenging.

You'll need to determine how often you will process orders, and build your infrastructure accordingly. If your front-end and back-end systems are tightly and smoothly integrated, you'll be able to handle real-time processing and increase your efficiency and responsiveness. In heavy sales situations, such as offering toys online during the holiday season, real-time order processing may be a crucial ability. Other merchants may find that processing orders on an hourly or a daily basis is acceptable.

Providing Customer Service

According to a report from Forrester Research, exceptional customer service strongly increases future sales through repeat visits and positive word-of-mouth. The study of 17,000 online consumers shows that 90 percent of satisfied customers are likely to visit again and that 87 percent will tell friends and family about the site.

The report also indicates that online shoppers expect Web sites to have customer service readily available throughout the buying experience. In 1999, 37 percent of online buyers used customer service on the Internet, a full 4.8 million users. More than 40 percent of online buyers have stopped shopping at a particular site because of unhappiness with the service received.

What's Preferred?

The study found that online shoppers had strong preferences when seeking customer service.

- 71 percent of users who needed customer service first turned to email, and 51 percent picked up the phone (multiple responses were allowed). Email and the telephone were the most used and the most preferred forms of contact.
- If only one channel was available, 46 percent of respondents chose email and 41 percent opted for the phone.
- When seeking help, 19 percent searched for information on the site, while 11 percent plowed through the FAQ section. Fewer than five percent of visitors preferred site searching and FAQs to other forms of customer service.
- Other forms of service, such as U.S. mail, fax, and chat, fell into the low single digits of use and preference.

Four Customer Service Needs

Most retailers view customer service as a problem-solving action *after* the sale. In e-commerce, however, customer service begins the moment a customer enters the Web site. Forrester Research's report identified four basic times of service need.

1. During shopping, 19 percent of customers used customer service to find products and inquire about product attributes.
2. During the buying process, 21 percent had questions about billing issues, receipts, and the check-out process itself.
3. Once the order was placed, 58 percent of users checked in on the status of an order in processing and its status in shipping.
4. Once the item was received, 19 percent of buyers had questions about returns.

Reactive and Proactive

The study also emphasized that solid customer service should solve problems, while anticipating difficulties before they arise. Quick response was the most preferred quality of reactive service, followed by easy returns and quick order tracking.

Among proactive service qualities preferred by online customers, delivery and shipping options were most important. These issues were followed by an interest in detailed product information and smart product recommendations.

Order Tracking, Order Status, and Updates

According to Forrester Research, online customers check order status an average of *seven* times to figure out when their item will arrive and who will deliver it! Why in the world do shoppers log on to check the whereabouts of their package that often? The answer is, *because they can*. This incredible stat (plus the research mentioned above) means that you simply must offer online package tracking at a minimum, and offer real-time order status (back order status, etc.) for real customer satisfaction. UPS and FedEx both offer free online tools to enable you to track packages through assigned shipping numbers.

If you use a third-party fulfillment center, you also need to tie in an automated notification system so that they alert you when an order is shipped (remember, you can't bill until it's shipped, so this is an important feature).

Another important feature to consider is how you'll offer the ability to update, cancel, or change orders, how often you'll update the information, and any restrictions on changes. Chapter 7 is dedicated to order fulfillment and addresses these issues.

Order Status Notification

The best sites don't force customers to log on every time they want to check order status—these sites proactively push order status information to the customer. A great example is Amazon.com. When you order a product, your order is immediately confirmed via email, and other emails are launched when the product is shipped or if the product needs back order authorization. If you haven't shopped in a while, you'll receive friendly reminder emails with suggestions. This kind of proactive contact saves a company a tremendous amount of money by preempting multiple calls to customer service.

Think about how proactive you want to be with your customers. Define the discrete events that will trigger notifications and determine the content of each email for each event.

Technical Support

Let's say that you sell technical products like computer equipment or specialized building equipment. Will you offer online technical support? Will you offer classes for using the building equipment? Will the support or classes be free, or will you charge for them? You can actually process orders for these services as if they were products in and of themselves. Look at various aspects of your business and see if you have some potential revenue streams such as classes that can be sold or even delivered online.

Product Returns

As you might suspect, products that are purchased online are returned more frequently than in the offline world. Chapter 10 will help you prepare for this big area of responsibility.

One of the first things to consider is the return policy itself. Will you accept product returns regardless of the reason? Where will you direct the customer to return the product? Consider each product and whether you will vary your policies based on the nature of the product, whether you will instruct customers to return a product to its corresponding manufacturer, and how you will pay for the return shipping. As with the other e-commerce infrastructure aspects, you have to carefully define all of your business rules surrounding each process.

Measuring Success

You can build the best site on the Internet, but you'll never know it unless you implement concrete techniques for measuring the site's effectiveness.

Site Metrics

There are many tools out there that will capture the statistics for your site's hits, visits, and page views, but is that really useful information? In fact, how will you measure success? I would suggest that you poll the major decision-makers within your company to find out what information would be useful to them. The sales management may want reports that compare online and offline conversion rates and data on which products were the best sellers. The marketing department may require information on advertising and promotional response. MIS will require reports from the hosting ISP or ASP to determine Service Level Agreement compliance. Chances are you'll require a lot more data from your e-business than you realize.

Developing the Customer Relationship

It's difficult to offer excellent pre-sales and post-sales customer support if you don't know who your customers are or what they want. There is a variety of ways to capture customer data and mine that data to become more effective at attracting and retaining customers.

Earning Trust

First and foremost, you have to earn the customer's *trust*. This is more important than any fancy marketing tactic or slick promotional campaign. No one will volunteer information about himself or herself if they suspect that the information might be used without their knowledge or permission, or to market unwanted products.

The key is to develop very comprehensive privacy, security, and marketing policies and prominently post these on your site. Also, have your site audited by one or more of the industry groups set up to police unscrupulous e-commerce practitioners. Seal programs such as those offered by Verisign®, Truste®, the Better Business Bureau Online®, and others require that you comply with their regulations to earn their seal, a valuable third-party endorsement. At the very least, you must obtain a digital certificate from Verisign to enable and verify that your transactions are conducted securely via Secure Sockets Layer (SSL). The Verisign seal has proven to be a seal trusted by online buyers.

Powerful collaborative filtering software, such as LikeMinds™ from Macromedia® *(http://www.macromedia.com/software/ likeminds),* can enable you to hone in on customer preferences and to present the products your customers will be most interested in. Developing good databases to capture shopper history and other transaction information is invaluable to successful e-commerce sites.

There is no substitute for classic market research. Good primary research (focus groups, interviews, face-to-face contact) and secondary research (published third-party studies, etc.) will help you answer questions such as

- How educated are your customers?
- Are they browsers or do they come to the site with a specific product in mind?
- Are they consumers, other businesses, or both?
- Are they brand loyal, and if so, which brands?
- Where are your customers located geographically?
- What products are most likely to appeal to each customer group?

It is very helpful to walk through each step of the sales cycle and determine what motivates your customer at each step.

Branding, Launching, and Promoting Your Site

A brand is not a catchy tagline—a brand is the entire *experience* someone has that is associated with your company. How do you want people to experience your e-business? As the most trustworthy? The most competent? The most innovative? What makes your site unique?

Think carefully about your value proposition. Why would someone shop at your site instead of a competitor's? What "pain" are you solving with your e-business?

There are tons of books about online marketing, so I won't cover specific techniques here. Just remember that you'll have to employ traditional marketing methods (radio, direct mail, public relations, etc.) in much larger measure than online methods (search engine listings, META tags, etc.). This is not inexpensive. Chapter 3 covers some of the cost factors surrounding e-business more in detail.

As we've seen, anyone can develop a pretty Web interface, slap it onto an electronic shopping cart, and say they're doing e-commerce. In truth, they haven't even started, and they will eventually fail. The remaining chapters explore the components of e-logistics in detail, including determining the Return on Investment, how to evaluate payment processors, order entry, and other software packages, global logistics, cost-effective shipping and handling, and a number of other topics. If, at the end of these chapters, you decide it would be easiest just to outsource the whole thing, Chapter 11 is dedicated to that topic.

Throughout the book you'll find checklists, challenging questions to ask yourself, and stories from the trenches—in fact, an entire chapter, Chapter 12, contains user perspectives. Wherever possible, I've enlisted the help of experts in each of the focused chapter areas and have drawn upon my own real-life experiences. At the end of each chapter, there are helpful resources and links for further exploration. In the next chapter, we'll discuss important rules and regulations and provide a useful checklist for implementing an electronic commerce infrastructure.

Resources

Articles

Atkinson, Helen. "Customers are sold on e-tailing, but sellers weren't as happy with holiday results." *Journal of Commerce, February 28, 2000.*

Evans, Philip and Thomas S. Wurster. "Getting Real About Virtual Commerce." *Harvard Business Review.* November-December, 1999.

McCullough, Stacie S. with Stan Dolberg, Liz Leyne, Andrew A. Reinhard and Jason Gatoff. "Mastering Commerce Logistics." Forrester Research, Inc. 1999.

Trade Journals

Commercial Carrier Journal
http://www.ccjmagazine.com

Inbound Logistics
http://www.inboundlogistics.com

Journal of Commerce
http://www.joc.com

Logistics Management
http://www.manufacturing.net/magazine/logistic

Transport Topics
http://www.ttnews.com

TrafficWorld
http://www.trafficworld.com

World Trade
http://www.worldtrademag.com

Organizations

Council of Logistics Management
http://www.clm1.org

International Warehouse Association
http://logistx.dartgc.com/

U.S. Department of Transportation
http://www.dot.gov

Transportation Intermediaries Association (TIA)
http://www.tianet.org

Intermodal Association of North America (IANA)
http://intermodal.org/

Institute of Logistical Management
http://www.logistics-edu.com

IOMA (Institute of Management and Administration)
http://www.ioma.com

WERC (Warehousing Education Resource Council)
http://www.werc.org

Other Logistics Links

The Outsourcing Institute
http://www.outsourcing.com

Outsourcing Center
http://www.outsourcing-center.com

Directory of Freight Forwarding Services
http://forwarders.com

TradeCompass
http://www.tradecompass.com

World-Wide Web Virtual Library Logistics Services
http://www.logisticsworld.com/logistics/

Yahoo Transport Industry News
http://biz.yahoo.com/industry/transport.html

Virtual Logistics Directory
http://www.logisticdirectory.com/logo.htm

Edgar Online
http://www.edgar-online.com

Logistics Online
http://logisticsonline.com

Building an E-Commerce Infrastructure

If you are contemplating offering goods for sale on the Internet, you have a number of decisions to make before you even get close to a computer. Don't be lulled into a false sense of confidence—building an e-commerce infrastructure for your business is a big challenge, even if you decide to outsource the implementation of the whole thing. As a merchant, you will be held liable for virtually everything, and some mistakes can result in pretty scary consequences in terms of the Federal Trade Commission (FTC) and other law enforcement entities.

In this chapter I'll define some basic terms, explain a few very important legal regulations, and then cover some e-commerce planning issues. At the end of the chapter, I've provided an E-Commerce Infrastructure Development Checklist to help you nail down some of your business processes. If you carefully answer all of the questions posed in the checklist, you will have the basics of a requirements document that you can use to guide in-house implementation or out-sourced service providers. First, let's start with a few basic terms.

Logistics

The Council of Logistics Management (http://www.clm1.org), the preeminent logistics professional organization, has adopted this definition of logistics.

Logistics is that part of the supply chain process that plans, implements, and controls the efficient, effective flow and storage of goods, services, and related information from the point of origin to the point of consumption in order to meet customers' requirements.

E-Commerce Logistics

E-commerce logistics, or e-logistics, therefore, is applying the concepts of logistics electronically to those aspects of business conducted via the Internet.

E-Fulfillment

E-fulfillment can be defined as the integration of people, processes, and technology to ensure customer satisfaction before, during, and after the online buying experience.

Important Rules and Regulations

Let's go through some of the legal rules you must comply with, whether you take an order over the Internet, by phone, by mail, or by carrier pigeon. In fact, as far as the FTC is concerned, it does not matter how the merchandise is advertised, how the customer pays, or who initiates the contact.

First, it would be wise to become thoroughly familiar with the FTC's Web site *(http://www.ftc.gov)* as well as the Web site for the Direct Marketing Association *(http://www.the-dma.org)*.

These sites offer a wealth of information, and clearly explain the many laws and regulations of doing business on the Internet. Many of the sections deal with mail or telephone ordering, but you should be aware that the same regulations apply to Internet commerce. In fact, when you apply for a merchant account, you will be applying for a MOTO (Mail Order/Telephone Order), or Card Not Present, account.

As far as banks and the government are concerned, the Internet is simply another channel for taking orders—in this case, without the buyer's card present for swiping through a credit card terminal or card imprinter. The following section on rules is from literature freely available from the FTC's Web site. I tried to make the language a little more friendly without changing its meaning.

The 30-Day Rule

The 30-Day Rule, or the Mail and Telephone Order Rule, is one of the most important rules to be aware of. According to the rule, you must have a reasonable basis for stating or implying that a product can be shipped within a certain time. If your ad doesn't include a shipping statement, you must have a reasonable basis to believe you can ship within 30 days.

If you can't ship when promised, you must send the customer a notice advising him or her of the delay and the right to cancel. For definite delays of up to 30 days, you may treat the customer's silence as agreement to the delay. For longer or more indefinite delays, and for second and subsequent delays, you must get the customer's consent. If you don't, you must, without being asked, promptly refund all the money the customer paid you.

You can give updated shipping information over the phone if your Internet ad prompts customers to call to place an order. This information may differ from what you said or implied about the shipping time in your ad. The updated phone information supersedes any shipping representation made in your ad, but you still must have a reasonable basis for the update. Be sure to train your customer service representatives to avoid giving the customer a delivery time on the phone that would contradict what you have stated online—you will be held liable for whatever the rep has promised, regardless of product availability.

What You Should Know Before You Make a Shipment Representation

When you offer to sell merchandise on the Internet, you must have a reasonable basis for

- any express or implied shipment representation, or
- believing you can ship within 30 days of receipt of an order—if you make no shipment representation, or if the shipment representation is not clear and conspicuous.

Whenever you change the shipment date by providing a delay notice, you must have a reasonable basis for

- the new shipment date, or
- any representation that you do not know when you can ship the merchandise.

Reasonable basis means that the merchant has, at the time of making the representation, such information as would under the circumstances satisfy a reasonable and prudent business-person, acting in good faith, that the representation is true.

The evidence you need to demonstrate the reasonableness of your shipment representations varies with circumstances. The following, however, are important:

- Anticipated demand. Is the demand for each advertised item reasonably anticipated?
- Supply. For each advertised item, is there a sufficient inventory on hand or adequate sources of supply to meet the anticipated demand for the product?
- Fulfillment system. For all promotions in the relevant sales seasons, can the fulfillment system handle the cumulative anticipated demand for all products?

- Record keeping. Are adequate records kept of the key events in each individual transaction to ensure that items can be shipped within the applicable time, as established by the rule?

Remember, whether you make a shipment representation or rely on the 30-day rule, your advertising should be unambiguous about when you will ship.

What You Must Know Before Making Shipment Representations in Sales Involving Credit Applications

If your customers apply to you to establish an in-house new credit account or to increase an existing credit line to pay for the merchandise they order, the rule provides the following:

- If you make no shipment representation when you solicit the order, you are allowed 50 (instead of 30) days to ship the order. The extra 20 days is to enable you to process the credit application. If you wish to use this provision of the rule, you must have a reasonable basis to believe you can ship in 50 days.
- If you do make a shipment representation when you solicit the order, you must have a reasonable basis for being able to ship in that time, regardless of whether the order is accompanied by an application for credit or extension of a credit line. You are presumed to have factored in the time needed to process the credit application or to have qualified your shipment representation appropriately.

When the Clock on Your Fulfillment or Other Obligations Begins

The "clock" on your obligation to ship or take other action under the rule begins as soon as you receive a properly completed order. An order is properly completed when you receive the correct full or partial (in whatever form you accept) payment, accompanied by all the information you need to fill the order. Payment may be by cash, check, money order, the customer's authorization to charge an existing account (including one you have created for the customer), the customer's application to you for credit to pay for the order, or any substitute for these transactions that you accept.

It is irrelevant when you post or deposit payment, when checks clear, or when your bank credits your account. The clock begins to run when you receive a properly completed order.

Note, however, that if a customer's check is returned or a customer is refused credit, the rule stops the shipment clock. It is reset at day one when the customer gives you cash, the customer's check is honored, or you receive notice that the customer qualifies for credit. At this point, you may take the amount of time you originally stated to fulfill the order.

What You Must Do If You Learn You Cannot Ship on Time

When you learn that you cannot ship on time, you must decide whether you will ever be able to ship the order. If you decide that you cannot, you must promptly cancel the order and make a full refund.

If you decide you can ship the order later, you must seek the customer's consent to the delay.

You may use whatever means you wish to do this—such as the telephone or the mail—as long as you notify the customer of the delay reasonably quickly. The customer must have sufficient advance notification to make a meaningful decision to consent to the delay or to cancel the order.

To ensure that their delay notices give all customers a meaningful opportunity to consent to the delay, some businesses adopt internal deadlines that are earlier than those set by the rule. If businesses fail to ship or give delay notifications by their internal deadlines, they automatically cancel the orders and make refunds.

In any event, no notification to the customer can take longer than the time you originally promised or, if no time was promised, 30 days. If you cannot ship the order or provide the notice within this time, you must cancel the order and make a prompt refund.

What a First Delay Option Notice Must Say

In seeking your customer's consent to delay, the first delay notice you provide to the customer (the delay option notice) must include

- a definite revised shipment date or, if unknown, a statement that you are unable to provide a revised shipment date;
- a statement that if the customer chooses not to wait, the customer can cancel the order and obtain a full and prompt refund; and
- some means for the customer to choose to cancel at your expense (e.g., by providing a postage prepaid reply card or toll-free telephone number).

The following information must be included when you cannot provide a revised shipping date:

- the reason for the delay, and
- a statement that if the customer agrees to the indefinite delay, the customer may cancel the order any time until you ship the merchandise.

If your first delay option notice provides a definite revised shipping date of 30 days or less, you must inform customers that their nonresponse will be treated as a consent to the delay.

Thus, your delay option notice might look something like this:

We will be unable to ship the merchandise listed above until [date 30 days or less later than original promised time].

If you don't want to wait, you may cancel your order and receive a prompt refund by calling our toll-free customer service number, (800) 555-1234.

If we do not hear from you before we ship the merchandise to you, we will assume that you have agreed to this shipment delay. In other words, if you want the merchandise, there is no need for you to call.

If your first delay option provides a definite revised shipping date of more than 30 days, or states that you do not know when you will be able to ship, you must tell your customers that if they do not respond, the order will be canceled automatically within the originally promised time plus 30 days.

For example, suppose you have a reasonable basis for being able to ship in 30 days and you have chosen to make no shipment representation in your advertising. Within the 30-day period after you receive the customer's properly completed order, you learn that you cannot ship in time and, although you believe you will be able to ship at some point, you don't know when. Your delay option notice to the customer might look something like this:

Because [explanation of back order problem], we are unable to ship the merchandise listed above. We don't know when we will be able to ship it.

If you don't want to wait, you may cancel your order and receive a prompt refund by calling our toll-free customer service number, (800) 555-1234.

If we do not hear from you and we have not shipped by [date 30 days later than original promised shipment time—in this example, 60 days after receipt of the properly completed order], your order will be canceled automatically and your money will be refunded.

If you do not want your order automatically canceled on [date 30 days later than original promised shipment time], you may request that we keep your order and fill it later. If you do request that we keep your order and fill it later, you still have the right to cancel the order at any time before we ship it to you. You may use our toll-free number, (800)

555-1234, either to request that we fill your order later or to cancel it.

Remember, you are required to explain the nature of the back order problem only if you provide an indefinite revised shipment date. This explanation should be detailed enough to permit the customer to judge what the possible length of the delay might be.

You also have the option of seeking your customer's affirmative agreement to the delay. In any event, you must indicate what will happen if the customer does not respond.

What Later Notices Must Say

If you cannot ship the merchandise by the definite revised shipment date included in your most recent delay option notice, then before that date, you must seek your customers' consent to any further delay. You must do this by providing customers a renewed delay option notice. A renewed delay option notice is similar in many ways to the first delay option notice. One important difference: The customer's silence may not be treated as a consent to delay.

A renewed delay option notice must include:

- a new definite revised shipment date or, if unknown, a statement that you are unable to provide any date;

- a statement that if the customer chooses not to wait, the customer can cancel the order immediately and obtain a full and prompt refund;

- a statement that unless you receive notice that the customer agrees to wait beyond the most recent definite revised shipment date and you have not shipped by then, the customer's order automatically will be canceled and a prompt refund will be provided;

- some means for the customer to inform you, at your expense (e.g., by providing a postage prepaid reply card or toll-free telephone number) whether the customer agrees to the delay or is canceling the order;

- the following information when you cannot provide a new definite revised shipping date:
  - the reason for the delay, and a statement that, if the customer agrees to the indefinite delay, the customer may cancel the order at any time until you ship.

If you have provided an appropriate and timely delay option notice and the customer agrees to an indefinite revised shipment date, no additional delay notices are required.

When You May Cancel an Order

Instead of seeking the customer's consent to delay, you can always cancel the order and send a refund. In that case, you must notify the customer and send the refund within the time you would have sent any delay notice required by the rule.

When You Must Cancel an Order

You must cancel an order and provide a prompt refund when:

- the customer exercises any option to cancel before you ship the merchandise;
- the customer does not respond to your first notice of a definite revised shipment date of 30 days or less and you have not shipped the merchandise or received the customer's consent to a further delay by the definite revised shipment date;
- the customer does not respond to your notice of a definite revised shipment date of more than 30 days (or to your notice that you are unable to provide a definite revised shipment date) and you have not shipped the merchandise within 30 days of the original shipment date;
- the customer consents to a definite delay and you have not shipped or obtained the customer's consent to any additional delay by the shipment time the customer consented to;
- you have not shipped or provided the required delay or renewed option notices on time;

- you determine that you will never be able to ship the merchandise.

The following is one example of a delayed order scenario:

1. You have a reasonable basis for believing that you will be able to ship the merchandise in 30 days. That being the case, you make no shipment representation in your advertising. When your prospective customer calls to place the order on July 1, nothing has happened to change your belief that you can ship in 30 days, so in accepting the order, you provide no updated shipment information. You plan to ship the order by July 31.

2. On July 10, you realize you cannot ship by July 31. Within a few days (reasonably quickly so the customer has time to make a decision), you send a delay notice with a revised shipment date. Based on factors such as customer demand for the merchandise and information you recently received from your suppliers, you reasonably believe that you will be able to ship 30 days from the original shipment date. The revised shipping date you provide in the delay notice is August 30, that is, 30 days from July 31. Your delay notice explains that, unless the customer tells you otherwise, you will assume that the customer is willing to wait for the merchandise until then.

3. Having heard nothing from the customer, on August 10 you realize that you will not be able to ship by August 30, so you promptly send a second delay option notice saying when you now reasonably believe you will be able to ship. The notice tells the customer that the order will be canceled automatically on August 30 unless you have already shipped by then or the customer expressly tells you not to cancel.

How Quickly You Must Make a Refund

When you must make a rule-required refund, the following applies:

- If the customer paid by cash, check, or money order, you must refund the correct amount by first class mail within seven working days after the order is canceled.
- If the customer paid by credit, you must credit the customer's account or notify the customer that the account will not be charged, within one customer's billing cycle after the order is canceled.

How Much You Must Refund

If you cannot ship any of the merchandise ordered by the customer, you must refund the entire amount the customer tendered, including any shipping, handling, insurance, or other costs. If you ship some, but not all, of the merchandise ordered, you must refund the difference between the total amount paid and the amount the customer would have paid, according to your ordering instructions, for the shipped items only.

For example, if you charge a flat fee for shipping and handling regardless of the total number or cost of the items ordered, you need not refund any shipping and handling charges if you ship some items. On the other hand, if your shipping and handling charges are indexed to the number of items or the dollar amount of the order, you can keep only those shipping and handling charges that are appropriate to the number or dollar amount of the items actually shipped.

When making rule-required refunds, you cannot substitute credit toward future purchases, credit vouchers, or scrip.

When the order is paid for, in whole or in part, by proofs of purchase, coupons, or other promotional devices, you must provide *reasonable compensation* to the customer for the proofs of purchase plus any shipping, handling, or other charges the customer paid. (The circumstances of each promotion may affect what is deemed to be reasonable.)

Why You Should Keep Records

Although you are not required to keep records, an accurate, up-to-date record keeping system can help show that you are complying with the rule. Your documentation should provide answers to the following questions.

- Substantiation for shipment representations. How is demand anticipated? How is inventory monitored? How is inventory acquisition coordinated with customer demand and order cancellation? How are demand needs communicated to and met by buyers, suppliers, and drop shippers?

- Fulfillment system. How is the fulfillment system designed to meet the requirements of the rule? Are the delay option notices in compliance? Does the customer's active or passive exercise of any cancellation option result in a prompt refund response?

- Record keeping. Are adequate records kept for each individual order, demonstrating the date you received the order; the contents of and date you provided any delay option notice; the date you received any exercise of a cancellation option; the date of any shipment and the merchandise shipped; the date of any refund and the merchandise for which the refund was made?

If you provide delay option notices by telephone, you may want to keep accurate records of the scripts you use. To help document your compliance with the rule, you may find it useful to maintain a chronological record of all calls you make, including the number from which the call is made, the called number, the party contacted, and the duration of the contact.

Businesses often ask how long they should keep their records relating to rule compliance. The statute of limitations on actions to enforce the rule is three years for consumer redress and five years for civil penalties. State statutes of limitations for individual customer or state actions are sometimes longer. Check the state laws where you plan to do business.

What the Rule Does Not Cover

The following sales are exempt from the rule:

- magazine subscriptions (and similar serial deliveries), except for the first shipment,
- sales of seeds and growing plants,
- orders made on a collect-on-delivery basis (C.O.D.),
- transactions covered by the FTC's Negative Option Rule (such as book clubs and music clubs).

The rule also does not cover services, such as mail order photofinishing. In the question and answer section that follows, you will notice other circumstances in which mail or telephone order merchandise may not be covered by the rule.

Why You Should Comply with the Rule

Merchants who violate the rule can be sued by the FTC for injunctive relief, monetary civil penalties of up to $10,000 per violation (any time during the five years preceding the filing of the complaint), and consumer redress (any time during the three years preceding the filing of the complaint). When the mails are involved, the U.S. Postal Service also has authority to take action for problems such as nondelivery. State law enforcement agencies can take action for violating state consumer protection laws.

Apart from this, most businesses regard compliance with the rule as simply good business practice.

Using a Fulfillment House or Drop Shipper

Q: *Who is liable for rule violations caused by a fulfillment house or drop shipper?*
A: The seller is.

This is because the person soliciting the order, not the agent fulfilling it, is the seller of mail or telephone order merchandise under the rule. The person soliciting the order can control— among other things—the shipment representations made in soliciting the sale. This should include the time needed to transmit orders to a fulfillment house and for the fulfillment house to respond.

However, FTC staff considers the following circumstances when deciding whether to recommend an enforcement action:

1. whether the merchant made all reasonable efforts to prevent violations, including, for example, contracting with the fulfillment house to require it to comply with the rule (or, at least, require it to promptly inform the merchant of any problems that could involve the rule), "seeding" orders with the fulfillment house to monitor its fulfillment time, and monitoring customer complaints for unusual surges;

2. whether the violations were genuinely unforeseeable and beyond the merchant's control to prevent;

3. whether the merchant, from all objective circumstances, did not know and did not have reason to know of the violations when they occurred; and

4. whether the merchant promptly took all reasonable steps to remedy the fulfillment, notification, or refund systems failures as soon as it discovered them, and to remedy any resulting customer injury.

"Bill me" Orders: Sales On Approval

Q: *We offer to ship merchandise ordered by mail or telephone and to bill the customer later. Are we covered by the rule?*

A: Whether the transaction is covered by the rule depends on whether you bill as part of a credit arrangement made with the customer.

For example, suppose you ship the merchandise under an arrangement in which the customer has an open account or a charge account you have provided, and the customer authorizes you to charge the account. This is a credit sale and is covered by the rule. The customer's authorization to place a charge on the customer's account meets the rule's test for coverage that the order is prepaid and thus properly completed when received by the merchant.

On the other hand, suppose you ship the merchandise along with an invoice payable upon receipt. This is not a credit or prepaid sale and is not covered by the rule. Of course, if you are unreasonably slow in shipping the merchandise or do not ship in the time you promised, the customer may have the right under state law to refuse to accept the merchandise.

Q: Does the rule cover sales on approval?

A: No. Sales on approval permit the prospective customer to return merchandise, usually after a "no obligation" or "free trial" period, even though it is exactly as represented in the merchant's advertising.

These sales do not require the customer to pay for the order until the merchandise is received and approved. Because the order is not prepaid with cash, check, money order, or charge, it cannot be treated as the receipt of a properly completed order—which would trigger the rule's requirements.

Unordered Merchandise

Whether or not the rule is involved, you must obtain the customer's prior express agreement to receive the merchandise in any approval or other sale. Otherwise the merchandise may be treated as unordered merchandise. It is unlawful to:

- send any merchandise by any means without the express request of the recipient (unless the merchandise is clearly identified as a gift, free sample, or the like); or
- try to obtain payment for or the return of the unordered merchandise.

Merchants who ship unordered merchandise with knowledge that it is unlawful to do so can be subject to civil penalties of up to $10,000 per violation. Moreover, customers who receive unordered merchandise are legally entitled to treat the merchandise as a gift. Using the U.S. mails to ship unordered merchandise also violates the Postal laws.

Insurance Charges

Q: *What are our responsibilities if we charge to insure delivery?*

A: Instead of directing customers to make claims against the common carriers who may be responsible for losing merchandise, most merchants reship for the sake of customer satisfaction.

To pay for these reshipment policies, some merchants ask customers to buy insurance, or they provide it as an option. By offering insurance, the merchant implicitly represents that it will honor any claim of nondelivery by providing prompt reshipment, or if reshipment is impossible, a prompt refund. It would be improper to collect fees from customers for reshipment insurance and not respond promptly and appropriately to their bona fide claims of loss.

Substitutions

Q: *If a customer orders an item that is back ordered, can we substitute an item of similar or better quality without the customer's consent?*

A: For back orders, the rule provides only two ways of responding to a properly completed order for mail or telephone order merchandise: obtain the customer's agreement to delayed shipment or provide a full and prompt refund.

Unless the customer expressly agrees to the substitution beforehand, you do not have the option of substituting merchandise that is materially different from your advertised merchandise. The term *materially different* means that the merchandise differs in some manner that is likely to affect the customer's choice of, or conduct regarding, the merchandise. Any product feature would be deemed material if it is expressly mentioned or depicted in advertising. Differences in design, style, color, fabric, or promoted end-use also would be deemed material.

Running Late? Overwhelmed with Orders?

The rule gives you several ways to deal with an unexpected demand.

You can change your shipment promises up to the point the consumer places the order, if you reasonably believe that you can ship by the new date. The updated information overrides previous promises and reduces your need to send delay notices. Be sure to tell your customer the new shipment date before you take the order.

You must provide a delay option notice if you can't ship within the originally promised time. The rule lets you use a variety of ways to provide the notice, including email, fax, or phone. It's a good idea to keep a record of what your notice states, when you provide it, and the customer's response.

General Offers and Claims: Products and Services

The Federal Trade Commission Act gives the FTC the tools it needs to act in the interest of all consumers to prevent deceptive and unfair acts or practices. In interpreting Section 5 of the Act, the Commission has determined that a representation, omission, or practice is deceptive if it is likely to mislead consumers and affect consumers' behavior or decisions about the product or service.

In addition, an act or practice is unfair if the injury it causes, or is likely to cause, is:

- substantial,
- not outweighed by other benefits, and
- not reasonably avoidable.

The FTC Act prohibits unfair or deceptive advertising in any medium. That is, advertising must tell the truth and not mislead consumers. A claim can be misleading if relevant information is left out or if the claim implies something that's not true. For example, a lease advertisement for an automobile that promotes "$0 Down" may be misleading if significant and undisclosed charges are due at lease signing.

In addition, claims must be substantiated, especially when they concern health, safety, or performance. The type of evidence may depend on the product, the claims, and what experts believe necessary. If your ad specifies a certain level of support for a claim—"tests show X"—you must have at least that level of support.

Sellers are responsible for claims they make about their products and services. Third parties—such as advertising agencies or Web site designers and catalog marketers—also may be liable for making or disseminating deceptive representations if they participate in the preparation or distribution of the advertising, or know about the deceptive claims.

Advertising agencies or Web site designers are responsible for reviewing the information used to substantiate ad claims. They may not simply rely on an advertiser's assurance that the claims are substantiated. In determining whether an ad agency should be held liable, the FTC looks at the extent of the agency's participation in the preparation of the challenged ad, and whether the agency knew or should have known that the ad included false or deceptive claims.

To protect themselves, catalog marketers should ask for material to back up claims rather than repeat what the manufacturer says about the product. Other points to consider:

- Disclaimers and disclosures must be clear and conspicuous. That is, consumers must be able to notice, read or hear, and understand the information. Still, a disclaimer or disclosure alone usually is not enough to remedy a false or deceptive claim.

- Demonstrations must show how the product will perform under normal use.

- Refunds must be made to dissatisfied consumers—if you promised to make them.

- Advertising directed to children raises special issues. That's because children may have greater difficulty evaluating advertising claims and understanding the nature of the information you provide. Sellers should take special care not to misrepresent a product or its performance when advertising to children.

Protecting Consumers' Privacy Online

The Internet provides unprecedented opportunities for the collection and sharing of information from and about consumers. But studies show that consumers have very strong concerns about the security and confidentiality of their personal information in the online marketplace. Many consumers also report being wary of engaging in online commerce, in part because they fear that their personal information can be misused.

These consumer concerns present an opportunity for you to build consumer trust by implementing effective, voluntary, industry-wide practices to protect consumers' information privacy.

Laws Enforced by the Federal Trade Commission

Free Products

A product that's advertised as free if another is purchased— "buy one, get one"—indicates that the consumer will pay nothing for the one item and no more than the regular price for the other. Ads like these should clearly and prominently describe all the terms and conditions of the free offer.

Negative Option Offers

The Negative Option Rule applies to sellers of subscription plans who ship merchandise like books or compact discs to consumers who have agreed in advance to become subscribers. The rule requires ads to clearly and conspicuously disclose material information about the terms of the plan. Further, once consumers agree to enroll, the company must notify them before shipping to allow them to decline the merchandise. Even if an automatic shipment or continuity program doesn't fall within the specifics of the rule, companies should be careful to clearly disclose the terms and conditions of the plan before billing consumers or charging their credit cards.

Testimonials and Endorsements

Testimonials and endorsements must reflect the typical experiences of consumers, unless the ad clearly and conspicuously states otherwise. A statement that not all consumers will get the same results is not enough to qualify a claim. Testimonials and endorsements can't be used to make a claim that the advertiser itself cannot substantiate.

Connections between an endorser and the company that are unclear or unknown to a customer also must be disclosed, whether they have to do with a financial arrangement for a favorable endorsement, a position with the company, or stock ownership. Expert endorsements must be based on appropriate tests or evaluations performed by people who have mastered the subject matter.

Warranties and Guarantees

Warranties

The Rule on Pre-Sale Availability of Written Warranty Terms requires that warranties be available before purchase for consumer products that cost more than $15. If your ad mentions a warranty on a product that can be purchased by mail, phone, or online, it must tell consumers how to get a copy of the warranty.

A written warranty is a legal document in which you set out what you promise to do if something goes wrong with your product. Clear organization makes it easier for consumers to compare what you promise in your warranty with what others promise in their warranties.

A written warranty is also a guide for customers to use to find out what to do when something goes wrong with the product.

When this happens, customers understandably want to find answers to specific questions quickly and easily.

Guarantees

If your ad uses phrases like "satisfaction guaranteed" or "money-back guarantee," you must be willing to give full refunds for any reason. You also must tell the consumer the terms of the offer.

What Your Warranty Should Include

By law, a written warranty must contain certain basic information about its coverage. Your warranty must include information about

- what parts of the product or what types of problems the warranty covers (and, if necessary for clarity, what parts or problems it does not cover);
- what the period of coverage is;
- what you will do to correct problems and, if necessary for clarity, what you will not do;
- how the customer can get warranty service; and
- how state law may affect certain provisions of the warranty.

In addition, if there are limitations or conditions on the warranty coverage you provide, you must include a statement of them in your warranty. You may want to consider what conditions and limitations you really need and eliminate those that are unnecessary.

If your warranty contains certain particular conditions or restrictions, you must include additional information.

Finally, the law requires that your warranty include a title that indicates whether it is *full* or *limited*.

Include Extra Detail in a Pro Rata Warranty

A special note is in order concerning what to include in a pro rata warranty. A pro rata warranty is one that provides for a refund or credit that decreases according to a set formula as the warranty period progresses or as the product is used. Because a pro rata warranty offers a remedy that is rather complicated, it should include certain detailed information so that customers can understand what the company will do if the product malfunctions. A pro rata warranty should include information that makes clear:

- what formula the company will use to calculate how much the refund or the credit will be at any time during the period of coverage;
- what the consumer will get—either a credit, a refund, or a choice of a credit or a refund, whichever is the case;
- that the only remedy is a credit toward an identical product, if this is the case; and
- what price the company will use as a basis to calculate the refund or credit—for example, the price the customer originally paid or the price at the time the product malfunctions, if different.

What Your Warranty Should Not Include

Promotional statements, instructions to service agents, and other extraneous material in a warranty may confuse customers about the purpose of the document. Include only necessary information in your warranty. A concise, straightforward warranty will promote your product better than a crowded document full of praise for your product.

If you feel that it is necessary to include promotional material about your product with your written warranty, keep it separate from the warranty. If possible, put it in a separate brochure.

If you put promotional statements on the same page as your warranty, clearly set apart your warranty, for example, by placing a border around it. The customer should be able to separate at a glance the warranty from the promotional material.

How to Organize Your Warranty

We suggest using as the headings for your warranty the information required by the FTC's Rule on Disclosure of Written Consumer Product Warranty Terms and Conditions.

Here are some examples of parallel, informative headings.

- What Does This Warranty Cover?
- What Does This Warranty Not Cover?
- What Is the Period of Coverage?
- What Will We Do to Correct Problems?
- What Will We Not Do?
- How Do You Get Service?
- What Must You Do to Keep the Warranty in Effect?
- How Does State Law Relate to This Warranty?

Titling a Written Warranty "Full" or "Limited"

The title "full warranty" is a shorthand message to consumers that the coverage meets certain standards for comprehensive warranty coverage set by Congress. By the same token, the title "limited warranty" alerts consumers that the coverage does not meet at least one of the standards that Congress set.

How to Determine Whether Your Warranty Is Full or Limited

Determining whether your warranty is a full or limited warranty is not difficult. Basically, if each of the following five statements is true about your warranty's terms and conditions, your warranty is a full one:

1. You will provide warranty service to anyone who owns your product during the warranty period.

2. You will provide warranty service free of any charge, including such costs as returning the product or removing or reinstalling the product when necessary.

3. You will provide, at the consumer's choice, either a replacement or a full refund if you are unable, after a reasonable number of tries, to repair your product.

4. You will provide warranty service without requiring that the consumer return a warranty registration card.

5. You will not limit the duration of implied warranties.

If any of these statements is not true, then your warranty is limited.

Your test should determine whether your warranty will be easy to understand and use in real-life situations.

The Children's Online Privacy Protection Rule

For those of you who may be thinking of marketing online to children, I would strongly advise that you reconsider. The FTC passed the Children's Online Privacy Protection Rule, which became effective April 21, 2000, and applies to the online collection of personal information from children under 13. Even if you operate a general-audience Web site and have actual knowledge that you are collecting personal information from children, you must comply with the rule. The new rule spells out what a Web site operator must include in a privacy policy, when and how to seek verifiable consent from a parent, and what responsibilities an operator has to protect children's privacy and safety online.

To determine whether a Web site is directed to children, the FTC considers several factors, including

- subject matter,
- visual or audio content,
- age of models on the site,
- language,

- whether advertising on the Web site is directed to children,
- information regarding the age of the actual or intended audience, and
- whether a site uses animated characters or other child-oriented features.

The Children's Online Privacy Protection Rule applies to individually identifiable information about a child that is collected online, such as full name, home address, email address, telephone number, or any other information that would allow someone to identify or contact the child. The rule also covers other types of information—for example, hobbies, interests, and information collected through cookies or other types of tracking mechanisms—when they are tied to individually identifiable information.

If you think that your site may deal with children as potential customers or even site visitors, please review the FTC's new rule very carefully.

Project TooLate.com: A Real-Life Horror Story

On July 26, 2000, the FTC hit seven Internet retailers with fines totaling $1.5 million for violating the Mail and Telephone Order Rule (the 30-Day Rule) during the 1999 holiday shopping season. It said that the retailers failed to provide buyers with adequate notice of shipping delays or they continued to promise specific delivery dates when timely fulfillment was impossible.

The seven online retailers, CDnow, Inc., KBkids.com LLC, Macys.com, Inc., Franklin W. Bishop d/b/a Minidiscnow.com, The Original Honey Baked Ham Company of Georgia, Inc., Patriot Computer Corp., and Toysrus.com, Inc., agreed to change their procedures to ensure that such violations would not recur in 2000, and to pay civil penalties totaling $1.5 million for the 1999 season's violations. The settlements were the culmination of Project TooLate.com, an FTC investigation of whether major online retailers delivered goods when promised during the 1999 holiday season.

The FTC emphasized that the requirements of the Rule apply to online and offline commerce equally, and added that the settlement shows the FTC takes violations of the Rule by e-tailers seriously and expects e-tailers either to comply with the law or face stiff penalties.

Here's a summary of the FTC actions.

- Didn't follow FTC rules when notifying customers of delivery times
  - CDnow.com: fined $300,000 ($200,000 waived due to company's poor financial condition)
- Failed to ship orders as promised and didn't notify customers of delays
  - The Original Honey Baked Ham Company of Georgia: fined $45,000
  - Patriot Computer: fined $200,000
- Took orders they likely couldn't fill; didn't ship as promised or notify customers of delays
  - KBkids.com: fined $350,000
  - Macys.com: fined $350,000 and ordered to fund an online consumer-education campaign
  - Minidiscnow.com (now defunct): must reimburse customers who ordered but didn't receive products
  - ToysRus.com: fined $350,000

The decrees also contained injunctive provisions prohibiting future Rule violations and required compliance reports, demonstrating that the necessary infrastructure changes have been put in place for full compliance with the Rule, to be filed within 120 days of the entry of the decree. Finally, the settlements contained a number of record keeping and reporting requirements to assist the FTC in monitoring compliance by the companies.

Since the ruling, several of the online retailers have upgraded their systems. KBkids.com dropped their third-party fulfillment company and is feverishly transforming its 300,000 square-foot facility in Danville, Kentucky, from a bricks-and-mortar fulfillment center to an Internet-only operation. CDNow.com, Inc. made changes in the policies governing its shipping and back order processes. Patriot Computer Corp. built an automated customer-response system that automatically sends a customer a letter if delivery will be delayed, and is negotiating with logistics companies to ensure on-time delivery. ToysRus.com Inc. will build a new customer-service operation based on software products from i2 Technologies Inc. and Siebel Systems Inc. They also hired a new executive team to lead its logistics, finance, IT, and customer-service efforts during the 2000 holiday season.

The moral of this horror story: The FTC's penalties could have been avoided if the retailers had invested in strong e-logistics and e-fulfillment infrastructures up front.

Defining Your Business Processes

After making sure you can comply with the FTC's rules, the fun is just beginning. Next, you must be able to clearly define your business processes. These are the myriad ways you engage customers, sell to them, fulfill their orders, provide ongoing service, gather valuable planning data, and establish your brand. These processes dictate how your entire infrastructure will be set up and operated. They are the "rules of the road" for your particular business. My advice is, don't even think about touching a keyboard or coding a single line until you can address each item on the following checklist—and this is by no means an exhaustive list.

The checklist below consists of questions that are meant to assist you in defining your business rules and processes. Use this as a springboard for your e-commerce infrastructure planning in conjunction with the other chapters in this book.

E-Commerce Infrastructure Development Checklist

Defining Your Business Processes

What Business Are You In?

- [ ] How would you define your business?
- [ ] What is the range of products that you plan to stock and offer online?
- [ ] What are the products that represent the top 20 percent of your business?
- [ ] Are all of your products physical goods?
- [ ] Will you offer intangible products, such as educational courses, warranties, service agreements, and guarantees?
- [ ] Will you offer Electronic Software Distribution (ESD)? Software and licenses that will be available for download through the Internet?
- [ ] How many unique products will you plan to offer?
- [ ] How many variations are there on each product (size, color, etc.)?
- [ ] Have you developed an SKU scheme?
- [ ] How often does product data and product mix change?
- [ ] Are any products hazardous and do they require special disposal?
- [ ] Are there any special packaging requirements?
- [ ] Are any products perishable?
- [ ] What are the care requirements for each product?
- [ ] Will any products require assembly?
- [ ] What are the dimensions and weight of each product?
- [ ] How many products fit in a case? How many cases to a pallet?

How Much Will Your Products Cost?

- [ ] Do you offer different prices to different customers?
- [ ] Which customer groups, if any, have different price structures?

❏ Do you want to have your online price information be dynamically generated, so that each user will see his or her specific prices?

❏ Do you ever have sales, special promotional prices, Buy One Get One Free (BOGO), or any other temporary price reductions?

❏ Have you considered possible channel conflict problems?

❏ Will you use online coupons?

❏ Do you support manufacturers' rebates?

❏ Will you offer volume discounts, "club" pricing, bundled deals, or other incentives?

Do You Want Fries with That?

❏ Which products can be logically grouped for the purposes of suggesting accessories, up-selling, cross-selling, or substitutions?

❏ Have you developed a set of contingencies if products are out of stock?

❏ How will you comply online with the FTC rule regarding substitutions?

Navigation

❏ What terms would your customers use to search for various product groups within your site?

❏ Will you offer navigation and searches by criteria, such as price ranges, brands, specific features, or other criteria?

❏ Will you have any special features that will make the site unique or particularly engaging (such as virtual dressing rooms, etc.)?

Custom Configurations

❏ Do you have any products that lend themselves to customization or component-based configurations?

❏ How will you lead customers through the configuration process? Will you use online configurators? Live customer service?

Online Diagnoses

❐ Will you offer complete product solutions online?

❐ How much information will you solicit from the customer online so that you can make automated product recommendations?

❐ Will you offer online product comparisons? What features will you compare? Price? Performance? Warranties?

❐ Will you present your company as an unbiased industry expert and provide product reviews or ratings?

❐ Will you allow your customers to provide product reviews or feedback on your site?

Customer Dialogs

❐ Who will answer emails from customers?

❐ Will you accept phone calls, faxes, and snail mail from customers asking questions or placing orders?

❐ What are the scripts you will use for the most frequently asked questions?

❐ Do you have written policies and procedures for handling customer inquiries?

❐ Will you offer live chat, online video conferencing or 24/7/365 toll-free customer service?

❐ What kind of response times will you offer?

❐ What are your escalation procedures to resolve problems?

Order Processing

❐ What kind of online shopping cart system will you provide so that customers can collect and review items before placing their orders?

❐ If you are selling business-to-business, will you offer automatic replenishment or other reordering functions?

❐ Will you provide registered users with their shopping histories or lists of previous purchases so that they can quickly reorder or buy compatible products?

Tax and Shipping Calculations

❏ Will you be offering real-time credit card authorization? If so, you must calculate tax and shipping in advance of the customer placing the order.

❏ Will you enable customers to choose shipping methods and delivery options online?

❏ Which items that you sell are taxable? In which states, regions, and cities will taxes be applicable?

Shipping

❏ Which items are small enough to ship with USPS? FedEx? UPS?

❏ How will you ship larger products? Truckload? Less Than Truckload (LTL)? Other carriers?

❏ Do you want your site to automatically calculate the most cost-effective shipping method for the customer?

International E-Commerce

❏ Will you be shipping internationally?

❏ Are the prices posted in U.S. dollars, or will you also post prices in other currencies?

❏ How long will it take for an order to be delivered to various worldwide locations?

❏ Will any unexpected taxes or duties be added to the cost of the orders?

❏ Are any products subject to export restrictions?

❏ How will you offer the customer a full, itemized list of costs involved in each sale, with a clear designation of the currency involved, terms of delivery or performance, and terms, conditions, and methods of payment?

❏ How will you handle international customer inquiries?

Paper or Plastic?

❏ Which payment options will you implement?

❏ What are the rates and policies for each of the credit card companies you will be dealing with (American Express, Visa, Discover, etc.)?

❏ Will you accept micropayments?

❑ Will you set up corporate credit accounts, and invoice customers?

❑ Will you be handling purchase orders? Automatic replenishment?

❑ Are you required by any vendors or customers to use EDI?

❑ Are there any other standards that you must comply with (RosettaNet, OBI, ICE, etc.)?

Fraud-Checking, Validation, and Transaction Clearing

❑ Will you employ any automated fraud-checking algorithms against your customers' credit cards?

❑ What types of authentication methods will you use? How stringent?

❑ How much risk do you want to assume?

❑ What services does your payment processor offer?

❑ Do you want to authorize cards and transaction amounts with a bank and reserve the funds before issuing the customer an order confirmation number?

Integrating with Inventory and Fulfillment

Product Availability

❑ Will you have enough immediate inventory to fulfill the first wave of online orders?

❑ Will you be drop shipping any orders direct from manufacturers?

❑ What agreements do you have in place with each manufacturer in terms of product availability?

Back Orders, Substitutions, Custom Orders

❑ How and when will you notify customers when products are out of stock or discontinued, or can be back ordered?

❑ How will you comply with the FTC rule about notifying the customer online, before the order is placed, that an item is out of stock?

❑ How will you comply with the FTC rules regarding product substitutions in those cases when the product ordered is out of stock?

❏ What are the online messages that you want the customer to see for each product situation?

❏ What policies do you have in place for custom orders? What are the delivery expectations? Product returns allowed?

❏ When will you pull a product off the site and stop sales? When the safety stock level is low or when there are none left in inventory?

❏ What are your reorder policies for each product?

Processing Orders

❏ What are the customer expectations you will set regarding the timing of order processing and delivery?

❏ Will you allow overnight orders up until 5:00 p.m., or will you set an earlier cutoff time?

❏ Will you outsource your order management or perform it in-house?

❏ Are you set up to perform real-time order processing, or will you send orders to order entry for manual re-input?

❏ How often will you process orders? Hourly? Daily?

Providing Customer Service

What's Preferred?

❏ Since email and phone are the most preferred form of customer contact with customer service, how will you handle these types of inbound communication?

❏ What kind of product information will you offer on the site? How easy is it to find and navigate through?

❏ What are your customers' most frequently asked questions? What are the answers?

Four Customer Service Needs

❏ How will your live customer service representatives handle questions about product attributes? What kind of product training and scripts will be provided?

❏ What are the most frequently asked questions about billing issues, receipts, and the checkout process? What answers will you provide online?

❏ How will you integrate information about order and shipping status online and offline? How will you provide that information in real-time to your customer service representatives?

❏ How will you answer questions about product returns?

Reactive and Proactive

❏ Which information will you proactively push to the customer (email notifications) and which will you force the customer to log on to the site to look for?

❏ Delivery and shipping options, detailed product information, and online product recommendations were the top four features customers wanted proactively communicated to them. How will you accomplish this?

Order Tracking, Order Status, and Updates

❏ How will you enable customers to look up the shipping status of their orders online?

❏ Will you tie in UPS or FedEx tracking numbers with the customers' order numbers so they only have to know one number?

❏ If you use a third-party fulfillment service, how will you implement messaging so that you are alerted when an order is shipped?

❏ What abilities will you offer for online order updates, cancellations, or changes?

Order Notification

❏ What messages will you automatically generate to notify customers of certain events? Which events?

❏ How will you alert the customer when the order is confirmed, the product is out of stock, or a back order needs to be authorized?

❏ Will you launch an email when a customer's order leaves your dock and enters the shipper's vehicle?

❏ How will you handle partial orders? What customer expectations will you set for incomplete product deliveries?

Technical Support

☐ Will you offer online technical support for any products?

☐ Will you sell customer training classes, service contracts, or other intangibles as products?

☐ Will these "product" sales need to be processed as orders?

Product Returns

☐ Will you accept product returns regardless of the reason?

☐ Where will you direct the customer to return the product?

☐ What are your return policies for each product?

☐ Will you instruct customers to return a product to its corresponding manufacturer?

☐ How will you facilitate product returns? Enclosed return-shipping labels? Paid shipping?

☐ How will you track the disposition of the returned products?

Warranties and Guarantees

☐ How will you comply with the FTC rules on offering warranties on products worth over $15?

☐ Do you have a 100 percent satisfaction guarantee?

☐ What legal product disclaimers must you make?

☐ What are the terms and conditions of each sale? Do these terms differ based on product?

☐ Will you offer full or limited warranties on products? Which products?

☐ Are there any locations where you cannot legally sell your products and services?

Measuring Success

Site Metrics

☐ How will you define success in terms of your e-commerce sites?

☐ What information will each manager in your company require regarding your customers, orders, conversion rates, site traffic, network performance, and other factors?

❏ What needs to be included on each report? How will the reports be formatted and delivered?

❏ How often will you need reports for each function?

Developing the Customer Relationship

Earning Trust

❏ How much do you know about your customers? Who exactly are they?

❏ What are your privacy, security, and marketing policies?

❏ What seal programs will you subscribe to?

❏ Will you employ any collaborative filtering or customer relationship management software?

❏ What types of market research do you use to determine your customers' needs and wants?

❏ How educated are your customers?

❏ Are your customers browsers, or do they come to the site with a specific product in mind?

❏ Are your customers consumers, other businesses, or both?

❏ Are they brand-loyal, and if so, to which brands?

❏ Where are your customers located geographically?

❏ What products are most likely to appeal to each customer group?

Branding Launching and Promoting Your Site

❏ A brand is the entire experience someone has that is associated with your company. How do you want people to experience your e-business?

❏ As the most trustworthy?

❏ The most competent?

❏ The most innovative?

❏ The most sophisticated?

❏ What make your business and your site unique?

❏ Why would someone shop at your site instead of at a competitor's?

❏ What "pain" are you solving with your e-business?

> ❐ What traditional marketing tactics will you employ (direct mail, radio, public relations, etc.)?
>
> ❐ What online marketing methods will you use (search engine listings, META tags, etc.)?

Resources

Articles

Bacheldor, Beth, and Steve Konicki, "Long arm of the law." *Information Week*. CMP Media, Inc. August 7, 2000.

Tillet, L. Scott. "E-Holiday Lesson: Start Planning Now for Crunch." *InternetWeek*. March 27, 2000. Issue: 806, Section: NEWS & ANALYSIS.

Helpful Links

American Express Company
http://www.americanexpress.com
The site provides a Customer Internet Privacy Statement, which provides a full description of Web site security, information about collection and use, and how to decline email offers.

Call For Action, Inc.
http://www.callforaction.org
Call For Action is an international, nonprofit network of consumer hotlines affiliated with local broadcast partners. Volunteers assist, educate, and solve consumer problems through free and confidential mediation. Help is available to individuals, small businesses, and the hearing and speech impaired via text telephone. The ABC's of Privacy, which describes how consumers can protect their personal privacy online, can be accessed at their Web site. You also can contact Call For Action at 5272 River Road, Suite 300, Bethesda, Maryland, 20816; 301-657-8260.

The Consumer Information Center
http://www.pueblo.gsa.gov
The Consumer Information Center publishes the Consumer Information Catalog, which lists more than 200 publications from a

variety of federal agencies. You can access the catalog and the full-text of all its publications at their Web site. You also can contact CIC for a free catalog at Consumer Information Catalog, Pueblo, CO 81009; (719) 948-4000.

The Direct Marketing Association
http://www.the-dma.org
The DMA is a trade association of catalogers, financial services firms, publishers, book and music clubs, online service companies, and others involved in direct and database marketing. The DMA's Mail Order Action Line acts as an intermediary between consumers and companies to resolve complaints. It can be contacted at 1111 19th Street, NW, Suite 1100, Washington, D.C. 20036. Or, you can contact the DMA by email at consumer@the-dma.org.

Federal Trade Commission
http://www.ftc.gov
Copies of the Project TooLate.com complaints and the proposed settlements are available from the FTC's Web site and also by contacting the Consumer Response Center toll-free at 1-877-FTC-HELP (382-4357), by TDD at 202-326-2502,or by mail at Consumer Response Center, Room 130, Federal Trade Commission, 600 Pennsylvania Ave, NW, Washington, DC 20580. To find out the latest news as it is announced, call the FTC NewsPhone recording at 202-326-2710. For information about the Children's Online Privacy Protection Rule, visit the FTC online at
http://www.ftc.gov/bcp/conline/edcams/kidzprivacy/index.html.

Benefits Versus Costs: The Real Costs Surrounding the Buy Button

Electronic commerce is a term that is increasingly being applied more narrowly to the process of conducting simple transactions online. Electronic *business*, however, is the total integration of electronic processes throughout the critical functions of an enterprise. A comprehensive electronic business site should be a total solution that takes into account e-logistics, e-fulfillment, supply chain optimization, enhanced customer satisfaction, and a combination of other tangible and intangible benefits. If you are in charge of "selling" such a solution to your top management, you'll need to present a business case that includes the factors business people care about.

Buy-in is crucial for any project. One of the keys to obtaining buy-in from the top is to show that the project will pay for itself not only in dollars and/or greater operating efficiency, but also in time to market, or greater market share—things that everyone knows will add to the bottom line and increase shareholder value.

This chapter explores the tangible and intangible benefits, cost savings, and expenses of implementing an e-business site, and offers a couple of methods for calculating return on investment (ROI). This is not a substitute for employing a financial analyst to perform heavy number crunching, but it will give you some checklists to start the process. Take the suggested benefits, costs, cost savings, and other elements listed, add any factors that are important to your company, and tailor the checklists at the end of this chapter for your use. The checklists should help you organize the data you gather before handing off the numbers to a financial expert for more sophisticated analysis.

Some Basic Methods for Measuring Financial Value of the E-Business Proposal

There are several techniques for measuring the financial value of a business proposal. Among them are the Payback Period, Net Present Value (NPV), and Internal Rate of Return (IRR). The Payback Period is a measure of how much time it takes to recover your initial investment. To calculate the Payback Period, divide the initial cost of the investment by the net annual cash flows the project is expected to bring back to the business. The result is the number of years it takes to recoup your investment. This makes the assumption that benefits accrue steadily over time, so that a $100,000 investment that brings in $200,000 in the span of one year will pay back the $100,000 in half of a year ($100,000/$200,000).

The Net Present Value method compares the present value of future cash flows expected from the project to the initial cash required for the investment. To calculate NPV for a project, multiply cash flows times the present value factor that reflects the time period over which you are evaluating the project and the rate at which your company is able to borrow money (also referred to as your company's cost of capital).

The Internal Rate of Return, a more complicated method, generates the discount rate at which the NPV of a project is $0. Leave this one up to the professionals, as it requires a sophisticated calculator or complicated spreadsheets.

A method that is being pushed by some IT consultants is the Modern Portfolio Theory (MPT), which financial managers have used for years to optimize investment portfolios on a risk-and-return basis. The philosophy here is that IT investments should be treated like any other financial investment.

Another method gaining popularity is called Economic Value Added (EVA). This is defined as cash-adjusted operating profit minus the cost of capital used to produce earnings. Calculating EVA is another task to leave to professional financial analysts, although it does yield some useful information that other methods lack.

For the purposes of this chapter, the simplest NPV method is suggested. Bear in mind that this traditional evaluation method is meant to be used with tangible quantities, and therein lies one of the many barriers to determining ROI[1] in today's scenario.

---

1. Please Note: The term ROI as used in this chapter refers to financial valuation methods, not to the ROI formula. The ROI formula relates net income to invested capital (total assets). It provides a standard for evaluating how efficiently management employs the average dollar invested in a firm's assets, whether that dollar came from owners or creditors. ROI is calculated most simply by dividing net profit after taxes by total assets. More detailed versions of the ROI calculation consider asset turnover. The ROI formula is a useful management tool and may not prove as useful in evaluating the financial profitability of a pending investment.

Barriers to Measuring ROI

The best minds in the industry seem to concur on two things:
(1) that a company's real sources of value are what customers
truly care about—intangible things like better business relationships and competitive differentiation, and (2) that intangible benefits are the hardest to measure.

Although you may gain a little comfort knowing there are a
lot of frustrated IT managers who share your challenge, you
will still have to come up with some measurements that will
satisfy your CFO. One of the big tasks is to answer: "What is
this particular benefit worth to my company?" Saving ten
phone calls per day to customer service may be worth $500
per day to your company, but only $350 per day to another.
And what value would your company place on an improved
image in the marketplace? Should you compare it to the company's existing public relations efforts, or is it completely
immeasurable? Questions like these are best answered by
opening discussions with the top executives of other departments within the company. The exercise of measuring ROI then
becomes a tool for discussing the cause-and-effect relationship
between an integrated e-business site and the achievement of
strategic business goals—and a good way to build business
buy-in.

Numerous studies have shown that interactive applications,
*particularly those that streamline the supply chain through
database access and inventory management*, showed a much
higher return than applications that merely publish information. One reason for the greater ROI is because supply chain
applications integrate Web technology more tightly with core
business processes, thus yielding greater benefits. E-commerce
logistics and e-fulfillment are at the heart of these supply chain
processes and offer some of the greatest potential for a high
return on investment.

E-Business Cost Reduction Potential

AMR Research extrapolated some e-business cost reductions based on a hypothetical company, assuming a $3,000 average order and 10 line items per order (see Table 3-1).

TABLE 3-1 E-Business Cost Reduction Potential
Source: AMR Research, 1999.

Order-processing costs	30% of customers to Web. Order-processing cost reduced by $25 per order.	$1,250,000 total cost savings
Marketing materials	30% to Web. Marketing costs reduced by 0.75% of sales.	$1,125,000 total cost savings
Customer service	Elimination of 25 call center staff at 40K per year (includes variable burden).	$1,000,000 total cost savings
Order accuracy	30% to Web. 1% of line items returns reduced by 50%. Cost of returns reduced from $150 to $120.	$450,000 total cost savings ($375,000 through the elimination of returns and $75,000 from reducing the cost of processing returns)
Back-order reduction	30% to Web. 2% of items back-ordered. $100 per back-order.	$1,000,000 total cost savings
Administrative processes	30% to Web. Processes represent 1.5% of sales and are reduced by 50%.	$1,125,000 total cost savings

As you can see, there are a number of benefits that accrue from process automation via the Internet, particularly from integrating transactions with the functions involved throughout e-logistics and e-fulfillment. As you review the benefits below, note which ones are particularly important to your company. Although you will be guessing most of the time, try to answer the question, "How much is this benefit/cost savings worth to my company?" Then try to quantify it in dollars, and plug it into your worksheets.

Reduced Cycle Times

If a firm can reduce the amount of time to complete a cycle, whether the cycle is from order to delivery, order entry to receipt of cash, or from idea to commercial product, significant gains from new business will result. And new business generates additional income and cash flow. By automating supply chain processes and making them Web-enabled, it is not uncommon for many firms to see cycle improvements on the order of 40 to 50 percent.

Order-Processing Costs

Every time a piece of paper is touched, it costs an organization money. The old ways of processing an order, such as manually entering the order into an order entry system, validating and processing credit cards, looking up previous records, and so on, led to many pieces of paper being touched. This adds up to greater costs, slower order-processing times, greater inaccuracies, and more disgruntled customers.

By automating the order-processing function and integrating it within an e-business site, the customer can order products, have the credit card authorized, check product availability, and perform a whole host of other functions in real-time. This creates tremendous cost savings and in-creased customer satisfaction.

Order Accuracy

Previously mentioned was the reduction in cost of order processing, but there are also cost savings brought about by a reduction of errors through greater automation and validation at the source of order entry. To the extent that order entry screens and processes are automated and validated, errors, duplicate orders, and other costly common mistakes are avoided. Greater order accuracy has another key benefit: reduced product returns, which is discussed in greater detail in Chapter 10.

Back-Order Reduction

One of the keys to a successful business is to have the right product available at the right time. Many companies that haven't automated their inventory management processes end up with a serious amount of redundant material in their safety stock intended to combat back-order situations. Savvy e-businesses are integrating real-time inventory control with Internet communications so that personnel (and sometimes customers) can quickly check stock availability. Automated systems can provide accurate forecasts and trigger events at key transaction points (e.g., purchases, messages, invoicing).

Better Forecasting

The manufacturing and delivery processes depend heavily on knowing how much demand exists. Through integrating Internet technologies and special software, such as those available from i2 Technologies and Manugistics, firms can work with their customers to maker greater use of historical data and to link current consumption information across the supply chain. Firms are finding that by moving to a shorter planning horizon in which current pull-through consumption information, rather than speculative data, is used, forecast accuracy can be improved by as much as 80 percent.

Scalability

A key benefit of an e-business site built on open industry standards is its ability to scale to encompass additional users, applications, servers, or even entire organizations without compromising the system's usability or integrity.

Versatility

A properly implemented e-business site has the versatility to accommodate the dynamic changes in goals and objectives a growing company faces. An e-business site can be built to serve overall business activities, such as database queries, discussion groups, and basic transactions, and still have the ability to be customized for a particular business purpose or a particular user group. The versatile quality of an e-business site also allows selective implementation—for example, one enterprise may choose to implement only back-office functions, whereas another may choose to implement an entire order entry system that spans multiple countries.

Security

Granted, no system is ever 100 percent secure, but the latest advances in security technology ensure that the content and transactions of all participants across a multi-organizational e-business site are protected. How much is a framework that exceeds industry standards for security worth to your company? Perhaps one way to answer that question is to estimate how much additional business can be accomplished with a secure framework in place, or how much business your company might be losing to a competitor that has a secure e-business site.

Immediate Access to Information

An e-business site allows immediate access to information, 24 hours per day, across time zones. With an e-business site, an organization can quickly and easily establish one-to-one, one-to-many, or many-to-many communication. The savings in time and money can be enormous. For example, e-business sites eliminate the need to wait for the next business day in order to respond to a message. Instant communication via e-mail or the Web eliminates costly phone calls, faxes, travel expenses, and face-to-face meetings. Content posted on an e-business site eliminates the costly postage and printing of mass mailings, and the cost of reprinting collateral material when information is updated.

Open Architecture—No Vendor Lock-in

An e-business site based on industry standards prevents your organization from being permanently tied to one vendor, as with a proprietary solution. This freedom allows you to try new software components from a variety of vendors. There are some excellent packages available out on the Net, which are from relatively unknown vendors, yet have better features and performance than many of the packages offered by the big players. This flexibility can save your organization thousands of dollars over the life of your e-business site. With open standards, the free enterprise system causes some healthy competition among e-business site solutions vendors. Your e-business site reaps the benefits.

Rich Formats

The rich variety of file formats that are usable within an Internet-based framework allows you to offer video, audio, animation, and a rapidly growing number of other forms of communication via an e-business site. Tools for creating content are plentiful and easy to use, enabling multiple content authors to contribute to the value of the e-business site.

Continuous Quality Improvement

The Internet community is constantly developing new technologies and enhancing existing product offerings so that a means of continuous quality improvement for your organization's e-business site is always available.

Global Collaboration

The collaborative project-based approach to doing business is becoming more popular than ever. This approach makes good sense to staff projects with virtual teams that come together for the purpose of the project, and then disband upon project completion. With an e-business site, these collaborative teams can be distributed throughout the world, never meeting face to face, but sharing their expertise through cyberspace. Since geographical and time constraints are minimized with an e-business site, entire virtual corporations have been built using an e-business site as a backbone.

Management of distributed teams is especially useful in projects involving multinational commerce, subcontractor relationships, worldwide associations or task forces, specialized development projects, and other activities that require interdepartmental cooperation and contribution from a geographically dispersed community.

Collaborative discussion groups can easily be set up on an e-business site to foster responsive, ad hoc, on-topic problem solving and joint project development.

Extended Enterprise Partnerships

Another benefit of an e-business site is in the creation of extended enterprise partnerships through improved channel communications and coordination. Setting up a secure e-business site with selective access to third parties improves supplier and franchisee effectiveness and fosters better central communication of corporate objectives and best practices throughout the extended enterprise. An effective e-business site empowers all parties for dialog, information access, and knowledge sharing, enhancing decision quality, understanding, and execution of decisions.

Self-Selection of Information

An e-business site can provide two means of disseminating information—push and pull. Pushed information can be useful, if the recipient has asked for it and it is not excessive. An overload of pushed information results in a glut of irrelevant information that is stored or deleted instead of used by the recipient. Pushed information can cause resentment by the recipient, partly because there is a loss of control on the user's side. The increasing frequency of junk e-mails is an example of an unwanted overload of pushed information.

Pulled information is at the heart of an effective e-business site. Information is selected on a need-to-know, empowered basis by users, who pull what they want, when they want it. An e-business site user can then gather all the information needed to make a decision on an ad hoc basis, and control remains with the user.

Costs of Acquiring Customers vs. Retaining Them

Shorter Sales Cycles

Traditional sales activities have relied on cost-intensive and labor-intensive meetings, phone calls, business trips, and sales calls. Paperwork, fax, and phone activities have been the mainstay of every salesperson and have long been considered the required cost of building personalized sales relationships. Now, with Internet-based technologies, repetitive, costly sales tasks have been reduced enormously. Individualized relationships have not been sacrificed, however—instead they are flourishing on the e-business site, while the time and effort involved in managing the sales process have been reduced.

The entire sales cycle, from prospecting, qualification, sales close, delivery, and ongoing post-sales support, can be performed securely through an e-business site. Customer histories and other useful information can be captured simultaneously, greatly enhancing support, maintenance, and the potential for add-on business and up-sell to other products.

An important benefit is the ability to create customized, one-to-one sales experiences, without any additional labor or expense to the enterprise. Customers and partners can access online product catalogs 24 hours per day and place orders easily using online shopping carts. The customer simply clicks a Buy button next to the product, and it is deposited into a virtual "shopping cart." At the end of the shopping session, the customer proceeds to a "checkout" area and is presented with a complete invoice, including any shipping charges. If the customer has previously completed an online customer profile, the system will automatically include all address and credit card information on the final invoice, and the customer simply clicks a button to process the order and bill the appropriate credit card. Throughout the shopping session, the customer can also be electronically tracked, and information such as purchasing patterns, total time spent shopping, frequently searched items, and other data can be gathered. These data are useful for offering the customer additional product alternatives, gauging inventory and demand, and providing an electronic mailing list in order to alert customers to promotional opportunities.

An e-business site can also be set up as an electronic broker-age by offering searchable information about goods and services, reducing the costs of searching for and dealing with customers or suppliers. This self-selection approach transfers more of the selling function to the customer, making transactions timelier and more cost-efficient.

By integrating e-business sites with existing order entry systems, point of sales terminals, and delivery systems, the costs of managing the buyer and seller relationship are greatly reduced. The ability to facilitate communication and interface processes across the value chain, as well as the degree of accuracy at all stages of transactions, is enhanced. Armed with the data and the capabilities of an e-business site, a merchant can capitalize on economies of scale, level the production load across many customers, and provide better sales and service, all at a fraction of the cost of traditional commerce methods.

Every stage of the sales cycle, from prospecting to closing the deal to account management, can be supported with information and sales materials. Any of your selected third parties can be granted managed access to your e-business site, and with their Web-enabled computer, they can download competitive information, data sheets, brochures, financial information, proposal boilerplate, articles, forms, pricing information, and other data, depending on their access privileges. Sales activities and downloads can be monitored, enabling top management to tailor data availability based on need and content.

Contact management systems, e-mail gateways, pager systems, and collaborative groupware applications can be integrated into an e-business site, enabling salespeople to proceed through the sales cycle without having to wait for traditional approvals, paperwork, or confirmations. A full-featured e-business site can maintain a constant stream of contact throughout the enterprise, so that important business deals are not compromised by missed calls or other frustrations. Contact management, calendaring, and other groupware applications can track a sales prospect through the sales cycle, instantly displaying where a prospect is in each stage of the sales process. Far from being a static Web site, an expertly implemented e-business site can be a vital, active vehicle for conducting business more efficiently.

The sales arena is a dynamic one of constant pressures of quotas, cold calls, sales visits, and follow-ups. Just learning the features and benefits of a product line can be daunting to a new sales representative or distributor. An e-business site lessens the learning curve by offering computer-based training, fast information access, and the 24-hour per day ubiquity of e-mail. Each day lost to training means another day of not reaching quota and lost prospecting opportunities. An e-business site can considerably lessen this pressure by providing a self-paced set of training materials that can be accessed at any time of the day for review. Some of the most common sales processes, such as quote generation or proposal creation, can be automated with fill-in forms and preprogrammed pricing formulas.

Shorter Time to Market

It is no secret that today's business environment consists of low profit margins, extreme competition, and intense deadlines. A delay in time to market for a new product can mean a potential loss of thousands, sometimes millions, of dollars. Reducing cycle times, supply chain and sourcing optimization, and better communication are critical to a business's survival. From order management and sourcing of raw materials through delivery and installation at the customer's site, the costs across the entire supply chain are a major portion of a manufacturer's balance sheet. An e-business site can improve communication throughout the supply chain and enable faster gathering and response to feedback, adaptation, and correction during the product development, manufacturing, and assembly processes.

E-business sites can adapt to and support virtually any business model or process, because they are truly industry and product independent. Whether your enterprise is a discrete manufacturer, publisher, or services firm, an e-business site can track performance, operational efficiencies, costs, and cycle times. Results gathered from e-business sites can drive up productivity while driving down costs. All participants of an e-business site can benefit from the increased efficiencies of even one of the member firms. In fact, a well-run e-business site is synergistic in its results—all parties benefit when positive changes are implemented inter-organizationally across the e-business site.

An e-business site has the potential to give firms producing soft goods, such as publishing, information services, or software, a market in which distribution costs or cost of sales shrink to zero. Hard goods dealers may eventually eliminate costly middlemen, allowing customers to order direct from the e-business site.

An e-business site can also streamline the channel by allowing suppliers, distributors, wholesalers, and retailers to access and contact each other directly, reducing marketing costs and cumbersome communications. By implementing uniform, automated management processes across e-business site participants, overhead costs can be reduced and the overall time to conduct business can be decreased.

Another benefit of e-business sites is increased visibility into potential problems and more rapid notification and response. With the integration of enterprise resource planning tools and supply chain management software, an e-business site can alert management to costly backlogs and delays and can notify the necessary personnel across multiple organizations to rectify a problem quickly. In this way, cost savings can accrue because small problems can be recognized and dealt with before becoming major disasters. Management reports can be generated and used to make productivity improvement decisions.

The monitoring and productivity tracking capabilities of an e-business site can assist in the selection, management, and retention of the best, most effective strategic partners, vendors, and suppliers. Future business development and product planning can be guided by the cumulative results gathered across all participants in the e-business site. By fully utilizing all of the capabilities of a robust e-business site, more competitive products and services can be designed and produced, thereby capturing greater market share, brand identity, and customer loyalty.

Customer Service and Support Benefits

Customers can become partners through an e-business site. The nature of the e-business site provides an environment for building stronger customer relationships through collaborative, semi-automated or fully automated customer service and support. An e-business site can provide a self-service model where customers can buy direct, entering their own orders and tracking their own transactions. Even though thousands of customers may be accessing your e-business site at any given time, the user experience each of them has is of a one-to-one relationship with you, which builds increased mindshare and loyalty. Profiles of each customer can be kept in a database and utilized to create dynamic views into the enterprise, customized to the user's level of access and needs. By enlisting the customer as a partner in collaborative product development or in product customization, user training and support are reduced, and customer satisfaction and the potential for add-on sales is greatly increased.

Other customer support functions, such as help desk, e-mail, voice mail, and order status and tracking, can also be greatly facilitated with an e-business site solution. At a fraction of the cost of traditional measures, a customer can be provided with their own private, customized workspace that can be automatically updated with information, such as online newsletters, tips for product effectiveness, promotional campaigns, customer surveys, and other client-oriented content.

Integration of back-office operations, such as call/issue logging, reporting, and analysis to evaluate employee effectiveness, can be achieved, giving customers a seamless interface with your enterprise. Customers can also play an active role in the quality of their own support through feedback mechanisms to report problems or questions to a customer support representative. These requests can automatically be forwarded to a corresponding Web-based conference, e-mail, or pager, and then be managed through the e-business site to resolution. If a customer requires a phone call or on-site visitation, the customer can simply fill out a form online, which is then automatically forwarded to the appropriate staff member for assignment and follow-up. Many enterprises implement the customer service function of an e-business site first—the results can be measured, and customer service is usually an area that experiences a great deal of pain, which can be quickly alleviated through an e-business site.

Reduced Need for Training

Since an e-business site employs a standard user interface—a Web browser—customer training is significantly simplified. Users have an immediate sense of familiarity, and network downloadable applets boost productivity immediately. Standard industry tools and software have further eased the training burden. Content has shifted from arcane, engineering-driven code to self-development of business content on standard, easy-to-apply platforms.

Better Learning and Knowledge Management

The self-service model of the e-business site applies to training as well. An e-business site provides a Just-in-Time training model that presents information on demand. Coursework can be completed at the learner's pace, within the learner's schedule. Online feedback and testing mechanisms can be built in so that a learner's competency can be tested, scored, and the results sent to management. Feedback also helps to continuously improve the quality of training materials and processes.

Cost Savings

Most of the benefits mentioned above also have some healthy cost savings built in; however, there are some additional cost savings produced by an e-business site that you can add to your ROI worksheets.

Reductions in Cost of Supply and Cost of Sales

Meeting, Travel, and Telephone Time Reduction

When labor, travel, and overhead are factored in, industry analysts figure the average sales call costs a firm in excess of $200. When you count up all of the salaries and other factors, a face-to-face business meeting can cost hundreds of dollars. Even the average phone call to the sales or support department ranges from $35 to $50. An e-business site reduces or even eliminates those costs, because it eliminates travel, phone tag, schedule conflicts, and most small talk. Participants in online interactive communications are generally more focused and productive, and since entire conversations can be captured, the "he said, she said" guessing about prior comments is minimized.

81

Printed Communications Cost Savings

An e-business site provides powerful information access tools that are instantly available on demand. Virtually anything that is now developed, printed, and mailed can be converted into electronic form and posted on an e-business site. This creates enormous cost savings by eliminating the printing, binding, and mailing of manuals, catalogs, brochures, technical documentation, press releases, advertisements, product specifications, and all other forms of written or graphic communications. For example, an employee manual must be written, duplicated, collated, put into three-ring binders, mailed or handed out to every employee, and then constantly updated. By putting all of that material on an e-business site, printing and assembly labor and costs are eliminated, postage is eliminated, and updates are done only once on the e-business site, ensuring that all employees see the latest version.

Strategic Alliances, Co-op Marketing, and Economies of Scale

The synergism that an e-business site can create among participants can produce economies of scale across all of the member organizations. Joint participation in activities such as buying materials and supplies, producing promotional campaigns, and sharing information can result in impressive hard and soft savings. Team selling through strategic alliances, and cooperative marketing with manufacturers can also contribute to cost savings. Most manufacturers will provide co-op marketing funding based on a percentage of the gross sales your company brings to them. These funds can generally be used for promotion or advertising. By applying the funds to building and maintaining an e-business site, the funds will be wisely used, and some of your e-business site-related costs will be offset.

Customer Retention

Everyone agrees that the time, effort, and cost of gaining a new customer far outweighs that of retaining an existing customer. If an e-business site can be strongly traced to retaining a number of customers, then the company has saved the costs of replacing those customers or "rescuing them" before they leave.

Costs of an E-Business Site

Designing, building and maintaining an e-business site involves both tangible (hard) costs and intangible (soft) costs. Sometimes these costs are easy to define and map to the e-business site project, but many times costs can be shared across projects and departments, making cost allocation difficult at best. Here are three ways to classify and allocate e-business site costs.

1. **Infrastructure Costs.** These are costs associated with doing business and include items directly related to the overall strategy of the company. Examples include telecommunications lines and equipment, office supplies and furniture—items that are part of the company's overhead budget. Has your company already built an intranet? If so, you can leverage that existing investment for the e-business site, basically eliminating many e-business site infrastructure costs.

2. **Direct Project Costs.** These are costs that you can map, dollar for dollar, directly to your e-business site project. You weigh these at a full 100 percent in your ROI scenario.

3. **Distributed Costs.** These are costs that can be spread across multiple projects or departments. The task here is to find which project or department will "own" most of the cost associated with a particular component of the e-business site. Sometimes Marketing will own all of the user interface and graphic design, Management Information Systems (MIS) will own the equipment and software, Sales will own some of the databases, and Accounting will own parts of the order entry system. The best approach is to split the costs and allocate a percentage of each to the appropriate project.

Hard Costs

Hard costs include tangible goods such as hardware, wiring, software, telecommunications lines, and the like. These are costs that, for the most part, should be fairly easy to quantify and allocate. Use the guidelines above to help allocate these costs.

Soft Costs

Soft costs include labor, training, loss of sales opportunities—intangible factors that are sometimes very difficult to quantify and even harder to allocate. Sometimes factors such as timing, seasons, prior training, and other issues can affect these cost figures.

Choosing a Project to Demonstrate ROI

As was mentioned in the beginning of this chapter, executive buy-in is best accomplished by demonstrating ROI through building a small "pain-relieving" e-business site scenario. To build your case *prior* to buy-in, it is smart to design a management presentation that directly addresses an area of pain in the enterprise. Most companies choose a problem that is high potential/low cost. Customer service is a good area to target, because chances are there are a few problems that are causing immediate pain. If you can demonstrate how an e-business site will save your company, say 50 customer service calls per day, and the average service call costs the company $50, then you can show an immediate cost savings of $2,500 per day—and that doesn't factor in the intangible benefit of increased customer satisfaction. If you can also demonstrate some Web pages that tie into your existing order entry system, you're probably well on your way to justifying an e-business site, even in the most hardened organization.

Sample ROI Calculation Worksheets

Here are some sample worksheets to help you estimate and allocate costs, savings, and revenues generated by an e-business site. These are rough guidelines only—take the worksheets and customize them to your business and your CFO's thought processes. As you implement your ROI demo scenario, you can use these worksheets to help top management see the big picture, and you can also fine-tune the figures with some preliminary data. Later on, when you are building the prototype, use these figures and compare them to actual costs that are incurred during the prototype phase. Then you can extrapolate some meaningful figures for the entire e-business site project.

As you are filling out these checklists, ask yourself these basic questions.

- What corporate objective/area of pain will this address?
- Has the company already invested in this item?
- If it exists, can I leverage it for the e-business site?
- Is this a one-time or recurring cost, savings, or source of revenue?
- What department in the company, or strategic partner outside the company, should "own" this?

When you've finished filling out the worksheets, simply add the total savings to the total revenues, and then subtract the total costs. This will give you an extremely rough idea of the Net Present Value, or profit, of the project. Then, convert the NPV to a percentage of the total costs, and you will come up with the ROI for the e-business site. Again, please realize this does not substitute for a formal financial analysis, but you should have enough ammunition for your ROI project presentation. You will continue to refine these figures throughout the life cycle of the e-business site, as you receive hard data over time.

How to Use the Worksheets

Take the sample NPV worksheet in Figure 3-1 and insert the line items that are the most relevant to your business from each category listed below. Under Revenues/Savings, for example, there is a list of descriptions (e.g., sales literature, product sales, etc.) that represent various areas of potential cost savings or revenue generation activities. The same is true under the heading of Costs. List the appropriate figures under each worksheet column heading next to its corresponding line item, and then make the final calculations.

For your convenience, you can find the worksheets in electronic form (Microsoft Excel format) at my Web site, *http://www.bayles.com*. Many thanks go to Julie Hoffman Walsh, CPA, for creating the Excel template and providing valuable expertise and insight throughout this chapter.

Revenues/Savings

E-Business Site Savings
Printing and Production Savings
❐ Sales literature
❐ Employee manuals
❐ Product catalog
❐ Direct mail
❐ Price lists
❐ Reference manuals
❐ Shipping documentation
❐ Financial documents
❐ Press releases
❐ Other literature
Transmission and Transport Savings
❐ Postage
❐ Telephone

Initial Investment Required ($)	$
Discount Rate Selected (%)	$
Number of months in NPV analysis	
NPV factor	
Company's Cost of Capital (%)	$

E-Business Cost/Revenue Description	Column A 100% of E-business Cost/Revenue	Column B % allocated to e-business site	Column C Amount ($) allocated to e-business site (col A x col B)	Column D One-time revenue? (Yes/No)	Column E Recurring? (Yes/No)	Column F Price/unit	Column G Anticipated Demand	Column H Total Revenue/ Savings or (Costs) for 12 months	Column I Projected One-time Revenues/ (Costs)	Column J Projected Recurring Revenues/ (Costs)	Column K Total
											$-
Revenues/Savings:											
Sales Literature											
Employee Manuals											
Product Catalog											
…											
Revenue/Savings Subtotal											
Present Value factor											
Present Value of expected Revenues/Savings											
Costs:											
Hardware…											
Software…											
Internet connection…											
…											
Cost Subtotal											
Present Value factor											
Present Value of expected Costs											
Net Present Value											
If NPV is positive, proposal is expected to generate net revenues											
If NPV is negative, proposal is expected to generate net costs											

FIGURE 3–1   Net Present Value Worksheet
Source: Julie Hoffman Walsh, CPA

☐ Fax
☐ Shipping
☐ Other savings

Travel and Meeting Savings

☐ Business travel, hotel, and airfare
☐ Sales meetings
☐ Partner meetings
☐ Sales calls
☐ Service calls

Time Savings

☐ Management time
☐ Sales rep time
☐ Service time
☐ Support time
☐ Other time savings

Resource Savings

☐ Equipment savings
☐ Research and development
☐ Other resource savings

E-Business Site Revenues

Electronic Commerce

☐ Product sales
☐ Subscription sales
☐ Services sales
☐ Profit from selling partner's products
☐ Other electronic commerce revenues

Advertising

☐ Advertising sponsorships
☐ Affiliate programs
☐ Other advertising revenues

Support Sales

☐ Per incident support services

❏ Support contracts
❏ Software upgrade subscriptions
❏ Other revenues

Costs

E-Business Costs

Hardware

❏ Servers
❏ Routers
❏ Workstations
❏ Hubs
❏ Digital camera
❏ Bar code equipment
❏ Other hardware

Software

❏ Server software
❏ Client software
❏ Database software
❏ Firewall software
❏ Version control tools
❏ Content development tools
❏ E-commerce software
❏ E-mail software
❏ Telecommunications software
❏ Accounting software
❏ ERP software
❏ Warehouse Management System
❏ Other software

Internet Connection

❏ Telecom line installation
❏ Telecom line monthly circuit usage
❏ Internet access installation

❏ Internet access monthly charges

❏ Other costs

Server/Site Hosting

❏ Server colocation/site hosting

❏ Site/server maintenance

Security

❏ Firewall machine

❏ Security audit

❏ RSA certificates

❏ Routers

❏ Site Security Officer (SSO) salary

❏ Other security and staffing costs

Development

❏ Graphic design and user interfaces

❏ Site analysis and design consulting

❏ Basic content coding

❏ Special applications

❏ Database integration

❏ Legacy integration

❏ Other development costs

Training

❏ Partner training

❏ Employee training

❏ Design of training courses

❏ Ongoing training

❏ Other training costs

Maintenance

❏ Server backup labor

❏ Server backup tapes/equipment

❏ Hardware servicing

❏ Software upgrades

❏ Other maintenance

Customer Service
- ❒ Call center design and consulting
- ❒ Call center implementation
- ❒ Call center system
- ❒ Call center salaries
- ❒ Toll-free phone lines
- ❒ Other costs

Management
- ❒ Project management
- ❒ Outside consulting
- ❒ Webmaster
- ❒ Other management costs

Electronic Commerce
- ❒ Merchant account setup
- ❒ Transaction fees
- ❒ Product catalog setup
- ❒ Systems integration
- ❒ Other electronic commerce costs

Product Fulfillment Costs

Warehousing

Distribution

Transportation

Taxes
- ❒ Depreciation
- ❒ Sales taxes
- ❒ Other taxes

Resources

Books

Poirier, Charles C. *Advanced Supply Chain Management: How to Build a Sustained Competitive Advantage.* San Francisco: Berrett-Koehler Publishers, Inc., 1999.

Tompkins, James A. and Jerry D. Smith. *The Warehouse Management Handbook.* 2d ed. Raleigh, NC: Tompkins Press, 1998.

Businesses

I2 Technologies
http://www.i2.com

Manugistics
http://www.manugistics.com

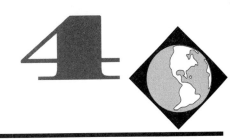

PAYMENT PROCESSING, FRAUD, AND OTHER TAXING ISSUES

What happens during the first fifteen seconds after the customer clicks on the Buy button can spell success or disaster for the online merchant. During this time, the customer's credit card information will go through eight or more validation and authorization processes and be transmitted back and forth among at least four different entities scattered throughout the world. Things can break down at any point in the process, creating not only customer dissatisfaction, but also legal liability for the merchant.

This chapter will cover the major aspects of credit card processing, Internet fraud risk management, and the quandary of Internet taxation.

Who's Who and What They Do in Credit Card Processing

In order to understand what goes on behind the scenes, let's walk through a simple credit card transaction. First, it's helpful to become familiar with who's who and the roles they play in credit card processing. You may think that the use of credit cards is confined to consumers, but corporate credit cards are on the rise. Most often, however, business-to-business (B2B) sites will spend a good deal of time setting up corporate accounts offline with individual business customers. Then, when credit terms have been set up, the corporate client will receive an authorized logon and password to be able to conduct business. This creates less opportunity for fraud and chargebacks—one of the advantages of B2B e-commerce.

Returning to the functions behind online credit card processing, there are several entities that play important roles.

- **Cardholder**: the individual or entity that uses a credit card to purchase goods or services from an online (or offline) store

- **Issuing bank**: the financial institution that issues a credit card to the cardholder. The issuing bank (also called the cardholder's bank) establishes and verifies the cardholder's credit line, provides the cardholder with monthly billing statements, and so on. American Express (Amex) and Discover issue their own cards, acting in a similar fashion to issuing banks. Interestingly, Amex and Discover also sign up merchants to accept their own cards, mimicking acquiring banks.

- **Card association**: an association such as Visa International or MasterCard International. The card association provides credit cards and other products for banks, who in turn privately brand the products, issue the cards to cardholders, and often set up programs for merchants to accept the cards. Card associations play a significant role in processing transactions by operating and managing worldwide authorization and settlement systems.

- **Card issuer**: an organization such as American Express or Discover, which (unlike a card association) offers credit cards directly to consumers and merchants.
- **Merchant**: the entity that is selling goods and services in exchange for payment. Goods can be either hard goods (tangibles), such as apparel and computer hardware, or soft goods (intangibles), such as service contracts or pay-per-view content.
- **Payment application**: the application used by the merchant to request credit card authorization and settlement of funds between the merchant and the acquiring bank. The application can be a self-managed application or an outsourced service.
- **Acquiring bank**: often referred to as the merchant bank or acquirer, the financial institution that enables merchants to accept credit card payments. The acquiring bank often works with a third-party processor to accept or decline the cardholder's credit card purchase request, deposits funds into the merchant's bank account, provides the merchant with periodic deposit statements, and so on. Acquirers are so named because they acquire a merchant's sales tickets and credit the order value to the merchant's account.
- **Third-party processor**: also known as payment processing networks, front-end processors, or just processors, the organization that works with an acquiring bank (merchant bank) to process credit card transactions via the card associations or card issuers. The third-party processor communicates to the card associations or card issuers to obtain authorizations and execute funds transfers. In some cases, the acquiring bank and the third-party processor may be the same entity.
- **Independent sales organization (ISO)**: an independent agent that solicits prospective merchants for merchant banks, ISOs are also referred to as merchant account providers. ISOs assist merchants in setting up merchant

accounts and ensuring that the accounts connect to third-party processors. ISOs may either assume partial or shared financial liability for merchant activity.

Anatomy of a Transaction

Now that you've been introduced to some of the players and functions involved in online credit card processing, let's walk through a simple transaction. Refer to Figure 4-1 throughout the following steps. Note: the example provides a generic overview of how credit cards are processed in the U.S.; the process varies by bank, card association, card issuer, and geographic location.

Maynard Jones has been making surf sandals since his hippie days in the 1960s, and has turned what was once a hobby into a booming beachwear enterprise with a storefront in Dana Point, California. After looking at the price of land, Maynard decided to build an online store rather than face the expense of brick-and-mortar expansion.

Being a hip kind of guy, Maynard knew that he wanted to use real-time (rather than batch) processing to process the credit card transactions from his store. Real-time processing enables Maynard to automate the work he would have to do to process transactions, gives him real-time fraud protection, and helps to minimize the data-entry errors that would occur if he had to reenter transactions manually.

The first thing Maynard did was find an ISO to help him set up an Internet merchant account. Even though he has an existing merchant bank for credit card transactions at his store, that account did not allow him to accept credit card payments from the Internet. The ISO set Maynard up with one of the many merchant banks (e.g., Humboldt Bank, National Bank of the Redwoods) and made sure the merchant account would connect to a major payment processing network, such as First Data Merchant Services (FDMS) in Nashville, Nova, Paymentech, or Vital.

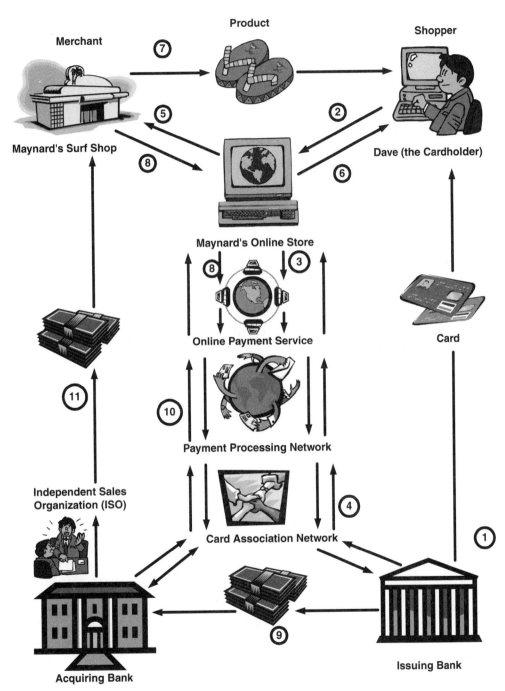

FIGURE 4–1   Anatomy of a Transaction

Maynard's Web site launch is a success. One of the first shoppers to come onto Maynard's site to buy a pair of surf sandals is Dave, who has always wanted sandals with tire treads on the soles.

1. **Card issued**. Dave has a Citibank MasterCard with a $5,000 credit limit. His available balance on the card is $1,000.

2. **Buy button.** Using a Web browser such as Netscape Navigator or Microsoft Internet Explorer (which supports Secure Sockets Layer (SSL)), Dave peruses Maynard's online catalog of sandals and selects a cool pair to add to his online shopping cart. Dave then proceeds to the checkout page and enters his Citibank MasterCard credit card information, expiration date, and billing address. He also selects the method of shipping. He lives outside California, so sales tax is not applicable (could be subject to change with legislation). With shipping, his order total is $50. He clicks on the Buy button to initiate the transaction.

   Behind the scenes, the information is transmitted to Maynard, who has set up an outsourced payment service, in this case, CyberSource. CyberSource receives the information from Maynard's secure commerce server, performs a fraud check on Dave's purchase information, and then initiates the process of communicating the billing information and purchase amount to the third-party processor.

3. **Authorization request**. CyberSource encrypts the purchase information and transmits it to the third-party processor, in this case FDMS-Nashville. FDMS receives the information and forwards it to the card association or card issuer.

4. **Authorization response**. In a matter of seconds, the issuing financial institution (in this case, Citibank, who issued Dave his MasterCard) verifies the credit card information and determines whether Dave has sufficient credit available to pay for the purchase. An authorization number is

generated and Dave's available credit (often referred to as *open to buy*) is reduced by the authorized amount (in this case, $50). If Dave's credit card information is not correct, or if Dave does not have available credit, then a message declining the transaction is generated.

In the same short span of time, Citibank also performs other operations, such as address verification service (AVS), whereby the billing information Dave entered online (specifically, the first three digits of Dave's mailing address and zip code) is compared to Dave's billing information stored in Citibank's database. An authorization message is returned to the card association and forwarded to the third-party processor.

5. **Merchant notification**. FDMS, the third-party processor in this example, receives the authorization message and other pertinent information from the card association or issuer and initiates the process of communicating the authorization message to Maynard, the merchant.

   The third-party processor uses CyberSource to encrypt the authorization message and transmits the encrypted information to Maynard's secure commerce server.

6. **Shopper notification**. Maynard's server receives the information and is programmed to immediately send a purchase approval or decline message to the cardholder, as well as other pertinent information (e.g., if the credit card was declined, a suggestion to check the accuracy of the billing information provided or to use a different credit card). Dave, who is still poised in front of his computer screen, receives the message that his purchase was approved, and is given an order confirmation number, which he prints out.

7. **Fulfillment**. It takes around ten seconds end-to-end from the moment Dave clicks on the Buy button until Maynard and Dave receive the authorization message. The authori-

zation process usually takes 10 to 30 seconds, depending on the merchant's payment application and procedures, Internet traffic, and other factors.

In the event of a successful authorization, the merchant begins the process of fulfilling the cardholder's order with the appropriate product or service. The authorization is a conditional pledge by the issuing bank, affirming the cardholder's ability to pay for the product or service (i.e., the account has adequate funds or has not been reported lost or stolen). Depending on rules and regulations of the respective bankcard association or card issuer, the authorization is usually valid for several days. If an order is fulfilled after the authorization expires, the merchant may have to request an additional authorization request and/or may not be able to obtain a settlement of that transaction.

As Dave's transaction is successfully authorized, Maynard proceeds to fulfill Dave's order and ship it out. Maynard, although hip, hasn't tackled the e-commerce fulfillment process, so he is still manually reentering information into his order entry and inventory systems and doing his own picking, packing, and shipping. Let's hope that Maynard's order volume doesn't suddenly overwhelm him—or that he buys this book and sees that there are better ways to do this!

8. **Settlement request.** Maynard compiles a batch of orders that have been fulfilled and begins the process of transmitting the batch to the third-party processor for settlement. Maynard performs this operation at regularly scheduled intervals. Maynard first transmits the batch to CyberSource.

Maynard's payment service, CyberSource, encrypts the purchase information and transmits the encrypted information to the third-party processor. The third-party processor receives this information and sends settlement instructions to the appropriate financial institution (via the card associations, as in the case of MasterCard or Visa).

In this case, CyberSource relays the settlement request to FDMS-Nashville, which instructs Citibank and Maynard's merchant bank to transfer the ticket amount from Dave's MasterCard account to Maynard's merchant account.

9. **Settlement.** For each credit card transaction in the batch, the appropriate financial institution is debited and the cardholder's credit card statement is updated.

   The acquiring bank receives the funds and makes a deposit into the merchant's bank account; $50 is subtracted from Dave's account and added to Maynard's account. The first week of the following month, Maynard's merchant bank subtracts $1.57 (2.44% plus $0.35 per transaction) from Maynard's account to pay itself and Maynard's ISO for establishing and maintaining the merchant account. Maynard's net is $48.43 on the transaction.

10. **Settlement response**. Maynard receives notification that funds have been deposited into his bank account. On a periodic basis, Maynard receives reports that can be used to reconcile batch settlement requests with his deposit activity.

11. **Funds available**. The interval between the merchant's issuance of a settlement request, transfer of funds, and funds availability can take up to several days, depending on the issuing bank, the acquiring bank, and the third-party processor. The settlement cycle time is affected by the acquiring bank's holding period on deposits, as well as other procedures and policies established by the acquiring banks and third-party processors.

The example above was a simple and generic online transaction processing, authorization, and settlement illustration. Many more potential steps and functions can enter into the picture.

The next section addresses some of the unique challenges Internet merchants face and includes some recommendations.

The Unique Challenges of Internet Merchants

The many unique benefits of shopping online (speed, convenience, privacy, relative anonymity) have created some unique challenges (Internet fraud, increased chargebacks and product returns, etc.). Because the Internet merchant deals with the shopper sight unseen, bankcard associations classify sales of goods and services over the Internet as *card not present* or *mail order/telephone order* (MOTO) transactions. There isn't a special classification yet just for Internet sales, so all of the policies of MOTO merchant accounts apply. The requirements for record keeping and the steps to avoid chargebacks are especially stringent, and the issues of merchant liability and risk management become paramount.

Recommendation 1: Employ a fraud screening system

Most people think that buyers are most in danger of being defrauded. The truth is that merchants are more often the targets of fraud. In most cases, the buyer is held liable only for the first $50 of credit card charges if the shopper's card is reported lost or stolen. On the merchant's side (in a card not present transaction), however, if the purchase was made using a stolen or fraudulently obtained credit card, the transaction is voided (a *chargeback*) and the merchant must issue a refund to the legitimate cardholder. *Even if the merchant obtained an authorization* (and a positive AVS message for U.S. cardholders), the merchant is still 100 percent responsible for refunding the amount of the chargeback.

This means a couple of things. First, AVS is only partially successful at fraud checking, and second, the only way merchants can potentially avoid chargebacks is to implement their own measures to deny fraudulent purchases up front. Several payment services offer fraud checking in addition to their other offerings.

For example, CyberSource Corporation is a payment service that has been addressing fraud risk management since the beginning of Internet sales transactions. Their Internet Fraud

Code Title	Code	Description
Fraud List Flag	F	a previous merchant has incurred a chargeback with no return of product
Velocity	V	this card has been used more than "X" times in the last "Y" minutes
Nonsensical Input (gibberish)	N	the customer input contains highly unbelievable data in the customer name and address fields
Geo-location Inconsistency	G	the correlation between the customer's phone number, billing address, shipping address and other factors has been determined to be suspicious
Internet Inconsistency	I	the correlation between the customer's e-mail or IP address (and possibly other factors) and stated billing address is suspicious
Obscenities	O	the customer input obscene words in the order form
Name Change	H	the customer using this card has 2 or more name changes in the last (timeframe)
High Count of Unique Credit Cards	C	the customer has used more than "X" credit cards in the last (timeframe)
Excessive Address Change	A	the customer has 2 or more billing address changes in the last (timeframe)
Product Category Frequency (Longterm Violation)	L	the customer is attempting to purchase a particular product more frequently than the merchant desires/would normally expect
Time		displays 00:00 format; the order time in the customer's local time
Host Severity		numeric 0-5 format; the risk associated with the customer's e-mail domain

FIGURE 4–2 Risk Profile Codes
Source: CyberSource

Screen (IFS) service runs a shopper's payment information through a series of tests to generate an overall IFS score. Risk Profile Codes are associated with 10 categories of tests that are included in the scoring process, as well as information regarding the customer's local time and risk associated with the customer's e-mail host. The Risk Profile Codes are shown in Figure 4-2. Merchants can set the threshold for how much risk they want to assume based on the IFS score.

Recommendation 2: Use online real-time authorization

Before the advent of real-time authorization, all credit card authorizations were conducted offline. The merchant captured and stored the customer's purchase information (think of the legal liability of storing that kind of sensitive data!). Sometime later, the merchant obtained authorization via voice, email, or a payment application. If the merchant received a declined authorization message, the merchant contacted the customer after the sale. Conventional industry wisdom suggests that 3 percent to 5 percent of authorization requests are declined, so those merchants using offline methods had to contact each and every one of those customers to pursue authorization or inform the customers of the merchant's decision to decline the order. Imagine the administrative headaches, the painful phone calls, and the poor customer experiences. Strangely, many so-called e-commerce providers today simply offer a crude electronic shopping cart that is attached to the merchant's Web site, without any kind of real-time authorization. The merchant is merely sent an email of all captured orders and forced to handle the authorizations offline.

With real-time processing, the customer clicks on the Buy button and the authorization status is provided to both the merchant and customer within seconds. The customer can receive immediate purchase confirmation, and in the event of a decline, the customer is immediately notified and is provided a choice of solutions (e.g., double check the accuracy of the information provided, use another credit card, call customer service, etc.). Make sure to find an e-commerce service provider that offers real-time authorization—the extra costs are well worth it.

Recommendation 3: Integrate credit card processing with your other back-office applications

Credit card processing is just one of several critical back-office applications. Your online business will be successful to the extent that you can integrate the payment application with your other back-office applications. Some payment applications easily integrate with other back-office applications, while others require middleware and/or extensive programming. In addition, some systems execute the applications in parallel, while other systems do not. If a system cannot execute these procedures concurrently, then transaction processing time is significantly increased—increasing the chances that more online shoppers will abandon the purchase process.

Unless you have an IT staff to dedicate to systems integration, you may want to consider an outsourced payment service to perform the other aspects of executing a transaction, such as

- **Fraud risk management**: the ability to assess the likelihood of a fraudulent transaction by analyzing several aspects of the cardholder's identity and the nature of the purchase.

- **Tax calculation**: calculating state, county, and city taxes, as well as Value Added Tax (VAT) for international transactions. With 7,600 taxing jurisdictions just in the United States, make sure you employ a tax information service or software solution, such as Vertex or Taxware, to keep abreast of the constantly changing tax tables.

- **Shipping and handling**: calculating the shipping cost of a given physical product, as well as providing customers with different shipping options (next day air, ground, etc.). Online shipping tools are described in Chapter 6.

- **Delivery address verification**: checking the accuracy of a shipping address or a logistically unacceptable address, such as a post office box. UPS and USPS offer online tools to perform these functions.

- **Export control and distribution restrictions**: depending on the distribution agreement with their vendors, resellers and other types of distributors may be allowed to sell only within a certain geographic territory. In other cases, merchants are banned by the U.S. from selling to certain countries and other entities. Export control is discussed in Chapter 8.

- **Physical product fulfillment**: notifying an organization's warehouse or a contracted fulfillment center to ship a product to a customer, in addition to tracking an order's fulfillment status. Fulfillment messaging becomes critical with outsourced fulfillment centers. In addition, since a merchant can't charge a buyer's credit card until after the order is shipped, it is imperative to have rapid shipment notifications.

- **Digital product fulfillment**: using a digital distribution system to download software, video, music, graphics, and other digital content to customers, as well as the ability to track download status.
- **Loyalty programs**: capturing purchase information in order to credit a customer's frequent flier account, rebate program, and other online incentive programs.

Recommendation 4: Make sure you have detailed credit card processing reports

With the high probability of chargeback disputes, attempted fraud, and product returns, an online merchant needs to have a payment solution that tracks every step of the settlement process and provides this information in a manner that can be rapidly retrieved and analyzed.

It makes good sense to have a system that rapidly generates a wide variety of reports. If a customer calls with an inquiry, a detailed credit card processing report enables the merchant's customer service staff to provide accurate information in a timely manner. In addition, it's much easier for a merchant to reconcile transaction activity reports—in particular, to reconcile their settlement requests with bank statements to ensure proper transfer of funds. Detailed reports are also mandatory for dealing with foreign banks. Once again, you can either integrate an existing payment application or contract an outside service to track the settlement process and generate the reports.

Serious Stuff

The topic of chargebacks was mentioned earlier, and this is a very serious problem for online merchants. Before we get into the next section, which covers Internet fraud, you should be aware of the strict conditions that merchant banks and payment processors impose on the merchant in order to minimize chargebacks from their end. Paymentech, one of the world's largest payment processors, has published a guide, shown in

Figure 4-3, for mail order/telephone order/Internet (MOTO) merchants.

Be sure to note the huge amount of responsibility that rests solely with the merchant. Because tax and shipping calculations, fraud checking, export control, and many other tasks are the merchant's responsibility, it makes extremely good sense to outsource those functions to a firm that specializes in electronic commerce services.

Paymentech's Operating Guide for Mail Order/Telephone Order/Internet Transactions

1. COMPLETION OF SALE

1.1 You must submit one Sales Data record for all goods and services sold in the same transaction. The collection and payment of all federal, state and local taxes is your responsibility. Taxes collected shall be included in the total transaction amount and not collected separately by another form of payment.

1.2 All available information about the sale, including handling and shipping charges, must be accurately recorded. You are responsible for determining that the purchaser is the person whose name appears as the Cardholder. If an account number is transposed into an invalid or inappropriate account number, the sale will result in a chargeback.

1.3 You will provide to the customer a true and completed record of the sale.

2. AUTHORIZATION/APPROVAL CODES

2.1 All sales shall require authorization. You shall request authorization for the total amount of the transaction.

2.2 An authorization/approval code indicates the availability of credit on the Card at the time of inquiry. It is not a promise or a guarantee that you will receive payment for the related transaction. It does not warrant that the person presenting the card is the rightful Cardholder.

3. REFUNDS AND EXCHANGES (CREDITS)

3.1 You shall prepare a credit Sales Data record for the total amount of the refund, including any shipping and handling charges being refunded. You shall record the credit with the same Card used to make the original purchase.

3.2 Paperwork is not necessary for an even exchange. For an uneven exchange, prepare a credit Sales Data for the total amount of the merchandise being returned and prepare a new sale for any new merchandise purchased.

FIGURE 4–3   *Operating Guide for Mail Order/Telephone Order/Internet Transactions*
Source: Paymentech

3.3 You may limit your acceptance of returned merchandise or establish a policy to make price adjustments for any transactions. If your refund policy prohibits returns under certain circumstances, you may still receive a chargeback relating to such sales pursuant to the Association rules and regulations.

3.4 You shall not process a credit without having completed a previous purchase transaction with the same Cardholder.

4. PRESENTATION OF SALES SLIPS AND CREDIT VOUCHERS

4.1 You must submit Sales Data to us on or before the next business day after the date of the transaction. Late submission may result in higher Association fees and/or a chargeback to you.

4.2 You must not submit sales slips for payment until the goods are delivered, shipped, or the services are performed (except as otherwise provided in the Merchant Agreement). If the Cardholder disputes being charged for merchandise or services before receiving them, the result will be a chargeback to you. We may from time to time contact customers to verify that they have received goods or services for which Sales Data has been submitted.

4.3 You shall not present for processing any transaction which was not originated as a result of an act directly between the Cardholder and you. You shall not present for processing any transaction you know or should have known to be (i) fraudulent or (ii) not authorized by the Cardholder. You shall be responsible for the actions of your employees.

5. CHARGEBACKS

The term "Chargeback" refers to the debiting of your Account or withholding of settlement funds for all or part of the amount of a particular sale as permitted by the Merchant Agreement. There may be a chargeback for the following reasons or as the Association rules and operational requirements dictate from time to time. Additions and/or deletions to this list may occur.

- Cardholder account number is incorrect or otherwise invalid

- Sale was not authorized or other required authorization was not obtained

- Sale was authorized but not for exact amount or wrong transaction date

- Cardholder never received merchandise/service requested or merchandise/service was not as represented by Merchant

- Cardholder's credit was processed as a sale

- Cardholder was charged incorrectly

- Cardholder was never credited for returned merchandise or a canceled order

FIGURE 4–3 Continued

- Card was expired, counterfeit, altered, or invalid at time of sale
- Cardholder's sales slip was deposited more than once
- Cardholder did not authorize or consent to the transaction
- Authorization code is invalid
- A Cardholder asserts any disputes, claim, counterclaim, defense or offset against you
- Sales Data is incomplete, inaccurate, or is not delivered to us within the required time limits
- Sales Data is fraudulent or does not represent a bona fide transaction in the ordinary course of your business, or is subject to any claim of illegality, negligence, dishonesty or offset
- You have failed to provide copies of sales drafts requested by us (retrieval request) within the prescribed time period
- Suspicious transaction or fraudulent transaction

6. DISPUTING CHARGEBACKS

If you have reason to dispute or respond to a chargeback, then you must do so by the date provided by us on our report to you. We are not required to investigate, reverse or make any adjustment to any chargeback when thirty (30) calendar days have elapsed from the date of the chargeback. All responses to chargebacks must be in writing, and must contain the following information:

- Date of Debit/Credit advice
- Company case number
- Total amount of chargeback
- Date and dollar amount in which the sale/credit was originally submitted
- If known, the date and authorization approval code
- Any supporting documentation to substantiate claim. You should include a dated cover letter detailing reasons for requesting a review of the chargeback. You should retain a copy of the correspondence and all documentation for files. You should retain proof that we received your response.

FIGURE 4–3 Continued

Internet Fraud

In the physical retail world, several built-in measures help deter theft. There is the face-to-face contact with the customer and the physical presence of the credit card. Embedded holograms, fine line printing, codes on the magnetic stripe, signature comparisons, and on-card photos help to effectively manage fraud and verify a card user's identity.

Purchases made through the telephone also have a degree of human interaction, which, although more anonymous than traditional retail, still acts as a deterrent. MOTO businesses use the AVS, train operators to detect "questionable" purchases, and use technology able to match the incoming phone number with the address and card number to validate identity.

Although merchant banks classify Internet merchants as MOTO businesses, there are significant differences between the two.

On the Internet, fraud can be executed in ways and at speeds not possible in the traditional retail or MOTO merchant world. The transaction is completely anonymous, requires no human interaction, and offers few apparent ways to verify purchaser identity (since email addresses can be anonymously obtained). Fraud attempts can be initiated simultaneously across several sites or in rapid succession at a single site.

The four most common methods used to commit fraud against Internet merchants are

- *Stolen Cards.* The card itself is stolen and used before the owner detects it missing; while traditional, this method is used less often than others to commit fraud on the Internet.

- *Identity Fraud.* The card itself is not stolen; thieves assume the identity of a cardholder, using information gained from credit card receipts, and email or phone scams prompting cardholders to voluntarily provide personal and bankcard information. Thieves use the advantage of anonymity on the Internet to commit fraud.

- *Card Generators*. Fraudulent credit card numbers are generated using software programs.
- *Post-Purchase "Ship To" Changes*. After a valid transaction has been made by the real card owner, thieves use the site's customer service screens to gain information necessary to assume the identity of the order owner and request a change in ship to information, having the goods delivered to an alternate address of their choosing. In each of these cases, fraud occurs because the perpetrator assumes the identity of another individual and completes the transaction using an anonymous medium.

The anonymity offered by the Internet makes it difficult to detect fraud and to correctly accept valid orders that share characteristics with fraudulent orders. To efficiently manage risk, a merchant should not solely rely on the protection offered by traditional card authorization systems that employ the AVS as their only fraud screen.

Address Verification Service

The AVS check, designed to support mail order and telephone order businesses, is usually run in conjunction with the bankcard authorization request. AVS performs an additional check, beyond verifying funds and credit card status, to insure that elements of the address supplied by the purchaser match those on record with the issuing bank. The following is a summary of responses merchants can receive from an AVS check:

1. The first five digits of the street address, the zip code, and credit card number match those on record at the bank (AVS=MATCH).
2. There is a partial match (e.g., street matches but not zip code, or zip code matches but not street) (AVS=PARTIAL MATCH).

3. The system cannot provide a response. This result is returned if the system is down or the purchaser does not reside in the United States (AVS is only available for U.S. residents) (AVS=UNAVAILABLE).

4. There is no match between the data elements (AVS= NON-MATCH).

While most merchants will not accept orders involving issuer declines or AVS=NON-MATCH, the automated nature of an online transaction requires merchants to implement policies and processes that can handle instances where the card has been approved, but other data to validate a transaction is questionable. Such instances include cases where the response is "Issuer Approved" and AVS =PARTIAL MATCH or UNAVAILABLE (e.g., the purchaser's bank approved the transaction, but it's not clear whether the transaction is valid).

Because a significant amount of legitimate sales are associated with AVS responses representing unknown levels of risk (or purchases made outside of the United States where AVS does not apply), it is crucial to find ways to maximize valid order acceptance with the lowest possible risk. Merchants have to find a balance between categorical rejection and blind acceptance in those instances where risk levels are unknown. Further, even AVS=MATCH responses carry some risk because stolen card and address information can prompt a MATCH response.

It is important to realize that AVS is by no means foolproof, and online merchants are still held liable for chargebacks even if the transaction was approved through AVS. This means that the merchant would be wise to employ additional fraud screening measures, as described under "Recommendation 1" in the previous section.

Internet Taxation

Online merchants in the United States have enjoyed an Internet tax moratorium while the various government entities scramble to figure out how to adequately apply tax policies to a new channel of sales and communications that has revolutionized business. This moratorium will soon end, and a tax compliance nightmare will begin.

Right now, there are approximately 7,600 taxing jurisdictions in the United States. A company has *nexus* if it is doing business within a taxing jurisdiction (i.e., maintaining an office location, leasing telephone lines, sending in sales reps on a repeated, frequent basis, etc.). For example, a manufacturer headquartered in Nevada, with nationwide sales offices, would have nexus in California if there were a sales office in Los Angeles. The manufacturer would remit California sales or use taxes on any transaction shipped into a California location.

It all starts to get very confusing. There are so many taxing jurisdictions that a purchase can be taxed differently based on what side of the street the purchaser lives. Added to that, certain states have occasional "tax holidays." Other states argue about what actually constitutes the triggering of a tax nexus for a merchant. One state wants to tax a merchant who sells software as soon as that software has been purchased and downloaded on more than 20 computers, arguing that the merchant will then be "doing business" in that state. Other states have proposed that a salesman with a laptop computer (not a sales office, just a laptop) should trigger a nexus, and the merchant should then remit sales tax for that state.

The first recommendation is obvious: find a competent tax advisor who has made Internet taxation a specialty. The second recommendation is to employ a system or service to calculate taxes on a real-time basis for online purchases. Here are some of the functions that should be performed behind the scenes, *before* the Buy button is clicked, but *after* the buyer has entered in all of the purchase information, including billing address and ship-to address.

- The payment application or service should identify appropriate tax jurisdictions by address rather than postal code. (Postal codes are not reliable for determining tax rates because they are subject to change and often do not correspond with state, county, and city designations.)

- When a customer's billing location is identified, the tax rate should be calculated according to interstate or intrastate sales; taxing jurisdictions involved; city/county, partial/full override rates; taxability of each line item; applicable maximum tax base; and excess amounts.
- Sales tax should be calculated for each product in the customer's shopping cart, unless tax has already been included in the product price.
- The applicable tax and product price should then be added to the total. If there are shipping charges, those should also be calculated and added to the total.

It is very important that the total price, including all taxes and shipping charges, be displayed to the customer *before* the customer is asked to click on the Buy button. The ability to perform these calculations in real-time is imperative for the shopper to gain the trust necessary to complete the transaction, as well as to provide the payment processor the correct order total.

Sales Tax Checklist

Figure 4-4, a sales tax checklist created by tax expert Julie Hoffman Walsh, CPA, can be used by a company to (1) determine if what it sells is subject to sales tax, and (2) identify company activities and operations that trigger sales tax liability in many states. A "yes" reply or an "x" in one of the location columns may indicate a sales tax obligation. This checklist is by no means complete, and the advice of a competent tax advisor is recommended to evaluate a company's sales tax issues.

Payment Processing and Credit Card Glossary

Acquiring Bank
The financial institution that enables merchants to accept credit card payments, sometimes referred to as the merchant bank or acquirer, the acquiring bank often works with a third-party processor to accept or decline the cardholder's credit card purchase request, deposits funds into the merchant's bank account, provides

In which state is your "home office"? _____

This is your "home state" and the sales tax rules in effect here will determine to what extent and how the business is taxed.

What do you "sell"?

Product *(other than software)?*	_____	Yes	_____ No
Software?	_____	Yes	_____ No
Internet Services?	_____	Yes	_____ No
Telecommunications Services?	_____	Yes	_____ No
Rents are collected on property or software?	_____	Yes	_____ No

Do you add the following charges to your sales invoice?

Freight?	_____	Yes	_____ No
Handling?	_____	Yes	_____ No

Please check the box for each column where the answer is "yes". List the other states, where appropriate. Sales to other states are not necessarily "tax free".	In Your "Home State"	In Other U.S. States	Outside the US	List Other States
Where in the value chain is your product sold?				
To manufacturers	Not Taxable in Certain Cases			
To distributors	Not Generally Taxable			
To retailers	Not Generally Taxable			
To end users				
To government(s), schools, nonprofits	Not Generally Taxable			
To foreign purchasers	Not Generally Taxable			
Do you use the product (transfer from inventory)?	State Use Tax May Apply			
Do you own, rent, lease, use/hire				
Office equipment?				
Telephone equipment?				
Telephone/cable services?				
Internet services?				
Software? (canned vs. custom)				
Business Inventory?				
Company cars?				
Trucks/vanpool vehicles?				
Employees?				
Independent Contractors?				
Do you arrange/coordinate more than once per year				
Sales conferences?				
Incentive trips?				
Seminars?				
Training sessions?				
Sales calls to key business partners?				
Offsite company functions?				
Does your sales force				
Install product at customer office?				
Train customer at customer office?				
Handle repair issues at customer office?				
Set up floor displays at customer office?				
Travel many days/year to customer office?				
Does your customer service center				
Handle sales calls from other state locations?				
Give product advice over the phone?				
Do you sell/service extended warranty contracts?				

FIGURE 4–4   Sales Tax Checklist

the merchant with periodic deposit statements, and so on. Acquirers are so named because they acquire a merchant's sales tickets and credit the order value to the merchant's account.

Authorization

The process of verifying that the credit card has sufficient funds (credit) available to cover the amount of the transaction. An authorization is obtained for every sale.

Bankcard

A MasterCard or Visa credit card.

Batch

The collective amount of transactions in the merchant's terminal or POS device that have yet to be settled.

Card association

An association such as Visa International or MasterCard International. The card association provides credit cards and other products for banks, who in turn privately brand the products, issue the cards to cardholders, and sometimes set up programs for merchants to accept the cards. Card associations play a significant role in processing transactions by operating and managing worldwide authorization and settlement systems.

Cardholder

The individual or entity that uses a credit card to purchase goods or services from an online (or offline) store.

Card issuer

An organization such as American Express or Discover, which (unlike a card association) offers credit cards directly to consumers and merchants.

Chargeback

A chargeback occurs when a cardholder disputes a charge, as in the case of fraudulent use of their credit card, and the bank is forced to reverse the charges.

Close

The process of sending the batch for settlement.

Commercial card

Credit cards used by businesses to cover expenses, such as travel, entertainment, and purchasing.

Corporate card

Credit card used for business-related expenses such as travel and entertainment.

Debit card
Credit card whose funds are withdrawn directly from the cardholder's checking account.

Discount rate
A collection of fees charged by the acquirer to process the merchant's transaction.

Electronic Cash Register (ECR)
A device used for cash sales, and ECR can also be integrated to accept credit cards.

Electronic Draft Capture (EDC)
Process of electronically authorizing, capturing, and settling a credit card transaction.

Fleet card
Private label credit card designed mainly for repairs, maintenance, and fueling of automobiles.

Interchange
The fees assessed a transaction by MasterCard and Visa.

Independent Sales Organization (ISO)
An independent agent that solicits prospective merchants for merchant banks, ISOs are also referred to as merchant account providers. ISOs assist merchants in setting up merchant accounts and assuring that the accounts connect to third-party processors. ISOs may either assume partial or shared financial liability for merchant activity.

Issuing bank
The financial institution that issues a credit card to the cardholder. The issuing bank, also referred to as the cardholder's bank, establishes and verifies the cardholder's credit line, provides the cardholder with monthly billing statements, and so on. American Express (Amex) and Discover issue their own cards, acting in a similar fashion to issuing banks. Interestingly, Amex and Discover also sign up merchants to accept their own cards, mimicking acquiring banks.

Merchant
The entity that is selling goods and services in exchange for payment. Goods can be either hard goods (tangibles) or soft goods (intangibles), such as service contracts, or pay-per-view content.

Merchant number
Identifying number assigned to each merchant.

Network
Company used to authorize and capture credit card transactions.

Payment application
The application used by the merchant to request credit card authorization and settlement of funds between the merchant and the acquiring bank. The application can be a self-managed application or an outsourced service.

Private Label
Credit or debit card that can be used only within a specific merchant's store.

Purchasing card
Credit card used by businesses to cover purchasing expenses.

Settlement
Process of sending the merchant's batch to the network for processing and payment.

Smart card
A credit-type card that electronically stores account information in the card itself.

TE card
Credit card used by businesses for travel and entertainment expenses.

Terminal
Equipment used to capture, transmit, and store credit card transactions.

Third-party processor
Also known as payment processing networks, front-end processors, or just processors, the organization that works with an acquiring bank (merchant bank) to process credit card transactions via the card associations or card issuers. The third-party processor communicates to the card associations or card issuers to obtain authorizations and execute funds transfers. In some cases, the acquiring bank and the third-party processor may be the same entity.

Resources

Articles

Alster, Norm. "Are we stealing from our schools?" *Upside Today,* March 23, 1999.
http://www.upside.com/texis/mvm/news/news?id=36e8186f0.

Andrews, Whit. "The digital wallet, a concept revolutionizing e-commerce." *Internet World,* October 15, 1999.

Andrews, Whit. "The new laws of dynamic pricing." *Internet World,* December 15, 1999.

Blumenstein, Rebecca. "Ecommerce group shifts how bills are paid." *Wall Street Journal,* April 27, 2000.

Briody, Dan. "Web currencies give cash a run for its money." *Infoworld,* April 17, 2000.

Cox, Beth. "A tale of two transactions." *Ecommerce Guide.* internet.com Corp., May 23, 2000.

Greenspan, Robyn. "Before the final click." *Ecommerce Guide.* internet.com Corp., May 31, 2000.

Greenspan, Robyn. "Prevent credit card insecurity from taking its toll." *Ecommerce Guide,* internet.com Corp., May 25, 2000.

Hillebrand, Mary. "Report: Online bill payment to reach $1B by 2004." *E-Commerce Times,* March 28, 2000.

Hoy, Richard. "Order tracking: slick and easy." *http://www.clickz.com,* June 2, 2000.

Johnson, David. "Establishing a merchant account for your Web business." *E-commerce Times,* June 17, 2000.

Kerstetter, Jim. "Online payments evolve." *PC Week,* August 23, 1999.

Merkow, Mark. "Evolving e-commerce to the next generation." *Ecommerce Guide,* internet.com Corp., September 8, 1999.

Norwood, David. "Solving the e-puzzle." *eAI Journal,* April 2000.

Rosen, Cheryl. "Electronic payments get personal." *Informationweek.com,* May 29, 2000.

Sapp, Geneva. "Online bill options mount." *Infoworld,* May 1, 2000.

Shesney, Glenn T. "Process online payments quickly and effectively." *E-Business Advisor,* June 2000.

Sturdevant, Cameron. "Present and accounted for: Standards evolve to support burgeoning online bill presentment market." *PC Week,* October 11, 1999.

Wasserman, Elizabeth. "Are Net taxes inevitable? With a deadline for reporting to Congress looming, the Internet Tax Commission will meet in Dallas to mull e-commerce taxes." *The Industry Standard,* March 20, 2000.

Links

Merchant Accounts and Payment Processing Links

1st American Card Service
http://www.1stamericancardservice.com

Acsmerchantservices.com
http://www.acsmerchantservices.com

Advantage Merchant Services
http://www.creditcardprocessor.com

American Express
http://www.americanexpress.com

American Information Services
http://www.qdebit.com

Authorize.Net
http://www.authorizenet.com

BankAmerica Merchant Services
http://www.bankamerica.com

Cardservice International
http://www.cardsvc.com

Charge.Com
http://www.charge.com

CheckVantage.com
http://www.checkvantage.com/index.html

CreditCardUSA
http://www.CreditCardUSA.com

Creditnet
http://www.creditnet.com

CyberCash
http://www.cybercash.com

CyberSource
http://www.cybersource.com

DigiCash
http://www.digicash.com

DTA Inc
http://www.datatransfer.com

Ebiz.com
http://www.getebiz.com

Electronic Payment Processing
http://www.eppinc.com

Electronic Transfer Inc.
http://www.paymentsystem.com

ePayments Resource Center
http://www.epaynews.com

Experian
http://www.consumerinfo.com

Globeset
http://www.globeset.com

GORealtime
http://www.gorealtime.com

Internet Billing Company
http://www.ibill.com

iTransact
http://www.redicheck.com

Mastercard Merchant Site
http://www.mastercard.com/merchants

Merchant Bankcard Network Services
http://www.bnkcard.com

Merchant On-Line
http://www.merchantonline.com

NetBill Central
http://www.netbill.com

Now Internet Tools
http://www.nowtools.com

OpenMarket
http://www.openmarket.com

Pay2See.com
http://www.pay2see.com

Paylinx.com
http://www.paylinx.com

PaymentNet
http://www.paymentnet.com

Paymentech
http://www.paymentech.com

Preferred Merchant Services
http://www.preferredmerchants.com

RemitNet
http://www.2.remit.net

ShopForRates.com
http://www.shopforrates.com

SET (Secure Electronic Transaction)
http://www.visa.com

Shoptek eCommerce
http://www.shoptek.com

Trintech
http://www.trintech.com

US Code Chapter 15 - Commerce and Trade
http://www.law.cornell.edu/uscode/15/ch41.html

Visa-Electronic Commerce
http://www.visa.com

Internet Taxation Links

A European Initiative in Electronic Commerce
http://www.cordis.lu/esprit/src/ecomcomx.htm

Citizens for a Sound Economy
http://www.cse.org/

Electronic Commerce Taxation
http://www.mshb.com/ec

Electronic Frontier Foundation
http://www.eff.org/

Guidelines for the Evaluation of EDI products
http://www.nist.gov/

National Electronic Commerce Resource Center
http://www.ecrc.ctc.com

Next Generation Internet Initiative
http://www.ccic.gov/

Organization for Economic Cooperation and Development
http://www.oecd.org/daf/fa/

Pdqtax.com
http://www.pdqtax.com

Sales Tax Clearinghouse
http://www.thestc.com

The Emergence of Electronic Commerce
http://www.oecd.org/subject/electronic-commerce/documents/emergence.htm

The Legal Risks of Setting Up Shop In Cyberspace
http://www.cism.bus.utexas.edu/

President's Information Infrastructure Task Force
http://www.iitf.nist.gov/

Department of Trade and Industry Website
http://www.dti.gov.uk/

Department of Trade and Industry Information Society Initiative
http://www.isi.gov.uk/

Army Electronic Commerce Center
http://www.armyec.sra.com

United States Government Electronic Commerce Policy
http://www.ecommerce.gov/

US Department of Commerce
http://www.doc.gov

CUSTOMER SERVICE

The functions of e-commerce fulfillment and e-logistics are vital threads in the tightly woven fabric that comprises the e-commerce continuum. However, interwoven throughout is the critical function of customer service. The quality of a firm's online and offline customer service determines the quality of a customer's entire experience with that firm. The customer experience starts before the first mouse click to enter a site and concludes long after the order has been delivered. It is no secret that faulty e-fulfillment and e-logistics creates a large part of customer service dissatisfaction.

This chapter will surface some of the key issues in e-commerce customer service, and include some tips for improving the customer experience, from preventing shopping cart abandonment to better post-sales support.

Chasing Empty Shopping Carts

In the e-commerce world, sales don't come easy. Customer conversion rates hover near 1.5 percent and abandoned online shopping carts have soared to as high as 88 percent. Why are these figures so dismal?

Resource Marketing conducted a research study of online customer service problems, which yielded some telling statistics. The marketing firm looked at 14 key factors, such as account administration, security, and returns. The chief complaints centered on customer service, as shown in Figure 5-1.

This is especially important data when you consider that the customers who access customer service online are also the ones that spend the most money. According to *InterActive Consumers,* a monthly report from Cyber Dialogue *(http://www. cyberdialogue.com)*, just over 26 percent of all online shoppers have sought customer service online. By comparison, 77 percent seek information on intended purchases, and 54 percent order goods and services online.

When the category of shoppers is restricted to those who order online, the percentage of customer service seekers rises to 33 percent. For shoppers who spend $500 or more online

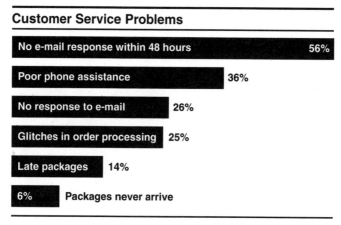

FIGURE 5–1   *Customer Service Problems*
Source: Resource Marketing, 2000

per year, 40 percent use customer service, as shown in Figure 5-2.

In fact, as Figure 5-3 shows, customer service is so important that the majority of online consumers actively look for Web sites that have good customer service. Roughly 57 percent make this a priority.

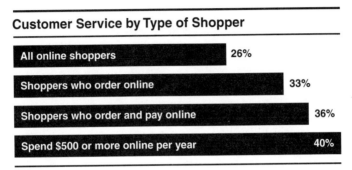

Customer Service by Type of Shopper

All online shoppers	26%
Shoppers who order online	33%
Shoppers who order and pay online	36%
Spend $500 or more online per year	40%

FIGURE 5–2 Customer Service by Type of Shopper
Source: *Cyber Dialogue, 2000*

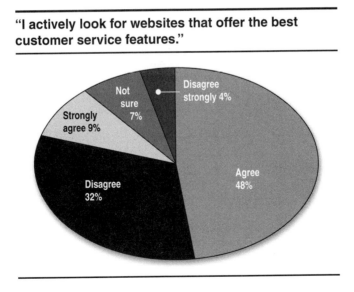

"I actively look for websites that offer the best customer service features."

FIGURE 5–3 "I actively look for websites that offer the best customer service features."
Source: *Cyber Dialogue, 2000*

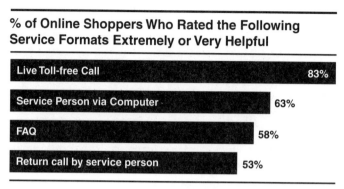

FIGURE 5–4   Percent of Online Shoppers Who Rated the Following Service Formats Extremely or Very Helpful
Source: Cyber Dialogue, 2000

In addition, consumers rated those forms of online customer service that involved communication with live humans more highly than other forms, as shown in Figure 5-4.

The most prevalent forms of customer service—email, self-service, Web-enabled contact centers (WECC) and e-CRM (electronic customer relationship management)—will be explored further.

Customer Service Creates Customer Loyalty

Customer loyalty programs have been receiving quite a bit of attention, with industry pundits espousing sophisticated ways to engender online customer retention through incentives, points, and coupons. The truth is, they don't work. The best way to engender customer loyalty is to provide good customer service.

Jupiter Communications found that although 75 percent of online consumers participate in some type of loyalty program, few said they were strong motivation to increase online purchases, as shown in Figure 5-5. In fact, the best way online merchants should reward loyalty is with improved service, such as priority service, personalized offers, or email updates.

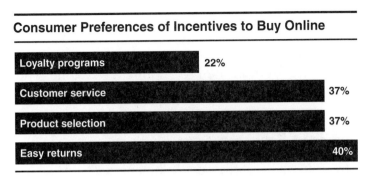

Consumer Preferences of Incentives to Buy Online

Loyalty programs	22%
Customer service	37%
Product selection	37%
Easy returns	40%

FIGURE 5–5   Consumer Preferences of Incentives to Buy Online
Source: *Jupiter Communications, 2000*

This was further underscored by the survey data that emphasized customer concerns about service.

- 72 percent of respondents said that customer service is a critical factor in shopping satisfaction.
- Only 41 percent indicated they were satisfied with the service they had experienced.
- 85 percent stated that returning merchandise is important to them, even though more than 50 percent were dissatisfied in this regard as well
- Even among consumers who participate in loyalty programs, there isn't a high degree of enthusiasm—only 35 percent belong to more than three programs.

In case you think that implementing comprehensive customer service is too expensive, consider the potential revenue that is lost without improved service. Researchers say U.S. retailers could leave up to $19 billion in potential e-commerce revenue on the table in 2000 unless they improve the online customer experience. According to a study by the consultancy Creative Good, total e-commerce sales could hit $57 billion in 2000, but only if enterprises pocket the forecasted $19 billion that hinges on significant improvements in customer care.

We've seen that the best way to increase customer loyalty is through improved customer service, and that customer loyalty is key to customer retention. Now, one last stat on the importance of customer retention on the bottom line: According to a study by Jupiter Communications, companies can boost profits by almost *100 percent by retaining just 5 percent more* of their customers. Add to that the fact that it costs considerably less to retain a customer than to acquire a new one, and you can see the role that post-sale customer support plays.

Multiple Contact Points

Customers not only seek e-business sites with good customer service, they also want to be able to interact with an online merchant through multiple channels. Today's "e-customers" want the ability to solicit information via phone, fax, email, Web sites, online chat groups, VOIP (voice over IP) calls, and even human face-to-face communication. E-customers are increasingly sophisticated and demanding—they want to determine how, when, and where they will be served. This need has given rise to a new *demand-based* business model in which customers expect the online merchant to be a central hub who will provide service via a multitude of channels.

Email Is Still the "Killer App"

In spite of the new, exotic technologies that are springing up, email is still the leading form of Internet communication and is expected to surge three to four times in volume over the next few years. By year-end, global inbound email and Web forms could reach 1 billion each month, with email processing likely to exceed 230 million hours.

With the overwhelming importance of email as the key channel of Internet customer communication, why do so many companies botch email management and response? As we've seen, studies have shown that online shoppers' most frequent complaint about customer service is that their email inquiries often receive no reply within 48 hours. If e-businesses are to succeed in the Internet economy, it is imperative that they streamline processes to control, route, and track email efficiently, and that they set response times and adhere to them.

Whether you outsource your email management or perform it in-house, you'll need to tackle defining the business processes and the human element before taking a look at automated email management systems.

Many of the practices, measures, and processes for inbound calls apply to electronic transactions. For this reason, electronic communication should be treated with the same principles applied to incoming call service levels and response times. Where you may find some differences is with staffing and scheduling. Although the processes are similar to those for handling inbound calls, you will need to pay closer attention to tracking and measuring email data. Here are some tips call center experts have developed to help you estimate your staffing requirements if you are hiring in-house customer service representatives, or to determine the number of agents necessary if you are employing an outside call center.

- Count or estimate the number of email messages you receive and the time spent on them to determine the number of agents you need.
- Be sure that the calculation includes incoming calls if agents are handling both.
- Identify the number of emails that are being generated daily over a given period of time.
- Break down the forecast by daily average and then by half-hours.
- Based on the average handle time, ascertain the number of agents required to manage the email volume projected while meeting service level and response time objectives.
- Take into account lunch, meeting, and vacation times, and schedule the agents accordingly.

The biggest challenge is not only capturing email information, but also integrating it seamlessly into the workload forecast. When forecasting workloads, try to schedule email management time by employing some of the following techniques:

- Assign 30 minutes of non-phone activity to each agent with the appropriate skill, but only when agents are exceeding the service level for incoming calls.
- Regardless of the impact on call service level, assign non-phone work to each agent at critical times to minimize the negative effect of poor response times on customer satisfaction.
- Assign the activity within a range of acceptable impact on service levels and empower the agent to manage response time.

Productivity Standards

You'll also have to create some email activity metrics, just as you would with an inbound call, and generate reports at both the call center and agent levels. Here are some productivity standards to consider.

- average time per email (per agent, cradle to grave)
- average time of email in queue
- number of customer callbacks via email
- number of customer callbacks via IVR (Interactive Voice Response)
- number of complaint emails
- number of phone callbacks
- number of emails handled by each agent
- number of emails handled by center
- time spent gathering information to close the email (similar to "not ready")
- number of emails routed incorrectly
- number of emails with problems that cannot be solved

Email response times, like service levels, measure the quality of service you are providing the customer. There are a couple of traps to watch out for, however, when you play the metrics game.

According to David P. Martin, II, C.P.L., a logistics expert, "The concept of customer contacts is a classic queuing theory problem. Arrivals to any system are usually distributed as a Poisson random variable. Just counting the number of emails without looking at the distribution could lead to some invalid estimates. The productivity standards would lead the reader to take the average number of calls and the average time to call to compute the overall workload, then divide that by the workload for one person to determine the number of people required. This usually ends up in too high an estimate (you're carrying more people than required). The second trap is to think that if the average number of calls per person is 30 per day, for example, then each person needs to complete 30 calls. This negates the idea of an 'average' because now it becomes a quota. The superior staff members will complete their 30 calls, then sit on their hands so as not to get peer pressure. The lesser staff members will cut corners and reduce customer service to make their quota. Bottom line: you end up hurting customer service!"

Finally, record the best examples of voice and email contacts for use by coaches and agents, and brainstorm the different types of contacts and how best to handle them. As email is highly dependent on written communications, create new positions in your organization for editors, proofreaders, and process owners to standardize templates and automated responses. Conduct periodic audits of the email response times and of a sample of the emails themselves. Develop an objective rating scale and score the email handling, the quality of the contacts, and the consistency of handling. These measurements will help you in recruiting and training, as well as in email script development.

Special Email Tips

Hiring and training customer service reps to handle email as well as contact center duties means that you'll have to look for agents that possess not only the skills necessary to handle incoming calls but also a wide range of other abilities, such as writing, editing, proofreading, grammatical accuracy, and knowledge of the subject matter. Most of your reps have to be excellent problem solvers, and you must give them the authority to make the decisions necessary to achieve first call or first email problem resolution. Here are some tips that have been compiled from a variety of organizations and experts.

- Answer all email questions. Answer the easy ones *fast*. Answer the hard ones carefully.
- Have a special panel of experts on hand to answer really tough questions.
- Let your customers know you by name. Have your employees personally answer and "sign" emails with their own names.
- Set up and foster relationships between employees and customers.
- Put a face to every name. Some Web sites feature photos of each employee alongside their name and a brief bio.
- Nurture your best members. Dedicate time and other resources to ensure these valuable customers stay satisfied.
- Enhance your training curriculum to include Internet training, independent and Web-based email response, business writing, keyboarding, and site navigation.
- Teach your agents "Netiquette," or the art of responding to customer email, using a professional writing style.
- Remember that an email sent to one customer may end up in the hands of several, so ensure that your agents steer clear of writing anything that may cause legal complications.
- You must also pay close attention to the format and wording of all email messages that your agents send.
- Responses to customers should be timely, accurate, clear, and complete, with short sentences.
- Use templates whenever possible to ensure consistency.
- Monitor agent responses—messages lost in cyberspace usually indicate an agent's lack of skill in a particular area.
- On your Web site, inform your customers about the response channels you offer and query them as to what they prefer: callbacks at a preferred time, email, voice mail, fax, regular mail, or call-in with a toll-free number.

- Treat email like an incoming live customer call and provide the same commitment to meet or exceed service standards.
- Decrease email response times by constantly gathering FAQs (frequently asked questions) and creating templates for quick responses.
- If you handle large volumes of email, you'll benefit greatly from hiring a manager to maintain and update all systems, training, practices, and procedures.

ERMS

Email response management systems (ERMS) are invaluable tools for automating and streamlining the many tasks involved in email communications. They can manage and track email from arrival through response, automating receipt, acknowledgment, routing, queuing, and reply, and including service level management and reporting. ERMS are capable of performing an enormous range of tasks, such as

- track and attach information relevant to customer Web activity;
- classify and route Web-generated emails based on origin;
- interpret, classify, and route independently generated emails;
- identify special handling for particular emails;
- create a contact record for every inbound message;
- associate a contact record with a customer profile;
- display contact record, history, and customer profile with an open email;
- alert agent when new message arrives;
- create an explanatory email to the customer if response time has changed;
- provide real-time monitor displays for agent and queue; and
- supply customized reporting.

Probably the largest benefit of email management systems is the relief they provide to service representatives by automatically sending brochures, price sheets, and other "canned" documents in response to literature requests. Through routing rules, ERMS also ensure that special customers or critical issues get special attention and that all messages receive a timely response. Messages that require human intervention are assigned case numbers, grouped according to priority, and tracked to prevent issues from being ignored or delayed.

For handling messages manually, email management systems allow customer service representatives to quickly and easily assemble responses from a variety of sources: a customer database that includes the history of email exchanges with each customer, a knowledge base of support documents and canned responses, and any number of enterprise resources. Many of these solutions can be integrated with traditional CRM (customer relationship management) systems, ERP (enterprise resource planning) systems, call centers, and other back-end data sources.

EGain Communications has a helpful flowchart, shown in Figure 5-6, that illustrates the processes their systems use to handle incoming messages.

Customer Self-Service

The Internet, unlike any other medium, can empower customers to try solving problems and responding to information requests on their own. This customer self-service capability not only saves time and money for the e-business, it satisfies many customers who prefer to do it themselves, in their downtime and in their own way.

Customer self-service can be provided by posting answers to FAQs and by providing the information and resources customers need to make purchasing decisions on your Web site. We all know that FAQs are usually not frequent, not asked, and rarely questions, but you should still monitor this area closely

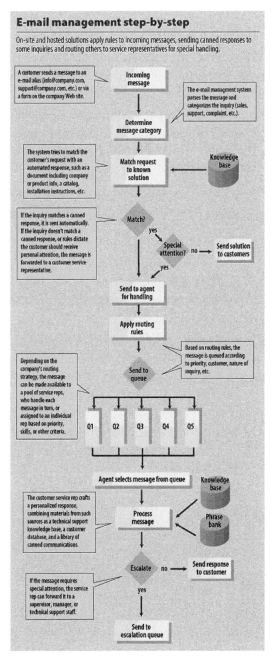

E-mail management step-by-step

On-site and hosted solutions apply rules to incoming messages, sending canned responses to some inquiries and routing others to service representatives for special handling.

A customer sends a message to an e-mail alias (info@company.com, support@company.com, etc.) or via a form on the company Web site.

Incoming message

The e-mail managment system parses the message and categorizes the inquiry (sales, support, complaint, etc.).

Determine message category

The system tries to match the customer's request with an automated response, such as a document including company or product info, a catalog, installation instructions, etc.

Match request to known solution

Knowledge base

If the inquiry matches a canned response, it is sent automatically. If the inquiry doesn't match a canned response, or rules dictate the customer should receive personal attention, the message is forwarded to a customer service representative.

Match?
yes

Special attention? no → **Send solution to customers**

yes

Send to agent for handling

Apply routing rules

Depending on the company's routing strategy, the message can be made available to a pool of service reps, who handle each message in turn, or assigned to an individual rep based on priority, skills, or other criteria.

Based on routing rules, the message is queued according to priority, customer, nature of inquiry, etc.

Send to queue

Q1 Q2 Q3 Q4 Q5

Agent selects message from queue

Knowledge base

The customer service rep crafts a personalized response, combining materials from such sources as a technical support knowledge base, a customer database, and a library of canned communications.

Process message

Phrase bank

If the message requires special attention, the service rep can forward it to a supervisor, manager, or technical support staff.

Escalate no → **Send response to customer**

yes

Send to escalation queue

FIGURE 5–6   Email Management Step-by-Step
Source: EGain Communications Corp.

and update it regularly, based on the type of products that are being sold.

Going one step further, automated self-service solutions, such as those from Software 911 and RightNow Technologies, give customers access to services such as online knowledge bases, product configuration utilities, interactive question-and-answer forms, discussion groups, and dynamically generated FAQs. This also stems the tide of repetitive emails so that customer service representatives are able to focus on other important matters.

The next type of basic level of interactivity on your Web site is via message threading by setting up online discussion groups. This has its pros and cons. Although these discussions can be quite helpful, I would highly suggest that you have your customer support staff moderate the threaded discussions for derogatory comments or profanity. This entails some time and labor dedicated to this task.

Another way to go is to host a Java-based chat room. The downside here is that chat services require even more development resources than discussion threading, and an individual within your company's customer support group would have to monitor the chat room and be able to provide any necessary technical support. Then, you'll either have to staff the chat room 24 hours a day, seven days a week, which isn't always feasible, or build in the ability to easily start and stop access to the chat room.

The good news is that if you are looking at implementing ERMS, a number of vendors integrate Web collaboration and other capabilities with their solutions, allowing chat sessions with customers to be recorded in their profiles along with email exchanges. And you don't have to buy an entire system all at once. The email management solutions from Delano Technology, eGain Communications, Kana Communications, and Talisma can be integrated one by one by purchasing separate modules, and you can provide them selectively—on a per customer, per transaction, or per service-level basis—so as not to overburden service representatives. An even better solution is to access these services on a hosted basis via the ASP (Application Service Provider) model, so you can deploy them without investing in infrastructure.

From Call Centers to Contact Centers to Commerce Centers

First, there was the call center, which centers on phone calls. Then there arose the contact center, which handles not only phone calls, but also multiple channels of contact, via the Web, fax, Voice Over IP, and other media. Now, there is the commerce center—and the emphasis on how customers are treated has shifted dramatically. In the call center model, the focus was on wrestling with issues like making sure not too many calls were being abandoned and that agents weren't spending too much time on each call.

In the commerce center model, the emphasis is being placed on the lifetime value of customers. Commerce centers are all about establishing relationships with each customer; learning more about each customer and his or her demographics so that he or she can be better served; and being able to intelligently cross-sell and up-sell products and services to them. This philosophy demands that customer service be consistent, whether customers reach the center through the Internet, by phone calls, fax, self-service on a Web site, or another method.

Multiple departments in an organization need to be able to look up customer records to see the most recent transactions with all departments, regardless of the means of communication. That means that departments like the help desk, marketing, sales, and customer service must share one database. These requirements have given rise to customer relationship management and e-CRM systems.

Customer Relationship Management Systems

The big CRM vendors—Siebel Systems, Baan, Lucent, Oracle, Remedy, and others—offer the most comprehensive solutions to the customer-support conundrum. A CRM system works on top of customer contact management, providing a consistent, *business rules-based* (not "routing rules"-based) means of controlling not just call center operations, per se, but the whole thread of operations involved in communicating with, selling to, servicing, promoting, and holding onto customers.

They are emphatically *workflow*-oriented products, occupying a large, still-generic niche, just below the level where highly customized business-process automation systems (SAP, PeopleSoft, etc.) begin to play. CRM systems profit from standing at a higher level of abstraction—the rules they process will be evolved by management as a coordinated and systematized expression of business goals.

With this in mind, organizations are turning toward e-CRM products as an option to help keep a watchful eye on their customer base. In addition to increasing customer service efficiency, these solutions can help grow brand awareness, foster product loyalty, and promote cross-selling and up-selling (the process of suggesting new, more expensive items to a customer based on what the customer has purchased in the past).

The Action Request System from Remedy Corporation is an example of an industry standard system that is morphing to give its customers, who are moving to "Clicks and Mortar," increased speed and agility. In use by more than 8,800 customer sites worldwide, Remedy's Action Request (AR) System allows enterprise-class workflow solutions to be created or updated in days, rather than months. Its latest release, version 4.5, provides more than a tenfold increase in scalability (as measured by the number of concurrent users of the system), and dynamically creates database logic, workflow business rules, and form layout without requiring programming.

Here's an example of how a properly implemented e-CRM system at an online bookseller might work. The system would automatically allow a customer to check on the status of a book order via phone or email (customer service), offer discounted coupons to other books by the same author (cross-selling), and provide free shipping on orders placed on a customer's birthday (brand loyalty).

Rolling out one of these enterprise applications can be quite costly and very resource-intensive. As an alternative, some sites are turning their attention to e-CRM services offered via ASPs. Under this guise, you can outsource some or all of your customer service offerings—usually for a much lower price.

Ultimately, the decision to place e-CRM in the hands of an ASP or roll out a product entirely in-house will depend on a number of factors, in addition to a quick price comparison.

In addition to its sales and marketing hooks, a main ingredient of an e-CRM solution is the capability to enhance customer service—a key to customer retention. For the most part, these customer service features fall into one of three categories—phone, Web, and email. Figure 5-7 shows that contact via the Web and email is poised to take over much of the current mode of phone contact.

As discussed, ERM solutions allow organizations to intelligently queue and route incoming email queries to appropriate customer service representatives for personalized responses.

Customer-to-business contacts by the numbers

The pervasiveness of the Internet and e-CRM will have a dramatic effect on the ways consumers interact with businesses.

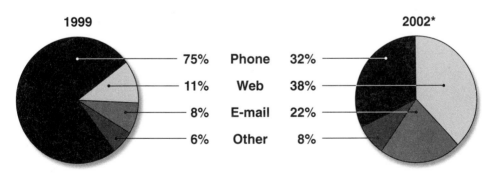

1999		2002*
75%	Phone	32%
11%	Web	38%
8%	E-mail	22%
6%	Other	8%

*Projection

FIGURE 5–7   Customer-to-Business Contacts by the Numbers
Source: Dr. Jon Anton, Director of Research, Center for Customer Driven Quality, Purdue University

Other products provide workflow-management capabilities as well as access to customizable knowledge libraries aimed at specific industries.

Finally, real-time solutions, such as those offered by Lipstream and LivePerson, provide collaborative customer services that are browser-based. These include text chat, VOIP, document and browser sharing, and shared application control.

Products such as Ask Jeeves' Jeeves Live service scale to meet the technical capacity of a customer's workstation and Internet connection. Low-end workstations will automatically be serviced via simple-text chat, while high-end systems with faster connections will be given the VOIP option.

A comprehensive CRM solution, such as that offered by PeopleSupport, shown in Figure 5-8, can be the best of all worlds. It can integrate seamlessly with a company's Web storefront to handle customer inquiries via email, telephone, online chat, and VOIP.

The ultimate goal of a successful e-CRM service or solution will provide transparency between your entire supply chain and your customers.

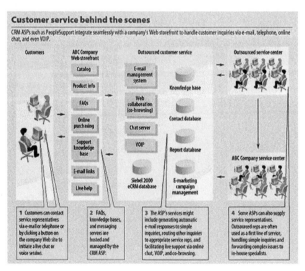

FIGURE 5–8   Customer Service Behind the Scenes
Source: PeopleSupport, Inc.

Outsourcing e-CRM

Follow this five-point strategy to successfully implement a hosted e-CRM solution.

1. Set realistic goals. Determine how you want to strengthen and maintain customer relationships and develop a sound strategy to achieve them. Creating customer satisfaction at all "touch points" requires support from all levels of management.

2. Involve all departments. Implementing e-CRM can and will have an impact on multiple departments in your organization. Secure department cooperation during the planning stages.

3. Let your strategy drive the technology. E-CRM is a process, not a product. Do your homework to find which ASP offers the services you need to implement your plan.

4. Consider an incremental rollout. Roll out your e-CRM strategy in managed stages and have each stage of implementation build on the previous one

5. Solicit feedback. Once your plan is implemented, keep employees in the loop. Encourage their input on how your strategy is working and make changes if it is not working.

Web-Enabled CRM

True Web-enabled CRM systems unify a customer's interactions with your business by creating one database for customer information and one flexible, extensible set of business processes that lets you better sell, market, and support your customers. This provides you with true transparency throughout the customer lifecycle. Here are some companies that can help out with e-CRM.

Aspect Communications
San Jose, CA, 408-325-2200, *http://www.aspect.com*

CenterForce Technologies
Bethesda, MD 301-718-2955, *http://www.cforcetech.com*

ELOYALTY
Chicago, IL 877-4-ELOYAL, *http://www.eloyaltyco.com*

E.PIPHANY
San Mateo, CA, 650-356-3800, *http://www.epiphany.com*

Hewlett-Packard Company
Cupertino, CA, 888-290-8950,
http://www.internetsolutions.enterprise.hp.com/frontoffice

HotData
Austin, TX, 512-646-6000, *http://www.hotdata.com*

IBM
Armonk, NY, 800-772-2227, *http://www.ibm.com/e-business/crm*

Lucent Technologies
Murray Hill, NJ, 888-4-LUCENT, *http://www.lucent.com*

mynetsales.com
Boston, MA, 617-350-0160, *http://www.mynetsales.com*

Nortel Networks Corporation
Brampton, ON, Canada, 905-863-0000,
http://www.nortelnetworks.com. See also *http://www.clarify.com*

Oracle Corporation
Redwood Shores, CA, 650-506-7000, *http://www.oracle.com*

PeopleSoft, Inc.
Pleasanton, CA, 800-380-SOFT, *http://www.peoplesoft.com*

Pivotal Corporation
North Vancouver, BC, Canada, 888-275-7486,
http://www.pivotal.com

Quintus Corporation
Fremont, CA, 510-624-2800, *http://www.quintus.com*

Recognition Systems
Chicago, IL, 312-382-8989, *http://www.protagona.com*

Remedy Corporation
Mountain View, CA, 650-903-5200, *http://www.remedy.com*

Saratoga Systems
Campbell, CA, 408-371-9330, *http://www.saratogasystems.com*

Siebel Systems, Inc.
San Mateo, CA, 650-295-5000, *http://www.siebel.com*

United Customer Management Solutions (UCMS)
Redwood City, CA, 610-650-7888, *http://www.ucms.net*

Xchange Applications
Boston, MA, 617-737-2244, *http://www.exapps.com*

Web-Enabling the Call Center

Contact centers are still the foundation of a successful service organization, but the definition of a "call" must be significantly expanded. A growing group of products, listed below, enables call centers to handle voice-over-IP, text chat, and email as effectively as they do phone calls.

Ask Jeeves, Inc.
Emeryville, CA, 510-985-7400, *http://www.corporate.ask.com*

AudioTalk
Mountain View, CA, 650-988-2040, *http://www.audiotalk.com*

BRIGHTWARE
Novato, CA, 800-532-2890, *http://www.brightware.com*

eFusion, Inc.
Beaverton, OR, 503-207-6300, *http://www.efusion.com*

eGain Communications Corporation
Sunnyvale, CA, 888-603-4246, *http://www.egain.com*

eshare communications, Inc.
Norcross, GA, 770-239-4000, *http://www.eshare.com*

Inter-Tel, Inc.
Chandler, AZ, 800-669-5958, *http://www.inter-tel.com*

Kana Communications, Inc.
Redwood City, CA, 650-298-9282, *http://www.kana.com*

MATRAnet, Inc.
Redwood Shores, CA, 650-598-4777, *http://www.matranet.com*

Net2Phone, Inc.
Hackensack, NJ, 201-530-4000, *http://www.net2phone.com*

PipeLive.com, LLC
Melville, NY, 800-768-0072, *http://www.pipelive.com*

Spanlink Communications, Inc.
Minneapolis, MN, 612-971-2000, *http://www.spanlink.com*

VocalTec Communications, Ltd.
Fort Lee, NJ, 201-228-7000, *http://www.vocaltec.com*

Call-Enabling the Web Center

While call centers are becoming Web-enabled, Web centers are becoming call-enabled. Unlike call centers, however, most e-businesses are starting customer support from ground zero and have little preexisting telephony or call center infrastructure. Fortunately, most of the newest CRM software offers sophisticated Computer Telephony Integration (CTI) capabilities and often includes call routing and workflow definition applications.

Apropos Technology
Oakbrook Terrace, 630-472-9600, *http://www.apropos.com*

Cisco Systems, Inc.
San Jose, CA, 408-526-4000, *http://www.cisco.com*

CosmoCom, Inc.
Hauppauge, NY, 631-851-0100, *http://www.cosmocom.com*

Davox Corporation
Westford, MA, 978-952-0200, *http://www.davox.com*

Ericsson
Richardson, TX, 972-583-0000, *http://www.ericsson.com*

Genesys Telecommunications, Inc.
San Francisco, CA, 888-GENESYS, *http://www.genesyslabs.com*

Interactive Intelligence, Inc.
Indianapolis, IN, 317-872-3000, *http://www.inter-intelli.com*

ISC
New York, NY, 877-472-4472, *http://www.isc.com*

Lightning Rod Software
Minneapolis, MN, 612-837-4000, *http://www.atio.com*

Nice Systems, Ltd.
Secaucus, NJ, 201-617-8800, *http://www.nice.com*

Noble Systems
Atlanta, GA, 404-851-1331, *http://www.noblesystems.com*

Wood Dale, IL, 630-227-8000, *http://www.ec.rockwell.com*

Swallow Information Systems, Inc.
Beverly, MA, 978-867-6000, *http://www.charter-2000.com*

Telephony@Work
San Diego, CA, 888-854-4224, *http://www.telephonyatwork.com*

Witness Systems, Inc.
Alpharetta, GA, 770-754-1900, *http://www.witness.com*

Xantel
Phoenix, AZ, 480-446-4000, *http://www.amapsplus.com*

Resources

Articles

Allimandi, Milton. "Web transaction and demand for live agents on the rise." *Call Center Magazine,* May 1999.

Coleman, David and Lewis Ward. "Hands-on e-business." *E-Business Advisor,* September 1999.

Coopee, Todd. "E-CRM calls customer king." *InfoWorld.com,* June 23, 2000.

Cummings, Elaine M. and Terri Haas. "Seeing green." *http://www.darwinmag.com,* June/July 2000.

Davenport, Tom. "Connect the dots: Get ready. E-services are coming to a business near you." *http://www.darwinmag.com,* June/July 2000.

Dinely, Doug and Jim Snyder. "Customer service meets the Web." *InfoWorld.com,* April 3, 2000.

Dunlap, Charlotte. "Connecting to a higher level of customer service." *Enterprise Partner,* June 28, 1999.

Littman, Jonathan. "Serving the customer." *Upside Magazine.*

McKendrick, Joseph. "Internet call centers: New era in customer service." *EC World,* February 2000.

Michael, Bill and John Jainschigg. "CRM for dot.coms." *Computer Telephony,* April 1, 2000.

Nichols, George W. "E-mail management: R.S.V.P." *Operations & Fulfillment,* May/June 2000.

Pachut, Michael J. "QRS offers a quick response when retailers come calling." *Investor's Business Daily,* May 21, 1999.

Piller, Charles. "Most Net retailers all sale, no service." *Los Angeles Times,* June 28, 1999.

Read, Brendan B. "Local and worldwide service bureaus." *Call Center Magazine,* January 2000.

Sarges, Cheryl. "Hey, wait—you didn't pay for that!" *Web Developer's Journal,* January 10, 1999.

Shelton, Ben. "Building customer loyalty on the Web." *EcomWorld,* March 1, 1999.

Wester, Gregory. "Customers are from Venus." *Newmedia.com,* May 1999.

Wilde, Candee. "Web-enabled call center services promise to let service providers put on quite a show—assuming they don't drop the ball." *CMP Media Inc., http://www.teledotcom.com/,* June 26, 2000, Issue: 513.

Windham, Laurie. "The customer loyalty puzzle." *E-Business Advisor,* December 1999.

Wood, Stephen. "Web-enabled call centers: The strategic why and how." *Call Center Magazine,* December 1999.

"Customer relationship management (CRM) & the call center." *CommWeb.com,* January 1, 2000.

"Is customer service getting left behind?" *Emarketer.com,* February 28, 2000.

"Customers seeking service." *Emarketer.com,* May 12, 2000.

"No easy way to customer loyalty." *Emarketer.com,* May 1, 2000.

E-CRM Resources

CRMCommunity.com
http://www.crmcommunity.com

Digitrends.net
http://www.digitrends.net

Conference for Help Desk Professionals
http://www.helpdeskconference.com

The Customer Relationship Management Daily Report
http://www.realmarket.com

IT Support News
http://www.servicenews.com

SupportGate.com
http://www.supportgate.com

SupportIndustry.com
http://www.supportindustry.com

Publications

Operations & Fulfillment
http://www.opsandfulfillment.com

DM News
http://www.dmnews.com

Catalog Age
http://www.mediacentral.com

Direct Marketing Magazine
http://www.mediacentral.com

Target Marketing
http://www.targetonline.com

Catalog Success
http://www.catalogsuccess.com

Call Center Magazine
http://www.callcentermagazine.com

American Demographics
http://www.marketingtools.com

Marketing Tools
http://www.marketingtools.com

Inside Direct Mail
http://www.napco.com

Marketing Software Review
http://www.schell.com/review

Forecast
http://www.marketingtools.com

Catalog-News.Com
http://www.catalog-news.com

IBC Toll Free News
http://www.ibctollfree.com

Direct Newsline Daily
http://www.mediacentral.com

SHIP HAPPENS

It's no secret that the instant product ordering capability of the Internet has created the expectation of instant gratification on the product delivery side as well. Online shoppers want their products delivered quickly, reliably, and for free. Table 6-1 shows the percentage of online purchasers who say that these and other factors would cause them to purchase more online. Other factors cited included free product returns, guaranteed delivery time, and quicker delivery—all elements that involve shipping. The ability to ship products reliably and inexpensively—whether to a consumer or to another business—can mean the difference between e-business success and failure. Needless to say, shippers are scrambling to meet this demand, and third parties are springing up to provide software and services to help shippers and online merchants alike.

TABLE 6-1 What Do Online Shoppers Want?
Source: Boston Consulting Group

Factor	Percentage
Free delivery:	95
Lower prices:	94
Free returns if I am unhappy with product:	91
Ability to make in-depth product comparisons:	75
Security features (encryption, digital certification, etc.):	75
Guaranteed delivery time:	75
Vendor agrees to insure any credit card losses:	74
Faster navigation (pages load more quickly):	73
More detailed product/vendor information:	71
Quicker delivery:	69
Simpler navigation at shopping sites:	64
Better means of "virtually" touching/feeling products:	64
Simpler ways of finding shopping sites:	62
Products I am interested in are sold exclusively online:	57
Ability to talk live to customer service rep for help:	57
Site has a store located near me:	46
Credit card used exclusively for Internet transactions:	44
Able to pay C.O.D.:	36

How to Offer "Free" Shipping

In a related report, Forrester Research, Inc. surveyed 5,831 online shoppers, 82 percent of whom said that shipping costs factor into their purchase decisions. The report concluded that free shipping will likely be a key factor in grabbing the 11 million households that began shopping online in 2000. Free shipping is definitely a factor that helps prevent online shopping cart abandonment at checkout time, especially for the less affluent users who are coming online in increasing numbers.

Free shipping was a ploy that many online retailers used to lure shoppers to their sites during the 1999 holidays. It was an expensive ploy, because now customers expect all online merchants to pick up the delivery tab. Free shipping seems to have become a simple cost of doing business—but how can e-merchants survive when they're the ones paying for all of this "free" shipping?

One way is to offer free shipping selectively, based on each order.

- By purchase size. Common sense says that margins on the products shipped must be high enough to cover the expense of shipping the item. Therefore, discount offers on shipping must be presented to customers only after a certain purchase dollar amount has been reached. E-tailers such as HomeRuns.com, Ashford.com and Office Depot use this tactic to generate more impulse purchases by offering free delivery at a specific purchase level.

- By customer. Only loyal, profitable customers should be rewarded with reduced charges or totally free shipping. Since retailers can usually get 20 percent discounts on shipping rates from carriers like Federal Express (FedEx) and United Parcel Service (UPS), the e-merchants can choose to selectively pass on the savings to good customers, and charge full rates to unprofitable or infrequent customers.

- By in-store pickup. Payless.com lets its customers pick up their online orders free of charge by having them come into any of its brick-and-mortar locations. While this eliminates the convenience of total at-home shopping, it does have the added benefit to the retailer of luring the shopper into the physical store. It's usually difficult to simply pick up a package and go—most shoppers will end up buying extra products once they have set foot in the store.

Finally, many e-merchants simply embed shipping charges into the item price and then offer "free delivery." Customers then get the perception that they are getting a deal. Of course, it's wise to remember that price comparison engines are getting more prevalent on the Internet, posing the risk that the customer will find the same product for less, perhaps because of a lower embedded "free" shipping charge.

How E-Commerce Is Changing Transportation and Logistics

Electronic commerce is forcing a fundamental shift in the structure and services of transportation and logistics businesses. Not only are these firms transporting more online-purchased goods, they are actually subordinating their individual business plans and identities and becoming an integrated part of their e-business customers' supply chains.

One key to this change is to become part of an extranet that links and allows all the trading partners—customers, warehouses, suppliers, drivers, rail partners—independent of their internal resources, efficient interaction with the supply chain. Information technology provides the underlying links as well as the logistics data collection and analysis platform for all these activities. The logistics data allows the transport companies to operate their businesses more and more precisely against demand. All that information has to be online and available all the time. These efforts are not inexpensive.

In fact, transportation and logistics companies spent $2,367 per employee on technology to support e-commerce over the past year, an increase of more than 11 percent from the year before, according to the Meta Group. The figures include expenditures on server hardware, operating systems, and client and server applications software, as well as systems and software dedicated to e-commerce applications. When you consider organizations like UPS, with 327,000 employees, or the United States Postal Service (USPS), with 760,000 employees, you can do the math and see the enormity of these expenditures.

Higher volumes of e-business shipments aren't the only reason for these organizations to boost spending. Aggressive e-businesses want their package carriers to participate fully in the just-in-time processes that enable manufacturers to fill orders as swiftly as possible while keeping inventory to a bare minimum. This means that the carrier's systems must become intertwined with all of the facets of the e-business model in a variety of ways, as shown in Figure 6-1. The role of the package delivery company is rapidly shifting to one that includes full-scale logistics, supply-chain management, and even warehousing.

As mentioned in the first chapter, studies have shown that online shoppers check the status of their package an average of seven times from the moment the Buy button is clicked until the package arrives. This incredible statistic means that an e-business must be able to initiate, track, and acknowledge shipments online or face a deluge of customer phone calls. The first task for the e-business, then, is to link its Web site to the carriers' host systems to obtain real-time tracking and tracing data. Fortunately, FedEx and UPS offer free tools that aid in tracking, tracing, and a whole gamut of other functions. The USPS is also feverishly trying to develop some tracking tools to meet the e-business imperative.

Both FedEx and UPS have released sets of application programming interfaces (APIs) to internal business applications that would link corporate networks, intranets, and Web sites directly to internal carrier applications. These tools range from simple tracking applications to sophisticated software that lets users manage inbound orders from consumers and trading

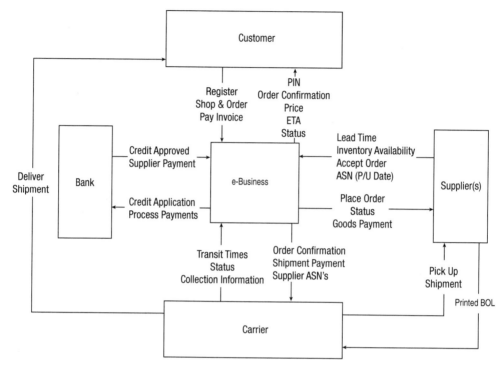

FIGURE 6–1   Carriers' Systems and Data Must Become Integrated with an E-Business's

partners in new ways. The ultimate goal in e-business is to achieve total end-to-end visibility throughout the supply chain, including delivery, down to the product component level.

Both FedEx and UPS are offering a particularly exciting answer to this challenge. The mammoth carriers have been racing toward offering software solutions that let corporate customers take a virtual peek inside packages in transit to reveal their contents and value. This means that a central administrator in a business can parcel out inventory, packing, and shipping instructions to appropriate departments and track not only the path of a package, but also the contents and value of the box. This total "package visibility" is also useful for international shipping, product returns, and repair shipments.

FedEx and UPS offer ways to integrate shipping, tracking, and distribution systems with the major enterprise resource planning (ERP) systems. FedEx has formed a broad strategic alliance with SAP AG that includes a direct interface between Federal Express applications and R/3 systems. This interface would mean that when an order comes into a warehouse, all parties involved inside the enterprise—as well as the customer—know exactly what items are on their way. For its part, UPS has made the move to integrate shipping, tracking, and distribution applications with PeopleSoft's ERP systems.

The Big Home Run

FedEx, UPS, and several start-up carriers, such as HomeGrocer.com, Kozmo.com, SameDay.com, and Webvan are racing to capture the home delivery market. All of these carriers are responding to the demand for better ground delivery service in the residential market—a sector that is expected to increase 119 percent by 2003, according to the National Research Federation. Online shoppers are now able to order such items as groceries, produce, video rentals, and even dry cleaning services. These orders create new demands for refrigerated trucks and other kinds of special handling. And that's just the beginning. Forrester Research projects online purchases will grow from $38 billion in 2000 to $184 billion by 2004. That means that business-to-consumer retailers will have to provide reliable, customer-friendly service, not just product, to their residential customers. It's a market fraught with challenges.

The biggest challenge is to find the lowest cost ways of getting the goods delivered. There are too many horror stories of consumers ordering a $10 CD, for example, only to be charged $12 to have it shipped. At the same time, business-to-consumer carriers are called on to provide more data about the contents and location of the packages they ship—another capability that affects costs.

The USPS and UPS combined handle about 75 percent of all business-to-home deliveries in the United States. UPS is famous for the amount of data it collects and its ability to scan packages and even trucks that are bar coded for tracking. In fact, UPS delivers about 12 million packages a day, about 7 million on which it electronically collects information.

The USPS is a different story. The USPS handles about half of the 75 percent home delivery figure, and that includes 3.4 billion pieces of mail each week. Although they have been working on a way to track each piece of mail via the Web, it's much more difficult for them, and the tools simply aren't there yet.

What about FedEx? FedEx has taken on the home delivery challenge in a big way, as part of a $100 million restructuring of the company. FedEx has acquired ground shipper RPS, renamed it FedEx Ground Packaging System, and has launched FedEx Home Delivery. The new unit will use regional contractors to deliver goods, and consumer-friendly options, such as evening delivery and the ability to specify the time a package should be delivered, will be added.

FedEx Home Delivery offers a host of premium service options—most of them unique to the small-package ground market.

- **Money-Back Guarantee**, a first in the residential ground market
- **Expanded Delivery Window** of 9:00 a.m. to 8:00 p.m., Tuesday through Saturday
- **Guaranteed Signature** service that ensures the capture of a signature for every package delivery
- **Guaranteed Select Day** delivery that enables recipients to choose the specific day of the week, including Saturday, for package delivery
- **Guaranteed Evening** delivery, which ensures that packages will be delivered between 5:00 p.m. and 8:00 p.m.
- **Guaranteed Appointment** delivery that confirms delivery within one hour of a specified time, which is designated by the recipient when contacted by the local FedEx Home Delivery terminal

Online Shipping Tools for E-Commerce Sites

Most of the major package delivery carriers offer online tools to help e-merchants not only provide package tracking and tracing to their customers, but integrate their internal systems with the carrier's for more efficient planning and data collection. A description of the major carriers' tools follows.

One word of wisdom, based on experience. Many of the tools that the carriers offer are free to download from their Web sites, but it really takes a savvy developer to actually implement the APIs into an e-commerce site. Plan on paying for a developer to spend about 20 to 30 hours per tool, at a minimum, to implement.

Airborne Express

Airborne Express is at the forefront of the air express industry. The first carrier to provide electronic data interchange (EDI) for customers, Airborne offers the following tools aimed at making all aspects of shipping fast, easy, and cost-effective.

- **LIGHTSHIP** Shipping and Tracking Software for Windows (U.S. shippers only). Prepare and print shipping labels, estimate shipping charges, determine delivery times, schedule pickups, track shipments, provide proof of delivery, and create shipping reports from a PC.

- **WORLD DIRECTORY** International Express Shipping Information Software for Windows. WORLD DIRECTORY provides the information needed to ship to more than 200 countries, and allows users to access transit times, acceptable commodities, documentation requirements, maximum declared values, customs requirements, and service and billing options.

- **LIBRA** Automated Shipping System. LIBRA is Airborne's free computerized shipping system for volume shippers. LIBRA weighs, rates, and labels each shipment in a matter of seconds. LIBRA also stores receiver addresses, prints invoices, generates management reports, tracks shipments, and more. For overseas shipments from the U.S., LIBRA simplifies documentation preparation, forwards export declarations to U.S. Customs, and cross-checks destination entries.

- **EDI: Electronic Data Interchange**. Airborne Express has EDI products to help increase efficiency and productivity in the transportation process. The e-tailer can process packages, create management reports, produce invoices, track shipments, pay bills, transfer funds, and more—all electronically.

DHL Worldwide Express

DHL Worldwide Express is the world's largest and most experienced international air express network, with service to 635,000 destinations in more than 233 countries and territories. DHL's 2,300 offices support the company's extensive worldwide coverage. Of that total, over two-thirds are owned and operated by DHL, far more than by any other company in the air express industry. As a result, DHL has a significant advantage over other air express carriers, who use third-party agents in foreign countries. DHL is also a licensed customs broker in more than 140 countries. These advantages result in faster transit times, streamlined customs clearance, effective tracking of shipments, and simplified billing.

DHL operates an unmatched global system of 34 hubs and 275 gateways. The network is serviced with a modern fleet of 101 aircraft in the U.S. and 222 aircraft worldwide. In addition to its own aircraft, DHL employs chartered and commercial airlines to move material. This gives DHL the flexibility to use the fastest possible means of transportation to any given destination.

DHL offers DHL CONNECT™, their version of software tools to help the shipper cope with the many vagaries of international shipping. Here are the functions DHL CONNECT offers:

- Prints plain paper airway bills
- Automatically prepares necessary Customs documentation
  – Commercial invoices

- – Certificates of Origin
- – Shipper's Export Declarations
- – Canada Customs invoices
- – NAFTA Certificates of Origin
- Schedules pickups
- Shipper's Address Book integrates with Symantec Act!®, Microsoft Outlook® and Lotus Organizer®
- Produces reports
- Orders DHL supplies
- Tracks DHL, FedEx, UPS, RPS, and Airborne shipments
- Offers shipment reporting
- Rates shipments
- Automatically assigns DHL routing (IATA) codes
- Links to helpful Web sites and email to DHL
- Can email prealerts to shipment receivers

Federal Express

With annual revenues exceeding $17 billion, FedEx Corp. is a premier global provider of transportation, logistics, e-commerce, and supply chain management services. The company offers integrated business solutions through a network of subsidiaries operating independently, including FedEx Express, the world's largest express transportation company; FedEx Ground, North America's second largest provider of small package ground delivery service; FedEx Custom Critical, the world's largest provider of expedited time-critical shipments; FedEx Logistics, an integrated logistics, technology, and transportation-solution company; FedEx Trade Networks, Inc., providing customs brokerage, consulting, information technology, and trade facilitation solutions; and Viking Freight, the leading regional freight carrier in the western United States. More than 2.5 million customers are connected electronically through the FedEx information network, and approximately two thirds of its U.S. domestic transactions are now handled online.

FedEx eBusiness Solutions are a combination of products and services in a customizable suite of business tools that help customers embrace new ways of 'doing business, from high-speed shipping software to Internet storefronts to the implementation of radically new business processes.

Some of the software and/or Internet-based tools include

- **FedEx interNetShip**®. Ship to over 180 countries, prepare FedEx shipping labels, arrange for pickup or drop-off, cancel shipments, track packages, and more—all online.
- **FedEx Ship**®. Delivers point-and-click addressing, label printing, package tracking, easy preparation of shipping labels, and more. A computer, a modem, and a laser printer are required.
- **FedEx Tracking**®. Track the status of up to 25 packages at one time at *http://www.fedex.com*.
- **Drop-off Locator**. Find and view maps of FedEx drop-off locations. Search by address, city, state, or zip code to find one of over 44,000 full-service and self-service locations worldwide.
- **Rate Finder**. Find the cost to ship from the U.S. to virtually anywhere.
- **FedEx Technology**. These are hardware-based tools that provide centralized control of a company's shipping process:
  - **FedEx PowerShip**®. Includes FedEx® shipping, online package tracking, recipient database, daily self-invoicing, and more.
  - **FedEx PowerShipMC**. Choose from multiple carriers, increase operating efficiency, enhance information access, and completely automate an organization's shipping processes with this hardware/software system.
  - **FedEx DirectLink**™. Receive and manage all FedEx invoicing data electronically.
  - **FedEx EDI Electronic Invoice and Remittance**. Designed to accommodate customers who want to be in complete control of billing data, processing invoices on their own computers and *using their own programs for integration with applications such as accounts payable and shipping transactions reporting.*

Customized FedEx solutions can also be incorporated into a business's infrastructure to allow real-time access to in-depth product information, shipment tracking, and other services.

- **FedEx PowerShipMC**. Multicarrier hardware/software system designed for mailrooms and shipping departments that 50 or more packages a day.
- **FedEx PowerShip**® **Server**. A complete hardware/software system designed for businesses where high shipping volume demands high-speed transactions, fully customized functions, and reliability. FedEx Powership Server can process an average of eight transactions per second, generate shipping labels, quote rates, produce activity reports, and bundle multiple shipments.
- **FedEx ShipAPI**™. Allows applications to be customized according to the operation's shipping needs. Connect to FedEx IT systems via the Internet, generate shipping labels, and track packages in real time.
- **FedEx NetReturn**®. An Internet-based returns management system, enabling management of the returns process from initiation to delivery.

Intershipper

Worldwide Merchant has updated its Web-based Intershipper software to offer real-time shipping information for most major parcel carriers. Intershipper lets users track packages sent via Atlanta-based UPS, Memphis-based FedEx, Seattle-based Airborne Freight, USPS, Silicon Valley-based DHL, and Pittsburgh-based RPS.

While most of the major carriers offer software that enables users to track packages, print labels and reports, and calculate rates for parcels sent via their specific service, Intershipper leverages information that is already available online and gathers it into a single location.

Intershipper may be useful for small businesses comparing rates domestically. The big companies all have negotiated fees with the large carriers that don't show up on public Web sites.

In industry, 80 percent or better have unpublished rates set up between customers and their carriers.

The latest version of Intershipper, which also lets users create shipping logs and find drop-off locations, can be integrated into Microsoft's Site Server software. It is available online and is free for the first three uses in a day.

Sameday.com

Sameday.com, formerly Shipper.com, is the first third-party logistics firm to offer same-day e-commerce fulfillment and delivery solutions to e-retailers nationwide.

- **Sameday Delivery**. Sameday's proprietary service delivers products to consumers the same day they are ordered online.
- **High-Speed Fulfillment**. Sameday's nationwide network of fulfillment centers and technological interface systems are designed for same day fulfillment and a broad range of high-volume peak demand products.
- **YourStore@Sameday.com**. Access to a turnkey Web site store in the Sameday.com Mall.
- **24-hour, 7 day-a-week Customer Contact Center**. Sameday's customer contact center features live chat, 24/7 coverage, and a professional staff trained in the e-tailer's business specifics.

SmartShip.com

Users can accomplish the following on this Web site:

- Obtain express shipping rates for the all the major carriers (Airborne, FedEx, UPS, and USPS).
- Decide whether it's best to drop off the package or to have it picked up by a carrier. In cases when drop-off is the best option, SmartShip provides directions to and deadlines for the nearest drop-off location. In cases when arranging a pickup is the better option, SmartShip provides a quick summary of the information needed to arrange the pickup via telephone.

- Use the services of lesser-known carriers by ordering the pickup and paying for the service entirely online, without having to pick up the telephone. These services are displayed alongside the services of the major carriers, to make decisions easier for the user.
- Track any package and view the results in the same manner every time, regardless of the carrier.
- Decide which carrier to utilize for a particular delivery requirement.

United Parcel Service

UPS, the world's largest express carrier and package delivery company, has formed a wholly owned subsidiary called UPS e-Ventures, aimed at researching, developing, and incubating new business related to e-commerce supply chain management.

One of the first companies UPS e-Ventures is developing, UPS e-Logistics, brings turnkey back-end solutions to small and midsize e-commerce start-ups that do not have the expertise to create a back-end system for their deliverables. UPS e-Logistics handles order fulfillment, payment processing, and customer care processes for their e-merchant customers' products and Web sites. Customers receive full reports that provide them with a vertical view of their companies. UPS e-Logistics also plans to serve dot-com divisions of traditional brick-and-mortar companies.

For merchants who want to incorporate UPS's shipping tools themselves, UPS offers the following free tools:

- **UPS OnLine Tracking** lets customers track their shipments from an e-commerce site, using a reference or order number. This functionality encourages customers to return to a site to track their shipments or to check the status of their order. This return traffic may lead to more sales. Customers can find out specific details about their shipments' status, including the time and location of each scan as the package moves toward its final destination.

- **Rates & Service Selection** lets online shoppers compare, price, and select shipping services that best fit their needs and budgets. For example, customers can choose express services, like UPS Next Day Air, when they need their packages delivered right away, or they can choose standard services, like UPS Ground, when they have more time for delivery. For single packages shipped from the U.S., the UPS Rates & Service Selection tool identifies all the available UPS domestic and international services and displays shipping rates based on a package's specifications. It can be used to generate a list of shipping services dynamically tailored for customers' shipments.

- **Address Validation** reduces shipping and billing address errors by validating the city, state, and postal code at the time of customer order entry, ensuring that errors are corrected long before orders leave the shipping dock. This reduces costly returns.

- **Time in Transit** enables customers to determine the number of business days it takes to transport a package using UPS Ground service between any two postal codes within the continental United States.

- **Shipping & Handling** lets an e-business institute its own shipping rates for the products their online customers order. The UPS rating information is downloaded and then tailored it to fit the business. Handling charges can be assessed, discounted shipping rates provided, or UPS's standards rates can be used.

- **Service Mapping** helps customers choose the best shipping service by providing a color-coded map that shows shipment transit time for UPS Ground service.

- **Electronic Manifesting** gives the flexibility of incorporating alternate billing options and reference number tracking capabilities, and transmits advance notice of shipping information via fax or email to shippers, receivers or third parties.

- **UPS Return Services** enables customers to generate an OnLine Call Tag. UPS drivers will bring the package label to the pickup location on the user-specified date and pick up the package. E-merchants can also generate a pickup label and send it to the customer with instructions to drop the package off at a UPS Customer Counter or Authorized Shipping Outlet.

Resources

Sample Shipping Contract

Terms and Conditions

1. In tendering the shipment for carriage, the shipper agrees to these TERMS AND CONDITIONS OF CONTRACT which no agent or employee of the parties may alter and that this Bill of Lading has been prepared by him or on his behalf by ACME Shipping.

2. In tendering the shipment for carriage, THE SHIPPER WARRANTS that the shipment is packaged adequately to protect the enclosed goods and insure safe transportation with ordinary care and handling, and that each package is appropriately labeled and is in good order (except as noted) for carriage as specified. The shipper further warrants to ACME Shipping that the content of the shipment may be lawfully carried over public highways and/or aboard airline aircraft and is not a prohibited commodity under any applicable law or regulation.

3. DECLARED VALUE AND LIMITATION OF LIABILITY. THE LIABILITY OF ACME SHIPPING IS LIMITED TO THE ACTUAL VALUE OF THE PACKAGE UP TO $100 unless a higher value is declared for carriage herein and a greater charge paid at the rate of $0.70 per $100 value. Shipments containing items of extraordinary intrinsic value such as money, currency, a fur, stones, works of art, and electronic components, etc. are limited to a maximum declared value of $500.

   When multiple packages are placed on a single Bill of Lading but the shipper has not specified the declared value of each individual package, the declared value for each individual package will be determined by dividing the total declared value on the Bill of Lading by the number of packages indicated on the Bill of Lading up to the actual value of each individual package or $100, whichever is less.

ACME Shipping is not liable for loss, delays, misdelivery, or non-delivery not caused by its own negligence or any loss, damage, delay, misdelivery, or nondelivery caused by (1) the act, default, or omission of the shipper, consignee, or consignor; (2) the nature of the shipment or defect or inherent vice thereof; (3) improper or insufficient packing, securing, or addressing of the package; (4) Acts of God, perils of the air, public authorities acting with actual or apparent authority, authority of law, riots, strikes or other local disputes, civil commotions, weather conditions, or mechanical delays of the trucks or aircrafts. ACME SHIPPING, SHALL NOT BE LIABLE IN ANY EVENT FOR ANY SPECIAL, INCIDENTAL, OR CONSEQUENTIAL DAMAGES, INCLUDING BUT NOT LIMITED TO LOSS OF PROFITS OR INCOME, WHETHER OR NOT ACME SHIPPING HAD KNOWLEDGE THAT SUCH DAMAGES MIGHT BE INCURRED.

4. CLAIMS. No action may be brought to recover damages for loss or injury to the goods UNLESS WRITTEN NOTICE OF LOSS DUE TO DAMAGE, SHORTAGE, OR DELAY IS REPORTED BY THE SHIPPER WITHIN 10 DAYS AFTER THE DELIVERY OF THE SHIP-MENT. WRITTEN NOTICE OF LOSS DUE TO NONDELIVERY MUST BE REPORTED BY THE SHIPPER WITHIN 30 DAYS AFTER ACCEPTANCE OF THE SHIPMENT OR CARRIAGE. No claim for loss to a shipment will be entertained until all transportation charges thereon have been paid. The amount of claims may not be deducted from transportation charges.

Claims for overcharges and refunds must be made in writing to ACME Shipping, within three (3) months of the billing date. All claims must be filed by the shipper.

5. Notwithstanding the shipper's instructions to the contrary, the shipper shall be primarily liable for all costs incurred in either returning the shipment to the shipper or warehousing the ship-ment pending disposition.

6. ACME Shipping assumes no responsibility for billing disputes resulting from inaccuracies contained in, or omissions from, the Bill of Lading.

7. All amounts due over 30 days shall accrue interest at the rate of 1.5% per month.

BILL OF LADING Page 1 of _____

SHIP FROM	
Name:	
Address:	
City/State/Zip:	
SID#:	FOB: ☐

Bill of Lading Number:_____

BAR CODE SPACE

SHIP TO	
Name:	Location #: _____
Address:	
City/State/Zip:	
CID#:	FOB: ☐

CARRIER NAME: _____
Trailer number: _____
Seal number(s): _____
SCAC:
Pro number:

THIRD PARTY FREIGHT CHARGES BILL TO:
Name:
Address:
City/State/Zip:
SPECIAL INSTRUCTIONS:

BAR CODE SPACE

Freight Charge Terms:
Prepaid _____   Collect _____   3rd Party _____

☐ (check box)   Master Bill of Lading: with attached underlying Bills of Lading

CUSTOMER ORDER INFORMATION

CUSTOMER ORDER NUMBER	# PKGS	WEIGHT	PALLET/SLIP (CIRCLE ONE)		ADDITIONAL SHIPPER INFO
			Y	N	
			Y	N	
			Y	N	
			Y	N	
			Y	N	
			Y	N	
			Y	N	
			Y	N	
GRAND TOTAL					

CARRIER INFORMATION

HANDLING UNIT		PACKAGE		WEIGHT	H.M. (X)	COMMODITY DESCRIPTION	LTL ONLY	
QTY	TYPE	QTY	TYPE				NMFC #	CLASS
							RECEIVING	
							STAMP SPACE	
						GRAND TOTAL		

Where the rate is dependent on value, shippers are required to state specifically in writing the agreed or declared value of the property as follows:

*The agreed or declared value of the property is specifically stated by the shipper to be not exceeding _____ per _____

COD Amount: $

Fee Terms: Collect: ☐   Prepaid: ☐
Customer check acceptable: ☐

NOTE Liability Limitation for loss or damage in this shipment may be applicable. See 49 U.S.C. _ 14706(c)(1)(A) and (B).

RECEIVED, subject to individually determined rates or contracts that have been agreed upon in writing between the carrier and shipper, if applicable, otherwise to the rates, classifications and rules that have been established by the carrier and are available to the shipper, on request, and to all applicable state and federal regulations.

The carrier shall not make delivery of this shipment without payment of freight and all other lawful charges.

_____ Shipper Signature

SHIPPER SIGNATURE / DATE	Trailer Loaded:	Freight Counted:	CARRIER SIGNATURE / PICKUP DATE
	☐ By Shipper	☐ By Shipper	
	☐ By Driver	☐ By Driver/pallets said to contain	
		☐ By Driver/Pieces	

FIGURE 6–2   Sample Bill of Lading
Source: Fran and David Barnes

SUPPLEMENT TO THE BILL OF LADING

Page _____

Bill of Lading Number: _____

CUSTOMER ORDER INFORMATION

CUSTOMER ORDER NUMBER	# PKGS	WEIGHT	PALLET/SLIP (CIRCLE ONE)		ADDITIONAL SHIPPER INFO
			Y	N	
			Y	N	
			Y	N	
			Y	N	
			Y	N	
			Y	N	
			Y	N	
			Y	N	
			Y	N	
			Y	N	
			Y	N	
			Y	N	
			Y	N	
PAGE SUBTOTAL					

CARRIER INFORMATION

HANDLING UNIT		PACKAGE		WEIGHT	H.M. (X)	COMMODITY DESCRIPTION Commodities requiring special or additional care or attention in handling or stowing must be so marked and packaged as to ensure safe transportation with ordinary care.	LTL ONLY	
QTY	TYPE	QTY	TYPE				NMFC #	CLASS
					PAGE SUBTOTAL		

FIGURE 6–3   Sample Supplement to the Bill of Lading
Source: Fran and David Barnes

Weship.net – Online Order Form

Your Name [_____](required)	
Your E-mail [_____](required)	
Your Phone [_____](required)	
Your Fax [_____]	

FROM:	**TO:**
Origin Zip: [_____]	Destination. Zip: [_____]
Pickup Information	**Delivery Information**
Contact	Contact Name
Phone Number	Phone
Address	Address
Address	Address
City, St Zip	City, St Zip
Package Ready To Pickup By	**Deliver By**
Time: [_____] Date: [_____]	Time: [_____] Date: [_____]

Description of Contents [_____]

Pieces / Weight / Dimensions / Insurance Value

			LxWxH	$
			LxWxH	$
			LxWxH	$
			LxWxH	$

Type of Service	Same Day / Next Flight Out ▾

Special Handling	☐ Sat. Delivery	☐ Convention Center	☐ Insure
	☐ Sun. Delivery	☐ Residence	☐ Do Not Insure
	☐ Lift gate Required		☐ COD $ [____]

FIGURE 6–4   *Sample Online Order Form*
Source: Fran and David Barnes

○ Bill Shipper   ○ Bill Consigner/Recipient   ○ Bill Third Party

Your Account Number

Billing Reference

New Customer
Click here to establish a.weship.net Account.

Third Party Billing Information

| Contact Name |
| Company Name |
| Phone Number |
| Address |
| Address |
| City St, Zip |

Special Instructions / Comments

Terms and conditions

Terms and Conditions

1.   In tendering the shipment for carriage, the shipper agrees to these TERMS AND CONDITIONS OF CONTRACT which no agent or employee of the parties may alter and that this , Bill of Lading has been prepared by him or on his behalf by Weship.net.

2.   In tendering the shipment for carriage, THE SHIPPER WARRANTS that the shipment is packaged adequately to protect the enclosed goods and insure safe transportation with ordinary care and handling, and that each package is appropriately labeled and is in good order (except as noted) for carriage as specified. The shipper further warrants to Weship.net that the content of the shipment may be lawfully carried over public highways and/or aboard airline aircraft and

| I have read and agree to the ter ms and conditions. ShipNow! | Clear Form / Start Over |

FIGURE 6–4   Continued

Articles

Ehrenman, Gayle. "What do online shoppers want?" *InternetWeek.* March 27, 2000. *http://www.techweb.com.*

"Free delivery is here to stay, research firm says." *ECommerce Guide,* January 14, 2000. *http://www.internet.com.*

Hudgins, Christy. "Logistics services: Governing who goes global." *InternetWeek,* November 15, 1999. *http://www.techweb.com.*

Joachim, David. "FedEx woos e-tailers with cheaper service." *InternetWeek,* January 19, 2000. *http://www.techweb.com.*

Krochmal, Mo. "Arizona company tracks package shippers." *TechWeb,* March 29, 1999. *http://www.techweb.com.*

Rosa, Jerry. "Subsidiary: Researching, developing new business—UPS unit aims e-commerce solutions at dot-coms." *Computer Reseller News*, February 21, 2000. *http://www.crn.com.*

Slaton, Joyce. "Delivering the goods." *The Industry Standard,* February 28, 2000.

Wilson, Tim. "Shippers repackaged as e-providers." *InternetWeek*, October 25, 1999. *http://www.techweb.com.*

Wilson, Tim. Transportation/Logistics—Shippers deliver the logistical goods." *InternetWeek,* October 25, 1999. *http://www.techweb.com.*

Shipping Resources Online

Airborne-Express
http://www.airborne-express.com

C@rgoNet
http://www.cargo-net.com

DHL
http://www.dhl.com

FedEx
http://www.fedex.com

FedEx Canada
http://www.fedex.com/ca/

Freightshipping.com
http://www.freightshipping.com

Newport Communications
http://www.truckinginfo.com

Sameday.com (formerly Shipper.com)
http://sameday.com

Shipping Magazine Online
http://www.shippingmag.com

SmartShip
http://smartship.com

TanData
http://www.tandata.com

The Internet Truckstop
http://www.truckstop.com

TruckNet
http://www.truck.net

United Parcel Service
http://www.ups.com

USA TRUCK
http://www.usa-truck.com

Xmessenger
http://www.xmessenger.com

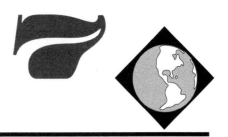

ACHIEVING TRUE FULFILLMENT

Online merchants rush to market, often focusing on the user or perceptual aspects of their e-commerce sites. This focus leads them to emphasize such activities as their appearance, content, and product organization. However, as we've seen, the "back-office" subsystems of e-commerce sites—those that provide the link between the user experience and the actual physical delivery of information and goods to the customer—continue to be a challenge. These parts, which include inventory management, order-capture and management, and reconciliation, often prove to be more difficult than the construction of the site itself.

The bottom line is achieving and sustaining increases in customer loyalty, and advantages and disadvantages accrue to each path you opt to take. A major consideration, however, is to set up your operation to minimize the cost of carrying inventory and subsequent shipping and handling. The most compelling reason for adopting one over another then becomes your business objective, which revolves around how you want to serve your customer.

Customer-sensitive trade-offs might deal with speed of delivery: same-day, which is important for perishables, or next day or thereafter, which reduces cost. Brand issues can force you to assess the appearance of product coming from your warehouse, and the attendant appearance of being more integrated. If you use an identifiable third party for any service (shipping, fulfillment, customer service, etc.), your responsiveness might be better, but the appearance of being "more virtual" might be a competitive disadvantage.

After all, what impression does a customer have of your operation when shipments arrive in a timely manner, but from different locations in packaging bearing different sources or origin? Are you the vendor or is that third party who supplies product or shipping the vendor in the customer's mind? That third-party logistics supplier might be the difference between near-term profit and loss, but your brand could suffer if packaging and aggregation issues are not dealt with.

These are some of the quandaries facing online businesses that are up against fulfillment bottlenecks. This chapter explores some of the most common fulfillment models and provides checklists for evaluating potential fulfillment outsourcers.

Offline Retail Fulfillment Models

In offline business-to-consumer (B2C) selling, merchants follow either of two business models. In one, the customer physically goes to a retail store, considers product availability and features, and then buys selected items to take home after conducting the transaction. There is usually some form of "instant" delivery at no additional cost. The offline merchant has to maintain some inventories to satisfy these customer requirements.

In this instance, while you might think that logistics (taking down inventory as needed from strategically located warehouses) is cheap and often inconsequential, the cost of brick-and-mortar locations, trained staff, and marketing can represent considerable expense. Since e-businesses don't have control of the manufacturing costs, the marketing and logistics costs are the only areas where they can reduce costs, and thus increase profit.

Alternatively, the customer buys product from a catalog and pays extra for shipping, sometimes with a hefty premium if next-day delivery is requested. Time of day of the order can be a factor if 24-hour turnaround is required.

While there are no "store" costs with the second model, back-end issues such as call centers, catalogs, and postage can be very expensive. Because orders are smaller and usually shipped directly to each customer's home, order picking and packing are more labor intensive, leading to backups on peak days or during peak seasons, and higher distribution costs compared to store delivery.

Online Fulfillment Models

Online merchants are taking the best of both models and adding their own spins to each to provide better availability, inventory selection, operating hours, customer service, and a host of other tangible and intangible qualities to differentiate themselves from offline merchants. However, to be competitive and survive, e-merchants such as online grocers must pare operating costs to the bone in hopes of attaining a slim level of margins. Ultimately, their plan is to become cost competitive by using technology to make many fulfillment costs borne by suppliers or customers less expensive while increasing customer service. True profitability then arises out of offsetting initially high customer acquisition costs with referrals and repeat business.

Therefore, WebVan, Amazon.com, and others are making fulfillment—the pick, pack, and ship process—a high priority part of their profit generation program. To achieve lower operating costs, WebVan invested millions in a state-of-the-art distribution center to reduce the time it takes to fill a customer's "shopping basket" and get it out the door into its network of delivery systems.

WebVan's fulfillment center in the San Francisco Bay Area, driven by a sophisticated IT system, features a specially designed conveyorized materials handling system. Aisles and storage racks are configured so one worker can manually locate, collect, and place customer orders on the conveyor in just under 20 minutes, one-third the amount of time the average consumer takes to push a cart through an offline store to acquire $120 worth of goods.

Online grocery shoppers buy off the Web for convenience. WebVan uses its back-end fulfillment system with enough automation to neutralize time as an issue for consumers and cost as an issue for the merchant. This homegrown fulfillment center is typical of steps taken by many of the pure-play dot-coms (companies without a brick-and-mortar presence) to establish a strategic capability around the least glamorous part of retailing, and the part easiest to screw up: fulfillment.

Getting a product from the virtual checkout counter into a customer's hands is devilishly difficult, as legions of novice online retailers can attest. Unlike WebVan, Amazon, and others, some Web stores are spending millions of dollars on site design, and then they neglect to put the same resources into fulfillment.

All too often, the smallest online retailers have such small-scale operations that they can stock and fill orders from the same converted garages that house their companies. Conversely, other retailers fill hundreds or thousands of orders per day by relying on distributors or original manufacturers to ship for them.

Supporting a sophisticated e-commerce effort often means using a warehouse, pulling inventory from shelves and packing it for shipment, retaining a delivery service, helping buyers track an order until it arrives, and taking returns. These all-important steps follow a customer's click on the Buy button.

The fastest-growing option by many going online is to hire an independent fulfillment house to store goods and provide "pick, pack, and ship" services. In fact, demand is so great for third-party fulfillment houses like Fingerhut Business Services, National Catalog, and Hanover Direct's Keystone Division that these companies are reportedly turning away new customers.

Even so, it's not always cost-effective to have someone else's warehouse crew stuffing your laptops into bubble wrap and boxing them for UPS pickup, as is the case for major OEMs. Many online retailers are struggling with the dilemma of whether to build their own fulfillment operations or to out-source order fulfillment, or having outsourced it, whether to bring it in-house. There is of course the bigger question: What's the most cost-effective and efficient way to get orders into customers' hands?

There are several ways to structure your operations to ensure proper fulfillment takes place. *Proper fulfillment* is whatever serves the customer best while preserving adequate profit margins to continue in business at a high level of customer satisfaction. Simply stated, if you can't meet these two requirements explicit in this model, then going online as a channel to support your venture is not the right one.

Most of the models that exist are variations of proven brick-and-mortar models—a single online storefront serves its customers from a central source of supply, one customer at a time. Alternatively, as in catalogs, a vendor makes transactions and parses fulfillment out to various suppliers. In the latter scenario, the sources of supply might provide drop-ship services, or may be fulfillment centers set up to take bulk shipment of products and then ship to order.

A third scenario integrates brick-and-mortar operations with online, allowing a customer to either buy or return through one or the other channel of supply, that is, buy online and, if needed, make a return offline, or buy offline and receive essential online support services after the purchase.

Each of the following online retailers demonstrates a different path.

Bringing It In-House

In 1998, Reel.com was one of those garage operations. They filled orders from a collection of 8,000 hard-to-find videos stored on shelves in the company's Berkeley, California, two-room office, in an old car dealership. Two distributors handled orders for the remaining 52,000 titles listed on Reel.com's Web site.

The arrangement served Reel.com well during its initial growth spurt. When the megahit *Titanic* debuted on video in September 1998, distributor Baker & Taylor used its 10-warehouse network to ship 300,000 copies to Reel.com customers—the day the video was released.

But the good times didn't last long. Two months later, Amazon.com opened its online video store in time to be competitive as they entered the lucrative holiday season, and other rivals soon followed. To differentiate itself, Reel.com decided to cut delivery times and expand the number of videotapes and DVDs carried. The only problem was that the company felt its distributors weren't up to the task. The distributors had so many clients that they didn't always meet the 24-hour to 48-hour turnaround demands; nor did they carry everything that Reel.com wanted.

Therefore, Reel.com, which became a division of video-rental chain Hollywood Entertainment, brought order fulfillment in-house. The company spent an undisclosed amount to lease a 30,000-square-foot warehouse not far from its new headquarters in Emeryville, California. Running its own distribution center meant the company could presell the latest DVD and video titles for delivery the same day they were released by the studios, a big plus for film buffs. It gave Reel.com the influence to negotiate purchase deals directly with video distributors.

However, the switch didn't translate into profits. Reel.com continued to rack up losses. Cutting out distributors helped boost gross margins, although company officials wouldn't say exactly how much. Management was confident that taking this important aspect of fulfillment in-house was a trend that would eventually push the business into the black.

Reel.com folded in mid-2000, partly because back-end operating expenses were too high.

Outsourcing It

If coordinating between one Web store and several distributors sounds daunting, imagine working with more than 100 suppliers.

For SkyMall.com, it's all in a day's work. Launched in January 1999, SkyMall.com is the online arm of SkyMall, the 10-year-old catalog placed in the seatbacks of major airlines. Like its offline parent, SkyMall.com collects placement and transaction fees in return for selling merchandise from direct merchants like Frontgate and Hammacher Schlemmer.

A typical SkyMall print catalog lists 2,000 items; however, SkyMall.com's Web site lists 15,000. It hit 30,000 by the end of 1999.

Since SkyMall.com does not maintain any inventory, the retailer relies on catalog partners to fill orders. For a few small vendors that don't handle their own shipments, the company contracts with a distribution center in Fremont, California, owned by fulfillment outsourcer Sykes Enterprises. For international orders, SkyMall.com leases space in Sykes' distribution centers in Scotland and the Philippines.

To coordinate the logistics of sending orders in a hundred directions, SkyMall selected Lowell, Massachusetts-based e-commerce order-management integrator OrderTrust. As orders come in, SkyMall conveys data to OrderTrust. OrderTrust then disseminates it to the appropriate vendor or distribution center and sends status reports back to SkyMall. SkyMall initially paid OrderTrust a fixed fee for the service, but switched to a per-transaction fee schedule.

SkyMall's smooth back-end order-fulfillment system enabled its online division, in only nine months, to grow to 25 percent to 30 percent of the company's total revenue.

E-Fulfillment Processes

E-fulfillment automates many processes, performing valuable functions that partly replace the need for manual activities and paper-based steps. These functions fall into several categories. The first stage is the moment of truth immediately after the sale is closed: the Notification. Concurrent with acknowledgement and confirmation is the behind the scenes process of physically moving product from warehouse through the handling stages and out into delivery channels. At its highest level of relation-ship intensity, e-fulfillment functions as the channel for actual physical fulfillment.

The Notification Process

Listed in order of relationship intensity are the all-important first moments of contact after a sale is apparently closed.

Acknowledgment and Confirmation

In a marketing world that has become depersonalized and automated, getting these types of acknowledgment in direct response to an action reassures customers that people still run businesses.

When calling a toll-free phone number to buy from an offline catalog, you interact with a human. This person takes your order, and confirms it over the phone. He or she will typi-cally repeat your credit card number, verify your name and address, confirm the items you just ordered, and tell you the total amount that will be charged to your credit card. You will also know, before you hang up, when you can expect to receive the items you ordered. Often you will be given an order confirmation number in case you have a problem with receiving the order.

If this scenario takes place at an online storefront today, the customer still needs to know that the order is confirmed. In fact, the need is greater, because there may be no person-to-person voice contact—the order is being placed computer-to-computer.

Today's leading Web merchants recognize this. Most of them therefore build in a number of confirmation contacts that help to reassure the customer that their questions are important and that the order was properly filled.

Consequently, immediate acknowledgement of an inquiry or order is powerful. When a prospect or customer completes a Web response form and clicks the Send button, an acknowledgment can instantaneously be sent with a message such as, *Thank you. We have received your inquiry and will process it immediately.*

Similarly, when placing an order, immediately after clicking on the Buy button, the customer can be notified the order was accepted: *Thank you for your order. In a few moments we will be confirming shipment of your selection, along with other details surrounding your transaction. We appreciate your doing business with (company name).*

At the point of sale, for example, the customer is led through a question-and-answer process, entering necessary data along the way. At the end of this process, a built-in autoresponder feeds back all of the data at once, asking the customer to review it and make necessary changes before pushing that Send button one last time. To assure privacy of sensitive information, the better sites use selected digits of credit card account numbers, "X-ing" out others in the sequence.

These are important steps in the confirmation process, because the customer is taking responsibility for the accuracy of the transaction and the merchant is assuring the customer it is okay to for them to do business with each other.

Any email to the customer restating the specifications of the order, confirming that it was understood by the company, and completing the confirmation loop by sending it directly to the user's mailbox enhances the sense of trust. Confirmation at this stage is important for another reason—if the customer did not place the order, or the order is incorrect, the individual can take corrective action.

Finally, some merchants are taking the confirmation process one step further by informing the customer when the order is shipped and when to expect its arrival. This is especially essential if there is a delay in the order, but it is just as useful and reassuring if the order is a normal shipment. Some marketers also include instructions for tracking the shipment at this stage. Others provide an online tracking component to their Web site.

Customer order confirmation is one application of trust-building, but confirmation is particularly useful in confirming a prospect's attendance at a seminar, for example. No product is involved, but registration often requires sharing sensitive personal information and frequently credit card account numbers to reserve a seat.

When Content Is Product: Information Fulfillment

What is content and what is product? When the first e-commerce shops went online, they were digital product catalogs. The content was the product, which was directly mapped to the stock-keeping unit (SKU) used by the online merchant's inventory system. As online merchants morphed from catalogs of passive information to active marketers, the distinction between content and product became blurred.

E-commerce sites must not only provide complete information about a product, but also be a source of relevant content to help sell the products. All of this content information must be fused with product information to produce an integrated browsing, shopping, and fulfillment experience.

Today, content ranges from product or content reviews to digital intellectual property, such as music, books, movies, and other forms of culture and art. Digital content must be seamlessly integrated with back-end fulfillment systems, especially if paper-based materials are used to support online operations.

Traditionally, *fulfillment of an inquiry* is most often handled through a paper-based transaction. In some cases, an inquiry may be fulfilled via fax, but most often, the inquirer receives paper fulfillment, which may include a letter, data sheets, and brochures. They may be packaged in a folder. All are frequently enclosed in a large envelope and mailed, or sometimes delivered via a package delivery service.

Even if the inquiry goes through multiple stages in the fulfillment process, the individual receives, at the very least, an offline mailing with some additional information and a reply device designed to further qualify that person's interest. If the individual responds to this step, he or she will receive additional information from the marketer.

Whenever the merchant sends the material, and by whatever method, there will be a time lag, unless the fulfillment is by fax only. That means a potentially hot prospect could cool off as days or even weeks go by before paper-based information works its way through the physical world.

Although it may be unrealistic to convert the entire paper fulfillment process to electronic fulfillment, moving toward fulfillment over the Internet has to be an attractive, long-term alternative. For one thing, electronic fulfillment is environmentally friendly.

Traditional fulfillment is paper-based and labor-intensive. Electronic fulfillment, on the other hand, does not waste trees, nor does it involve ink. It does not have to be produced in quantities of 1,000, 10,000, 50,000, or 100,000, and stored. It does not have to be cut, folded, stapled, and inserted into folders and envelopes. It does not burden your staff (or Postal Service workers). In short, it saves time, money, and natural resources. In addition, it does not have to be "trashed" because of obsolescence.

In today's electronic fulfillment environment, printed literature can have a longer shelf-life. Time-sensitive information can be just as easily conveyed electronically, on the Web. Collateral materials can also be mirrored electronically to leverage copy and artwork. This extends far beyond the point of a casual convenience for prospects and customers.

Electronic fulfillment is a desirable means of delivering information almost instantaneously—at a cost too low to ignore. The need for printed literature may still exist in certain circumstances, but it can be substantially reduced with electronic fulfillment.

Electronic fulfillment also provides customers and prospects with a new kind of instant gratification. They can immediately receive information electronically and either view it online, print it, or save it for later handling. They can just as easily unlock or download information of perceived high value or software that they can demo, try, and/or buy, right from the computer desktop. Information can even be personalized to meet the individual's specific needs and delivered free and on a regular basis to the individual's computer. Based on the individual's feedback, electronic fulfillment can be further tailored.

Electronic fulfillment thus becomes the beginning and support of a relationship. You can engage your prospect or customer in a dialogue, which allows you to continuously learn more about the individual's real needs. You can collect data from the prospect or customer by asking questions on electronic surveys and response forms, and turn the answers into marketing intelligence. By linking the information to a database, you can then use this intelligence to build a highly effective communication program, tailored to individual needs.

Database-driven electronic fulfillment ultimately meets the informational needs of many individuals, one person at a time. Meanwhile, you drastically reduce the costs and lag time of traditional fulfillment. You develop an ongoing, one-to-one relationship with the prospect or customer, learn more about that person's specific needs, and reap the financial and timesaving benefits of electronic fulfillment.

Getting Physical: From Click to Pick

Even if operating "virtual," in the real world there are warehouses, products, people, and deliveries of physical goods. And whoever develops an e-commerce capability must be able to deal with issues that synchronize product inventories with pricing, inventory status, invoicing, and final reconciliation. Here are the stages any merchant must go through, whether in-house or using a third party, to ready an operation for rapid-turn fulfillment. After all, one of the reasons B2B and B2C customers shop is for convenience, and an important ingredient of convenience is ease of ordering and quick receipt of frequently hard to locate goods and services.

There are many interrelated steps that must be coordinated to bridge the gap between a customer browsing an e-commerce site and actually purchasing and receiving an ordered product.

- The site communicates information about products that are available for sale.
- Next, customers purchase (via a shopping cart or some other transaction method) by selecting from a database of products so they can place an order.
- The order is then transmitted to the fulfiller or fulfillers, who complete the delivery of goods to the customer.
- Finally, someone must handle any post-delivery activity to ensure customer satisfaction, such as returns or exchanges, and be prepared to perform transaction reconciliation.

Setting up the Back-Office Functions

Online merchants and others who require shipment of goods from inventory maintain a product catalog database that contains a brief description of each item, pricing, availability, SKU, and any appropriate variations in models or configurations. Each database element represents a product entity that can be sold and shipped. To make the customer experience efficient, relationships must be made between products to be sold and content elements with which they are associated.

Product-to-content mapping is often offered in multiple formats (e.g., PCs are available with CD-ROMs and/or DVD drives, with hard drives of varying capacities, with or without monitors, and so on). Each configuration or variation in format must be properly linked to the correct piece of content.

As the size of these databases grows, the e-merchant encounters database complexity issues. Product counts for large sites can be upwards of hundreds of thousands of SKUs, with content, such as supporting data sheets, an order of magnitude beyond that. Each different data set is interdependent with others, and each must be consistently updated or refreshed to stay current.

It's not customer friendly for a site to advertise a product to a user and then discover that the merchant or fulfillment house does not carry that item. Sites that offer 24/7 availability need to stage databases to refresh and synchronize data sets.

Ideally, database routines such as loading, mapping, linking, and indexing must be done offline at a staging site, and then monitored as the information is added to the live site. Someone, either internally, at the hosting service, or with the fulfillment house, is usually entrusted with managing these updating routines to avoid disturbing the site itself or any in-process transactions. One vendor claims to employ over 100 scripts and programs to clean, load, and link data from its content and product data providers. Most run automatically on daily schedules, with exception reports generated for items that require manual attention.

The Hand-off from Buy Button

When the customer adds a product to the shopping cart, the product as represented on the site and the SKUs in the inventory database are matched. Each third-party fulfillment house usually has its own series of SKUs to represent a given product. Some use Universal Product Codes (UPC). What is added to the shopping cart is a virtual product ID that is then mapped to the appropriate SKU at order time.

When the customer clicks the Buy button, he or she enters the order-capture pipeline. The digital order pipeline consists of a sequence of processing steps that vary with the many different shopping cart products that exist in the e-commerce product marketplace (such as Open Market's Transact™ and Microsoft's® Commerce Server 2000™).

In the first pipeline stage, the system collects product information from the shopping cart or other transaction mechanism. Next, the site must map each virtual product to the SKU in the database and determine where the customer order is fulfilled. Some products are dropshipped from the OEM, for example, rather than fulfilled from the merchant's inventory. The pipeline must contain business rules to determine the source of supply for the customer's order.

A business rule may require that all goods be sourced from one location, simplifying the order process so the complete order can be drop-shipped from a single location. Another business rule may require shipment from a location with the lowest shipping cost because of proximity to the customer. Unfortunately, when using sources for an order, such as when Amazon.com must pull books from different distributors, the customer might receive separate shipments from each.

When buyer information is collected and item prices and applicable discounts are applied, the order subtotal is computed. Site queries on inventory status of the items ordered can be performed earlier in the order pipeline, if required.

If whoever manages the product catalog database does not handle real-time inventory queries, the merchant may have to rely on batch-processed, after-the-fact inventory profiles. This often invalidates the reason for being online to provide immediate order status to customers! See Chapter 4 for more reasons to handle transactions in real-time.

Business rules provide a consistent way to determine whether the quantity-on-hand estimate supplied for a SKU is within acceptable tolerances to be considered "available/in stock." If there are real-time inventory queries, then the system can compose an order message and transmit the request to the inventory location.

Each transaction requires mapping data from the site's order management system (and pipeline) into messages understood by whoever maintains the product inventory database. How the data is represented could be a problem because there are wide variations in formats, ranging from the American National Standards Institute's (ANSI) Accredited Standards Committee (ASC) X12 electronic data interchange (EDI) format to proprietary batch-file data formats. The current trend is toward eXtensible Markup Language (XML) to represent electronic data, and many standards bodies are considering various draft format proposals. See Chapter 9 on emerging data exchange standards for more about the standards bodies.

The Electronic Commerce Modeling Language (eCML) is another effort toward standardizing electronic wallets that contain frequently requested bill-to and ship-to information, credit card data, and so on. The XML/EDI initiative's goal is to wrap the several decades-old legacy investments in EDI with XML to provide a schema more appropriate for today's e-commerce environment.

Shipping address and delivery method are the next pieces of information to be collected. Ideally, if the buyer has purchased before, the site displays a list of ship-to addresses from the buyer's address book, and presets the shipment method based on existing buyer-preferences. Depending on decisions made upstream in the pipeline, the available shipment options are determined by the product source chosen to handle and ship the order to the customer.

If multiple sources of product are involved, then a shipping carrier shared by each source, such as UPS or FedEx, can combine and ship the order. If there is a single source, then the system queries that source for current delivery options. Complications at this process point include support for multiple ship-to addresses for the same order, special handling instructions, possibility of gift wrapping and messages, time-of-day delivery, and so on. Order totals are computed once the buyer has selected all shipping and special handling.

Next, credit card or other transaction-intensive information is entered or retrieved from the customer database, and the credit card and purchase order or other document is authorized for the order total. If a consumer transaction, the system interacts with a credit card clearinghouse to validate the address verification and to determine whether the buyer has sufficient credit available. Communicating with merchant banks and/or credit card clearinghouses could require a dedicated line and a modem to transmit the requests using clearinghouse's proprietary protocol. A standard in this area is Secure Electronic Transaction (SET), which unfortunately lags in adoption. Alternatively, a site can use a third party like CyberCash or CyberSource to broker the transaction between the site and the clearinghouse. Refer to Chapter 4 for more information on the steps in transaction processing.

A word of caution, though: most who set up an e-commerce venture think they can connect to CyberCash, bill the credit card, and then immediately ship the item. Often overlooked by the novice online merchant is the need to make sure they have inventory at their operation or in the third-party fulfillment center. Then, and only then, should they authorize the credit card to charge, or *settle*, the transaction, which can only be done after the item is shipped. Chapter 2 goes into the FTC rules surrounding shipping before settlement.

If you've ever charged the account and then found out you were unable to ship, you can appreciate the sticky situation: by law, no transfer of funds from account to account can take place without verification that product has gone out. Once the transaction is approved and the buyer has clicked on the confirmation button, the order is accepted by the site's order-management system. Most sites offer the buyer the opportunity to cancel the order within a specified time frame, which delays referring the completed order to the holder of the product. If the source doesn't support a real-time protocol, then the order is transmitted during the next batch-file generation cycle. If real-time order processing is supported, then the site can transmit an XML message over secure HTTP, including all necessary information for the source of supply to process the order. To assist in the reconciliation process, the XML document includes the merchant order number, which links the store's order management system and the suppliers' order/warehouse management systems.

Reconciliation

After an order has been captured and transmitted to the warehouse, there's still a lot of work to be done. The fulfiller processes the order, starting first with allocation of inventory to complete the transaction. In a fully automated environment, work orders are issued to pick products and package them.

The products are then shipped to the shipping address, using the selected carrier. If some of the items requested by a customer are not available, the customer's order is placed on hold or back order, until the fulfillment house inventory is replenished with new stock from the e-merchant.

During these steps, the better merchants keep the buyer informed about the status of the order. As at Amazon.com and other such sites, the buyer can go to the site and bring up the order history, requesting a real-time order-status query. If it's supported, the site communicates with the fulfiller via secure HTTP and requests the status of an order. A typical message includes details of all shipment data, cancellation requests, back order status, and other transactions that have taken place while processing the order.

Many third-party logistics services transmit their order status files nightly via FTP or encrypted email, describing the day's order activity (shipment, cancellations, etc.) and order items that are on back order.

This starts the reconciliation process, that is, how the outsourced service performed in filling the customer's order and requirements mandated by the merchant. It is illegal for anyone, a site or a third-party fulfillment house, to charge or settle a credit card transaction until the order has been fulfilled, either in full or partially. This means the order fulfillment information returned to the merchant by the fulfillment house must be verified for accuracy before the credit card settlement request is issued.

Here is a partial checklist for merchants to use to determine if reconciliation should proceed.

- Were the correct SKUs shipped for the right quantity and cost?
- Were the correct shipping, tax, and handling charges accurately allocated?
- Did the third-party fulfillment house put order items on back order?
- Were the actual item, shipping, packaging, and other charges/costs sent to the merchant correctly?
- Was the customer notified correctly and promptly of the order status at each stage?
- Who is to notify the customer of how partial shipments are to take place?

Without valid information, merchants can't post a shipment invoice to the order management system. Settlement tasks, which run periodically to process shipment invoices that need collection, are electronically communicated to the clearinghouse to charge the buyer's credit card. When the order is originally placed, funds are only allocated or authorized, but not disbursed. If the merchant and third-party fulfillment house don't agree on order details, buyers may be charged the improper amount.

Order information is then transferred from the order management system to the merchant's financial system for purchase order generation, accounts payable to pay the third-party fulfillment service—who in turn might make payments to carriers, tax authorities, and so on. All of the data must accurately reflect what transpired while processing a given order, and must be timely. Otherwise, the merchant can't provide a customer with accurate order status information or develop routine metrics, like margin analysis, inventory forecasting, and site traffic.

Fulfillment Sources

There should be no surprise: different fulfillment services offer a variety of different options. Finding one to fit your needs and your online store scale of operations requires lots of research.

Some fulfillment houses handle not only distribution, but also order processing, call center, customer service, and financial and marketing reporting. Often the most important feature to opt for is an email customer service system. This capability answers customer inquiries (i.e., disposition of product, questions about billing, special orders).

Checklist to Prepare Yourself before Choosing a Fulfillment Service

Questions to ask yourself:

- ❏ How large is our inventory?
- ❏ What is our inventory?
- ❏ How much can we budget for fulfillment?
- ❏ How fast do we need to get our products delivered?
- ❏ How fast must inventory be replenished?
- ❏ What terms are available from suppliers?
- ❏ What are the prices for credit card merchant services?
- ❏ How do we allocate fulfillment costs?
  - ❏ Non-finished goods freight costs?
  - ❏ What shipping/handling can we lay off against the transaction and remain competitive?
- ❏ Do we need customer, promotional, or marketing support?
- ❏ Is our business data system compatible with that of the fulfillment service?

Is Third-Party Fulfillment Right for Your Venture?

Large companies, more than ever, are outsourcing many tasks to third parties so they can concentrate on their core strengths. Nike, Hewlett-Packard, and hundreds of others are choosing third-party fulfillment or third-party logistics (3PL) firms as another link in a lengthening chain of outsource services.

Fulfillment houses, operating as 3PLs, were developed to use expertise in process management tracking and warehousing for both manufacturers and retailers. Retailers are using fulfillment services to maintain a "deep" (large) inventory (titles normally not stocked), reduce inventory costs, and drop-ship orders directly to customers. Manufacturers use them for direct marketing campaigns like mail order catalogs.

The term *fulfillment* describes a "horizontal tier" of services, from the beginning of a job through delivery to distributors or end users.

Some fulfillment houses, such as Fingerhut, create and service their clients online, as well as provide printed catalogs that let sales representatives and customers order literature and merchandise via the Web. These firms provide such services as inventory warehousing, order processing, shipping, and inventory management.

This type of 3PL provides whatever services are contracted for at an up-front, agreed-upon price, leaving the merchant free to concentrate on selecting products, selling goods, and serving the customer. The 3PL receives purchased goods, stores them, picks them to fill customer orders, and then packs and ships them by the method that the merchant or customers choose.

Under the terms of your contract, the 3PL works for you by labeling the cartons, setting packing lists that carry your name and logo, and handling delivery and even returns, so there is no doubt who sent the package.

Because this 3PL option is lucrative for vendor and merchant alike, there has been a rush to start new Internet order fulfillment companies. Some of these companies previously provided similar services for catalog sellers. Others, like Sameday.com and ifulfill.com, were launched to serve Internet merchants.

Sameday.com

Sameday.com, formerly shipper.com, is a large, well-financed operation designed to serve serious e-tail Web sites. It targets companies with $10 million to $50 million a year in sales volume. Clients usually have their own Web-based shopping cart and credit card processing.

Sameday.com has two large fulfillment centers and is developing several more in large, key cities in the U.S. As a means of differentiation, Sameday.com uses best-of-breed distribution and supply chain software. Consequently, its systems interface directly with the merchant's server to pick up orders and drop off shipping confirmations.

Sameday.com services are complex and comprehensive. Pricing is based on the merchant's exact requirements. When built out, their nationwide distribution network will be able to offer one-day and two-day delivery service for merchants' key, high-moving items for ground UPS rates. This is done by holding duplicate inventory at each site and shipping from sites located within one-day and two-day UPS delivery zones of the customer.

Sameday.com plans to provide same-day delivery for orders that are placed by noon in their key market cities, at $10.00 to $15.00 per delivery. In March 2000, Sameday.com opened a 114,000-square-foot location in Chicago. The company said in a press release that with the addition of the new facility, it will be able to provide same-day delivery to four of the largest markets in the U.S., encompassing all suburbs and cities surrounding Los Angeles, San Francisco/San Jose, New York City, and Chicago.

Opening an average of one new facility per month, Sameday.com said it could then begin servicing customers from centers in Dallas; Atlanta; Washington, DC; Memphis; and Seattle by the third quarter of 2000. The company also plans international locations by the end of 2000.

Each facility is complemented with a proprietary fleet of delivery vans.

ifulfill.com

ifulfill.com aims at the large and untapped market of small merchants who have no credit card processing, fewer than 50 items, and who sell 1 to 50 items per month. Everything about the ifulfill.com system is designed to make IT management and physical inventory handling easier for the unskilled or small vendor.

Signup for ifulfill.com is handled online with a "code snippet" generated for each item. This snippet, or *bot*, is cut and pasted directly into the merchant Web site. Then, when a customer clicks on a product description, the selection is sent to the ifulfill.com shopping cart. When all selections are made, the shopper enters name, address, and credit card information. The customer also learns that the purchase will appear as an ifulfill.com charge on the next credit card statement.

The merchant is hit with a 7 percent credit card fee, plus a sliding per-order fee that ranges from $4.00 for the first 10 orders per month to $1.00 for anything over 50 orders per month. An additional $0.30 is charged for each extra item on an order.

There is a minimum monthly charge of $4.00 for each item listed. With this pricing model, a musician selling five CDs would have a $20.00 minimum monthly charge, which would be covered by the first five orders placed each month.

Certainly, when added to all other fees incurred by a small online merchant, the $4.00 per order fee is expensive. As sales per month increase, the cost per order quickly drops. When inventory runs low, the merchant is automatically notified to reorder. Other than selling and depositing checks, this is all the online merchant must do to run the business.

This is a good solution for part-time Web entrepreneurs. It is also a good example of a business model custom-tailored for the Web.

What to Look for in a Fulfillment House

A good starting place to locate a fulfillment house is to find one that stocks the depth and breadth of product types that your site sells. A solution used by many online merchants is to locate distributors used by the traditional brick-and-mortar retailers selling the same products to an established industry group.

Factors to consider when evaluating a fulfillment house include:

- inventory levels, that is, the number of SKUs in stock
- order fill rate, which is the percent of orders that get processed the same day
- cut-off time to process a same-day order
- number of shippers supported
- cost of goods to the retailer
- support for real-time communication of inventory level checks, orders, and other information as opposed to batch-file communication
- availability of credit card processing on the retailer's behalf
- level of customer service on the retailer's behalf
- capability to offer frequent and consistent email contact with the customer
- capability to handle product returns

To sum up, as the flood of merchants coming online continues, often the speed and efficiency of how fulfillment is handled can be a major differentiator against competition. However, to be truly successful, each must use the appropriate sources to integrate marketing and sales-driven front-end commerce sites with back-end fulfillment houses.

Here is a set of summary checklists that can be used to prepare your e-business for a fulfillment service, as well as to select a fulfillment service.

Checklist to Prepare for a Fulfillment Service

- ❏ How large is your inventory?
- ❏ What is your inventory?
- ❏ How much can you budget for fulfillment?
- ❏ How fast do you need to get your products delivered?
- ❏ How fast must your inventory be replenished?
- ❏ What terms are available from suppliers?
- ❏ Is your business data system compatible with that of the fulfillment service?
- ❏ Can your Web site's order page be linked directly, in real-time, to the fulfillment center?
- ❏ Who will handle the payment processing? Does the fulfillment house offer credit card processing services? What are the prices for credit card merchant services?
- ❏ How do you allocate fulfillment costs?
  - ❏ Non-finished goods freight costs?
  - ❏ What shipping/handling can you lay off against the transaction and remain competitive? Can you offer "free" shipping and stay in business?
- ❏ Who is to notify the customer of how partial shipments are to take place?
- ❏ Do you need customer, promotional, or marketing, support?

Checklist for Selecting a Fulfillment House

- ❏ Does the fulfillment house stock the depth and breadth of product types that your site sells?
- ❏ What kind of inventory levels are they handling, that is, the number of SKUs in stock?
- ❏ What percent of orders get processed the same day? (order fill rate)

❏ What is the cutoff time to process a same-day order? If a customer gets an order in by 5:00 pm, can it be shipped the same day, if desired?

Real-Time Processing and Communication

❏ What kind of support for real-time communication of inventory level checks, orders, and so on can be provided? Alternatively, does the fulfillment house only offer to batch-file communication?

❏ Does the fulfillment house offer credit card authorization and processing online, so that the order is instantly available for filling?

❏ What kind of customer service can the fulfillment house offer on your behalf?

❏ Can the Web inventory be constantly verified, so if it can be seen and ordered, it is in stock?

❏ Are orders bar code-scanned during picking and check-weighed at the manifesting scale to insure complete picking accuracy?

Shipping

❏ How many shippers does the fulfillment house support?

❏ If an order will take more than two days to deliver by UPS ground or other local services in the U.S., then are special lower rates offered to the customer?

❏ If an order cannot be shipped the same day, is it shipped the next day with free upgrade to next-day delivery to be sure it is received within two days?

❏ Will barcoded return labels and documents accompany each part of the shipment for use if any part of the order must be returned?

Email Communications

❏ Is an email sent to the customer as soon as the shipment is manifested, showing shipping date, expected arrival date, final costs, and tracking number?

❏ If the order is to be shipped from multiple sites, does an email confirm each part of the shipment?

❐ Is another email sent the day after expected delivery for verification that delivery was made and accurately fulfilled?

Accountability

Ask these questions of the fulfillment house's reference customers.

❐ Were the correct SKUs shipped for the right quantity and cost?

❐ Were the correct shipping, tax, and handling charges accurately allocated?

❐ Did the third-party fulfillment house put order items on back order?

❐ Were the actual item, shipping, packaging, and other charges/costs sent to the merchant correctly?

Resources

Articles

Avery, Art. "Reinventing order fulfillment for the Internet age." *Ezine,* July 29, 1999. *www.ELogistics101.com.*

Staff. "Bluelight.com selects submitorder.com for fulfillment." *Ecommerce Guide,* April 11, 2000, *http://www.internet.com.*

Kapsinow, Steve. "Using fulfillment services for e-commerce." *ECommerce Guide,* April 15, 1999. *http://www.internet.com.*

Mesrobian, Edmond and Brian Ringer. "Toward successful e-fulfillment: It's all in the SKU." *Web Techniques,* January 2000.

Rafter, Michelle V. "The art of fulfillment." *The Industry Standard*, September 13, 1999. *http://www.thestandard.com.*

Spears, Mit. "Capitolisms: Unfulfilled promises." *Upside Today,* March 30, 1999.

Fulfillment Links

Consolidated Marketing Services
http://www.cmsassociates.com

Fingerhut
http://www.fingerhut.com

iFulfill.com
http://www.ifulfill.com

OrderTrust
http://www.ordertrust.com

Retail Tech Online
http://www.retailtech.com

SameDay.com
http://www.sameday.com

SubmitOrder.com
http://www.submitorder.com

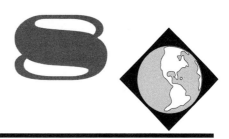

GLOBAL LOGISTICS

The Profit Potential of Going Global

The moment your e-commerce site goes live, you become a worldwide entity. You are also faced with an important decision: should you accept orders worldwide? With 30 percent of online shoppers located outside North America, you may be passing up tremendous revenue opportunities if you don't accept and fulfill international orders. The growth in the international Internet population means more potential business for U.S. companies, particularly from consumers who are eager to buy products they cannot obtain in their countries.

By 2003, International Data Corporation (IDC) estimates 60 percent percent of Internet users will be outside the U.S. and the non-U.S. share of e-commerce will reach 46 percent, up from 26 percent in 1998. IDC projects the compound annual growth rate of European e-commerce at 138 percent, which will take it from a mere $5.6 billion in 1998 to $430 billion by

2003. Runner-up to Europe in Internet growth, the Asia and the Pacific region will see near quadruple growth, from 21 million users in 1998 to 81 million users in 2003.

Also, consider these stats from research firm Forrester Research, Inc.

- North America lost its majority share of the world's Internet user population in first quarter 1999.

- Worldwide e-commerce revenues will grow from $98.4 billion in 1999 to over $1.2 trillion by 2003, with the U.S. continuing to enjoy a majority share of global EC (electronic commerce) dollars in that year.

- After the U.S., Germany has the second-highest level of e-commerce revenues in the world, at $1.5 billion in 1998 and $4.4 billion projected for 1999; the United Kingdom follows with $1.49 billion in 1998 and $3.7 billion in 1999.

- The number online in South America will rise from 4.1 million in 1999 to 26.6 million in 2002, an increase of 550 percent.

- More than 75 percent of the world's Web sites are in English.

eMarketer projects a similar shift in the global share of e-commerce revenues. As the pie chart in Figure 8-1 indicates, the U.S. share will decline from 76.8 percent in 1998 to 52.6 percent in 2003. The chart is in billions of dollars.

It is clear that ignoring orders outside of the U.S. is extremely shortsighted, but how do you navigate the many obstacles that international commerce presents? Although entire books have been written about international trade, customs clearance, and shipping, this chapter will focus on an overview of the top issues in global logistics. Then we'll drill down in detail on the subject of international taxation of electronic commerce—a thorny topic that is currently garnering great attention.

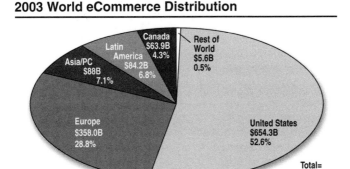

2003 World eCommerce Distribution

FIGURE 8–1   2003 World E-commerce Distribution
Source: eStats, 1999

The Pitfalls of Going Global

One of the first television commercials in the U.S. that promoted international electronic commerce featured a tourist couple that stumbled upon an old woman working in an olive orchard. Assuming the old woman was an unsophisticated peasant, the couple inquired about buying olive oil. The old woman went on to say that she was now selling olive oil worldwide over the Internet, all through implementing some IBM technology. In truth, global e-commerce and logistics is far from easy.

In one survey conducted by Forrester Research (see Figure 8-2), a whopping 46 percent of the interviewees said they turn away international orders because they do not have processes in place to fill them. Obstacles range from an inability to handle direct international orders, to language and cultural barriers that hinder basic communications, to varying stages of Internet adoption and infrastructure.

In yet another study, Forrester Research found that 85 percent of the firms they surveyed couldn't fill international orders because of the complexities of shipping across borders (see Table 8-1). Of the 15 percent that did handle global orders,

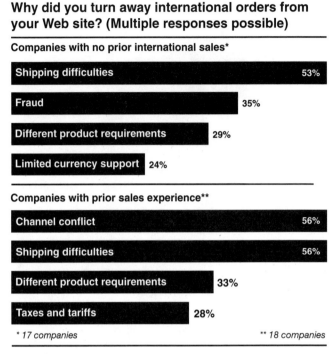

Why did you turn away international orders from your Web site? (Multiple responses possible)

Companies with no prior international sales*

Shipping difficulties	53%
Fraud	35%
Different product requirements	29%
Limited currency support	24%

Companies with prior sales experience**

Channel conflict	56%
Shipping difficulties	56%
Different product requirements	33%
Taxes and tariffs	28%

* 17 companies   ** 18 companies

FIGURE 8–2   Why did you turn away international orders from your Web site?
Source: Forrester Research

most shipped only to a few countries in Europe and Asia, where orders can be filled out of local warehouses. Three-quarters of the firms that didn't ship globally stated the main reason was system inability to register international addresses accurately, or the price of total delivery cost.

The same group cited a sizable list of fulfillment challenges facing them by the year 2003 (see Table 8-2). These challenges include distributing globally, lowering fulfillment costs, managing volumes, accepting online returns, decreasing order-to-receipt cycles, increasing order visibility, projecting demand forecasts, and a host of other issues.

Such challenges are expensive to solve. In fact, Forrester says companies must sell $1 million or 10 percent of sales—whichever is larger—to cover just the costs of internationalizing a site and offering telephone support to customers outside the United States.

TABLE 8-1 "Do you ship globally?" Percent of 40 companies responding
Source: Forrester Research, Inc.

Yes 15%	All origins, All destinations	▄ 10%
	Some origins, some destinations	▪ 5%
No 85%	US origin to 1 to 2 destinations	▄ 15%
	US origin to military/ government addresses	▪ 5%
	US origin/ destination only	██████ 65%

TABLE 8-2 "What will your biggest fulfillment challenges be in 2001?" Percent of 40 companies responding (multiple responses accepted)
Source: Forrester Research, Inc.

Distributing globally	38%
Lowering fulfillment costs	35%
Managing volumes	30%
Accepting online returns	30%
Decreasing order-to-receipt cycle	25%
Increasing visibility of orders	25%
Projecting demand forecasts	15%
Other	28%

In terms of preparing to handle international shipping, most experts recommended that if the products are small enough to affordably send by airplane, companies should outsource distribution to express shippers such as DHL Worldwide Express, Federal Express, and United Parcel Service. For large items, shipping with a freight forwarder may make more sense.

Export Controls

One of the first challenges faced in conducting international e-commerce is U.S. export controls. For example, the U.S. Department of Commerce Bureau of Export Administration *(www.bxa.doc.gov)* maintains a list of Denied Persons, which comprises the people or entities that you can't export to. This means any type of goods—software, office supplies, clothes, music albums. The penalties for violating U.S. export controls are severe: a fine of $100,000 for each incident, plus an audit by the government. Interestingly, many people on the Denied Persons list have U.S. addresses, so technically, you aren't exporting to them, but the rules still apply.

Some U.S. export restrictions are obvious—others only arise when you try to ship. Most people know that U.S. companies cannot sell to Cuba. However, other rules are not so simple. In November 1998, for instance, the U.S. Department of Commerce restricted exports to 300 Indian and Pakistani entities and subordinate entities believed to be involved in Indian or Pakistani nuclear programs. IBM got nabbed by U.S. export laws in July 1998 when a district court judge fined IBM East Europe/Asia $8.5 million for exporting computers to a Russian nuclear weapons laboratory, according to the Department of Commerce.

But U.S. export laws are minor compared with the legal requirements, tariffs, and customs authorities encountered in 190 nations of the world. In some third world countries, you have to get as many as 25 to 30 stamps from various customs officials before you can get a high-value package released.

There is help out there, however. Express delivery and freight forwarding companies are set up to help companies comply with import/export laws and tariffs—without assuming legal liability. In addition, logistics software vendors such as Rockport, Syntra, Nexlinx, and Vastera help simplify documentation and provide current trade regulation information. Some of these independent software vendors (ISVs) also provide global regulatory compliance and actual landed cost calculations.

Getting Paid

Another issue is setting up payment mechanisms. Americans are becoming increasingly comfortable with giving credit card information online—but most of the world still doesn't use credit cards, *anywhere*. The high rate of stolen credit card number usage, particularly in Eastern Europe, adds risk to international credit card payments. Many Europeans prefer debit cards to credit cards, and the Japanese and Chinese will only use their credit cards on a very limited basis. And imagine trying to collect on a bad debt in Russia—or in any country where language, communication systems, and culture make it difficult to even contact someone. In spite of this, many experts say that credit cards are still the most expedient means of setting up international payments when companies go global. Software and services from online payment processors such as CyberSource offer automated international currency conversion and export control checks.

Channel Conflicts

You can't sell something online without saying how much it costs, and this can trigger some nasty channel conflicts, especially when a globalized site makes pricing disparities apparent. If people in Hong Kong see they can buy a product in U.S. dollars for less, it can be a real issue, especially for large companies. In addition, the whole issue of Internet taxation can present some built-in competitive pricing conflicts. If someone can buy a product on the Web from a country (or in the U.S., from a state) that won't charge sales tax, that total cost savings will be a great incentive for the purchaser.

Speaking of taxes, no chapter dealing with international electronic commerce and logistics issues would be complete without addressing the baffling subject of international taxation. One of the top experts in this challenging field is tax attorney Wendy Kennedy, of the firm of PricewaterhouseCoopers. Wendy shares some invaluable insights that could potentially save you millions of dollars in tax compliance fees.

Taxation of International E-Commerce Transactions

Wendy Kennedy

PricewaterhouseCoopers

The global nature of e-commerce creates opportunities for tax avoidance, as well as double taxation. Vendors are faced with the choice of ignoring potential taxes on transactions outside their home countries or incurring the very substantial costs of compliance. Competitive advantage can be lost if the cost of the good reflects the tax liabilities. The danger of ignoring possible tax liabilities, however, is that there is no statute of limitations if returns are not filed. A vendor can be faced with an assessment for taxes going back for many years. If the tax is sales tax, the vendor or service provider will have lost the opportunity to collect the taxes from the purchasers of its products or services.

Tax liability can be classified into two distinct categories: direct and indirect. Each should be considered separately.

Let's first examine *direct* taxation, how it's triggered, what is taxed, and ideas on how to minimize its impact. Then we'll look at *indirect* tax liability, what triggers a duty to collect and remit it, what transactions are affected, and how to minimize its impact.

Direct Tax	Indirect Tax
Business Profits	Sales and Use Tax
Withholding Taxes	*VAT*
Royalties	Customs Duties
Interest	Consumption Tax
Distributions	Business Registration

Direct Taxation of International E-Commerce Transactions

There are three primary concepts that trigger jurisdiction to assess income tax: 1) *citizenship or residency*; 2) existence of a *permanent establishment* or other fixed place of business; and 3) the *source of income* arising from within the country. These concepts are important to both vendor and service provider, who may unexpectedly find business profits subject to taxation in a number of countries, and to the consumer, who may be required to withhold and deposit tax associated with payment to the vendor or service provider. From an e-business perspective, the ability to sell goods online does not require a local presence in the jurisdiction of the customer.

Permanent Establishment

Most bilateral tax treaties grant jurisdiction to tax income based on specific criteria. The threshold issue arising under these treaties is whether activities undertaken or performed by the vendor or service provider create a permanent establishment in the host country. This determination is vital for countries that customarily tax income based on whether that income arises in their country, but by virtue of a treaty have given up the right to tax that income if there is no permanent establishment or fixed base of operations in that host country. Thus, a permanent establishment in the host country must be found to exist before that country has jurisdiction to tax the business profits arising from sales in their country.

A permanent establishment, as used in most treaties, means "a fixed place of business through which the business of an enterprise is wholly or partly carried on."[1] A place of business is *fixed* if there is a physical location linked to the enterprise for the conduct of business and the location has a certain degree of permanence.[2] A *place of business* has been afforded a broad interpretation, encompassing any tangible asset(s) used for carrying on the business, one asset (a laptop, fax machine, or telephone) alone, located in the host country, would be sufficient to constitute a place of business.[3] Finally, there must be a business activity in which the asset serves the enterprise's overall business purpose. Notwithstanding the existence of a fixed place of business, certain activities of an agent of the business enterprise, performed in the host country, can also cause a permanent establishment to be created.

Activities creating a permanent establishment need not necessarily be performed by a human being. A permanent establishment can be created where the business is carried on "mainly through automatic equipment," with activities of personnel restricted to setting up, operating, controlling, and maintaining the equipment.[4] This arguably covers computer equipment; in particular, a server owned by a vendor will most

---

1. UN Model Convention Art. 5(1); US Model Convention Art. 5(1); OECD Model Convention Art. 5(1). Specifically identified as creating a permanent establishment are a place of management, a branch, an office, a factory, a workshop, or a place of extraction of natural resources.

2. If the place of business was not set up merely for a temporary purpose, it can constitute a permanent establishment, even though it existed, in practice, only for a very short period of time, because of the very special nature of the activity of the enterprise.

3. Each of these requirements is not further defined in the treaty. Many treaties reference domestic law of the country whose tax is to be determined when needed to interpret undefined treaty language. For example, the Service held that entering a single horse in a single race in the United States did not create a permanent establishment, even though racing a horse would constitute a business. The ruling hinted, however, that entering more than one race during the year might create a permanent establishment. Rev. Rul. 56-63, 1958-1 CB 624 (under the former French treaty).

4. OECD Model Convention Comm. Art. 5(1); and see Explanatory Notes "...vending machines and other automated devices..."

likely trigger a permanent establishment,[5] as the equipment, in some instances, is seen as an agent of the business enterprise.

An additional complexity surrounding e-commerce transactions is the difficulty of identifying the country or countries in which the economic activities generating the income occur. If, for example, a U.S. company operates a Web site through which it advertises and solicits sales by offering online ordering, it is difficult to conclude whether the economic activities generating the income occur in the U.S where the Web site is created and operated, in Ireland where the Web site is accessed on a server, or in the U.K. where the customer uses his computer to access the server and interact with the Web site.

Specific activities that do not create a permanent establishment include: maintaining stock of goods or merchandise solely for the purpose of storage, display, or delivery of the goods or merchandise (warehousing and delivery);[6] maintaining a stock of goods solely for the purpose of processing by another enterprise (assembly); and maintaining a fixed place of business solely to carry on "auxiliary or preparatory"[7] activities. Auxiliary and preparatory activities can include advertising, supply of information, scientific research, servicing of a patent or a know-how contract, and construction, assembly, or installation projects. The decisive criterion will be whether the activity forms an essential and significant part of the activity of the business as a whole. Whether advertising, solicitation, use

---

5. The Organization for Economic Cooperation and Development (OECD) drafts model treaties and commentaries used to interpret the treaties in the form of treaty commentaries. It recently revised the commentaries regarding permanent establishment and Web servers to indicate that a server owned and/or leased by a company creates a permanent establishment in the host country; however, a server holding the same Web site information, which is not owned or rented by the business enterprise, would not create a permanent establishment.

6. The UN Model Double Tax Convention Art. 5(4), however, departs from the OECD Model Convention and the U.S. Model Convention in that it fails to exempt stocks of goods maintained for delivery by a dependent agent from constituting a permanent establishment—by stipulating that an agent who maintains stocks of goods for delivery shall constitute a permanent establishment, even if he has no authority to conclude contracts.

7. Activities that are considered auxiliary when performed are so remote from the actual realization of profits that it is difficult to allocate any profit to the fixed place of business.

of independent agents or contractors, and use of a database are considered auxiliary or preparatory can be of vital importance to an e-commerce company.

Advertising and Solicitation

Mere advertising[8] is generally characterized as an auxiliary or preparatory activity; thus product or services advertising alone, particularly brochureware, should not give rise to a permanent establishment. Web advertising, including direct mail campaigns, sales promotions, or affinity programs implemented via email or via Web sites or pages not belonging to the business enterprise itself (i.e., banner advertisements placed on unrelated company Web sites) would similarly not trigger permanent establishment status. The answer becomes muddied, however, where Web advertisements contain click-throughs allowing consumers to browse for merchandise, request information, and interact with the business enterprise.

Activities performed by traditional mail-order companies, located in one country, processing orders received by mail, facsimile, or phone from consumers located in other countries, and that have no physical presence would not give rise to a permanent establishment in that other country by virtue of those activities alone. If service companies are hired, however, in that other country, to process orders and to clear payments, these additional activities may create a permanent establishment.

E-commerce companies often perform the same or similar activities as traditional mail order, except that processing orders and payments occurs online. The Web site may be accessed by the consumer, the order taken, the payment processed, and delivery scheduled in a visually seamless transaction. In reality, behind the online transaction the purchase information may be sent to several different servers hosting different process functions.

---

8. Utilized, by content, any company not engaged in advertising as its principal business.

First, credit card, debit card, and soon e-cash information may be processed and approved on a server maintained by a bank, credit card provider, or other service company. Following payment approval, the purchase information is sent to a server, owned by or maintained for the company's use, for processing and delivery.[9] Servers can be located anywhere in the world. Mirror sites, designed to hold a duplicated batch of information closer to the consumer, are common. The software essentially performs activities traditionally performed by company employees or agents. The presence of a server that holds software capable of performing these activities may create a permanent establishment in the host country, particularly if that server is owned by the business enterprise.

Brokers, Commission Agents, and Independent Contractors

Another class of activities typically excluded from permanent establishment status is the use of brokers, commissioned agents, or independent contractors, so long as the independent agent is both legally and economically independent of the business enterprise and is acting in the ordinary course of its own business. Take, for example, a foreign researcher who sells information over the Internet through a Web site hosted by a U.S.-based Internet service provider (ISP). Since the foreign researcher's relationship with the U.S. ISP would be considered independent, neither the foreign researcher's activities nor use of the U.S. ISP would create a U.S. permanent establishment.

Database as a Warehouse

Could server-based access to information and other content—music, for example—stored in a database or a data warehouse, which provides access to large volumes of content or information, be considered a "warehouse" and therefore be

---

9. Software loaded on the server provides the functionality, company information, and processing or delivery instructions.

excluded from permanent establishment status? A software company located in the U.S. contracts with a service company in the UK to maintain and run its database. Will the activities performed by the service company create a permanent establishment of the software company in the UK? It could be argued that the service company is only providing the software company with the use of facilities solely for the purpose of storage, display, or delivery of goods.

In view of the difficulties of applying the permanent establishment concept to e-commerce, other nexus criteria may be developed by tax authorities. For example, the nexus criterion used by the IRS is "substantially engaged in business" or "actively targeting a market," a legal concept applied to subject foreign businesses to domestic jurisdiction.

Source of Income Rules

In the absence of a tax treaty, the U.S. and many other countries use the concept of source-based income to tax activities that generate income from within their borders, whether or not a permanent establishment exists. If the source of income arises within a particular country, then that income may be subject to taxation in that country, even if there is no other contact or nexus with that country. The UK, for example, taxes nonresidents not otherwise covered by a tax treaty on their UK source income. The source rules are used not only to determine whether a particular country has jurisdiction to tax business profits (direct tax), but also to determine the applicability of consumption tax (VAT and sales and use tax).[10]

Using source of income rules, each transaction is characterized as the sale of goods, the use of intangibles,[11] or the provi-

---

10. VAT accounts for 18.6% of the tax revenues of EU member states 6 JOIT 106 (March 1995). VAT is also the most important source of income to the EU as its own resource, amounting to 40.9% of the EU's total budgeted income in 1998 (based on information obtained from the Dutch Ministry of Finance). See European Commissions "Interim Report on the Implications of Electronic Commerce for VAT and Customs," DG XXI 98/0359, April 3, 1998 (Interim Report).

11. *Intangible* is broadly defined and specifically includes a patent, copyright, formula, goodwill, and franchise. IRC S 865(d)(2).

sion of services. This characterization will ultimately determine whether a country has jurisdiction to tax the income, require collection and remittance of sales tax and use of VAT, and will also determine the availability of foreign tax credits. What becomes problematic is that the same transaction can be characterized differently by different countries.

For example, the Inland Revenue (UK) characterizes all software delivered over the Internet as a service, for which VAT becomes payable. The IRS, however, has taken the position that software subject to a shrink-wrap[12] license should be characterized as a tangible product for which sales tax, and in the case of a cross-border sale, customs duties, will be payable, regardless of the method of delivery. Revenue Canada's position with regard to shrink-wrap software delivered online tracks the IRS position; however, most other software sales are considered sale of a literary work for which royalties are paid, and therefore, royalty withholding tax (but no consumption or sales tax) must be collected by the purchaser. Until treaties, protocols, and domestic regulations specifically address these issues, income generated in cyberspace will continue to raise difficult questions concerning which country has the jurisdiction to tax Internet transactions.

Characterization of the transaction can have a significant impact on its tax treatment. Revenues arising from a transaction can be treated as royalty income, rental income, sales proceeds, or income from the provision of services. It is possible to structure a transaction in several different ways, the result of which changes the character of the income recognized, the source of income, and the direct and indirect tax liability. For example, in the UK, transactions characterized as a sale of tangible property would be subject to customs duty and VAT, but not normally to tax on business profits or royalty withholding

---

12. *Shrink-wrap license* is a business term referring to the nature and extent of rights transferred in the context of mass marketed or off-the-shelf software; when shrink-wrap license software is sold over the Internet, it is also known as a "click-wrap" license.

tax, provided the vendor has no permanent establishment in the UK and is located in a treaty country.

Royalty income derived from the use of intellectual property is sourced where the intellectual property is used. Income arising from the provision of services is generally sourced to the place where the services are performed.[13] There are exceptions to the general rules; for the purposes of consumption tax or VAT,[14] the income arising from the provision of services may be attributed to the place where the services are used. Income received from the sale of tangible property (inventory or personal) is generally sourced to the place of sale, determined by reference to the place where title to the property is transferred.[15] This characterization can alter the taxable liability, withholding requirements, tax rates, and the extent to which consumption tax applies—and forms one of the most contentious issues in international trade.

Tangible Property Sales

Generally, the source of income arising from the sale of personal property, including inventory property, is the place where the title passes.[16] If the title passes outside the U.S., the income from the sale is considered foreign-source. The sale of tangible property is consummated at the time when, and the place where, the seller transfers all right, title, and interest in the property to the buyer.[17] Title passage can be determined by the

---

13. IRS 861(a)(3) and 862(a)(3).

14. Business consumers of e-commerce goods are required to pay levies on their purchases when they file returns.

15. IRC SS 861(a)(6) and 862(a)(6).

16. IRC S 865(b).

17. Reg. S 1-861-7©; cf. United States v. Balanovski, 236 F2d 198 (2d Circumstances. 1956), cert. denied, 352 US 968 (1957) (title passes at place where seller performs last act demanded by buyer). Where bare legal title is retained by the seller, the sale is deemed to have occurred at the time and place of passage to the buyer of beneficial ownership and risk of loss. The regulations warn that if a sale transaction is arranged in a particular manner for the primary purpose of tax avoidance, the substance of the transaction will determine where the sale occurred. Relevant factors include where negotiations occur, where the agreement is executed, and the location of the property.

contract for the sale of the goods, agreed to by clicking the acceptance button; however, in the absence of such a term, legal title passage rules of the countries involved will be applied to determine where and when title passed from the vendor to the customer.

The following example illustrates the difficulty of determining which country has jurisdiction to tax revenue derived from an e-commerce transaction. Company X maintains a Web site offering downloadable content to consumers all over the world. The delivery of the content is immediate, and is actually stored on the host server that sends copies to consumers upon receipt of payment. One of the host servers is located in France, while the consumer is located in Canada. If where the contract and delivery are made were determinative of title passage, would Company X be taxable as carrying on business in Canada?

If an analysis of the transaction is inconclusive, the general rule deems a contract to have been accepted once it is first mailed. The consumer makes a decision to purchase while visiting a Web site. Generally, when a purchase decision has been made, the consumer will indicate the product desired, enter payment information, and send the information back to the vendor by clicking acceptance. Should the product information contained on the Web site be deemed an offer, acceptance will be said to have occurred the moment the consumer sends his purchase order over the Internet.

Alternatively, if the Web site is deemed a solicitation to make an offer, then acceptance does not occur, and thus the contract is not made and title does not pass until the vendor has approved the sales, perhaps by complete verification of the payment information and return confirmation to the buyer. The delivery issue is more problematic. The consumer receives the content at his computer sent from the host server located in France.

Intangible Property

Income arising from a sale of intangible property and royalty income that is contingent on the productivity, use, or disposition of an intangible is sourced where the intangible is used.[18] For example, a transaction generating royalty income from a licensee located in the UK will be subject to royalty withholding tax, but not to customs duty or VAT.

The transfer of both customized and standard software generally is considered a license if the right to use the computer program is transferred for a limited period in consideration for regular royalty payments. Custom software developed under a work-performance contract generally comprises the full transfer of the copyright to the customer, which generally excludes a further licensing agreement. However, if the copyright is not fully transferred, the agreement may specifically provide for a licensing arrangement. This will typically be the case if custom software developed under a work-performance contract in the developer's company is transferred to the customer, and the customer has the right to distribute the program (to a specific group) for a limited period of time.

Payments made under mixed contracts are usually categorized separately according to the types of transactions. If separate categorization is impossible, categorization is determined according to which transaction prevails. Separate prices generally indicate different transactions. However, a transaction may not be categorized separately if it is of an auxiliary nature compared to the main transaction.

Provision of Services

Income earned for the performance of services is generally sourced to the location where the services are performed.[19] Thus, performance of services might not be subject to tax as long as services are provided by a foreign company and

---

18. IRC S 865(d)(1)(B), 862(a)(4), 861(a)(4).

19. See, for example, IRC SS 861(a)(2)(A) and 862(a)(2).

are performed outside the country. There are exceptions, however—downloaded software and/or content in the UK will be treated as supplying services in the UK.[20]

Indirect Taxation of E-Commerce Transactions

VAT (Value Added Tax) is a sales and use or consumption tax chargeable to the final customer on most goods or services made within a particular country or imported into that country. Most VAT legislation distinguishes between the sales of tangible goods and services, primarily because different rules may apply to determine whether a particular sale will be within the scope of the VAT territory or regime. VAT regimes vary from country to country, although some harmonization is occurring in the EU.

Due to the difficulty of factoring in the different legislation and rates around the globe, products are often priced on the Internet before sales taxes or VAT. This can be irritating for the buyer, who may find he has to pay an additional amount to obtain delivery. For the sellers, failure to charge sales taxes/VAT can lead to penalties and interest. It might be advisable to quote a single price for worldwide sales with import charges and local taxes identified as extras for which the customer is to be responsible. In practice, this method of pricing is normally adopted for business-to-business transactions in which, if the purchase were for resale, the transaction would be exempt from VAT. However, it is not normally the model for retail business, as it is generally accepted that retail customers want to know the price that they will pay and do not want to have to deal with tax formalities. Two strategies appear to be emerging to address this concern.

The first is to appoint a shipping agent to deal with tax issues. The supplier sets a price covering the tax liability for

---

20. EU VAT rules, Sixth VAT Directive, article 9(2)(e) designates certain services subject to VAT, including services performed by accountants, lawyers, and other advisors, provision of information, leasing of movable property, advertising services, transfer of intellectual property rights such as copyrights, patents, and licenses, and financial services.

each country, and bills in local price—thus variations stemming from differences in VAT rates are not so obvious to the customers.

The second is to operate a local fulfillment or distribution center. The conventional wisdom is that customers prefer to deal with a local source, and more importantly, when competing with a locally based competitor, speed of delivery may be vital. This of course means a local VAT registration. Although it may be necessary to establish "local" distribution centers, trade volumes may require that the distribution center serve several countries. Thus, the distribution center faces a mix of VAT issues, partly dealing with the VAT registration and other requirements where the distribution center is located, and partly having to deal with the distance-selling issue in the customer's country.

Where sales over the Internet are of tangible goods, the VAT implications are generally the same as for traditional sales channels. Collection of VAT from the suppliers of services will not be easy if the supplier is located outside and does not have a presence in the EU. If the customer is an EU-registered business, existing UE VAT rules require that customer "self-assess" local VAT that becomes payable in connection with the purchase of certain supplies and services from a foreign supplier (the "reverse charge mechanism"). In this situation, the VAT is remitted by the customer rather by than the supplier. The benefit to the foreign supplier is that it is not burdened with charging local VAT, filing local VAT returns, and remitting VAT to the local tax authorities. The effect is that it is possible for a business to supply VAT-free services to an EU customer by locating itself outside the EU.

Unresolved Issues

It might be reasonable to argue that online delivery of a custom-designed newspaper to a foreign customer should be characterized as use of intangible property—thus the income would be sourced to place of use by customer. Alternatively, should the online delivery of the newspaper be characterized as services performed primarily within the host country, giving rise to source income in that country? Or, should the transaction be treated as sale of goods manufactured in the origin country, perhaps subject to the 50-50 U.S. and foreign allocation rules?

Application of existing tax law to e-commerce transactions remains problematic. For example, a Tokyo customer makes an online purchase, delivered from a server in Tampa—unless traffic is heavy, at which time a mirror server in Sydney provides delivery. The product was created by a collaborative effort of individuals located in Seattle, Singapore, and Beijing, who are all employed by a Cayman company. Does the income even have a source?

What Can We Expect in the Future?

Ongoing discussions are taking place to determine whether new international standards are needed to tax global e-commerce. Recent U.S. Treasury reports identify the growing concerns related to electronic commerce. The continuing difficulty remains in determining which country has jurisdiction to levy tax on e-commerce transactions. There is an increasing importance of residence-based taxation (residence of vendor or provider) over the more traditional source-based concept of taxation. Then there is the difficulty of applying traditional notions of how to characterize the nature of the income itself as sale of goods, royalties, or services. Finally, the difficulty of tracing or auditing Internet transactions is expected to create real compliance issues. These concerns are shared by revenue agencies worldwide.

Guidelines proposed by the European Commission are designed to ensure that taxation will be certain, simple, and neutral in order to avoid market distortions and encourage growth of e-commerce. The Guidelines call for no new taxes—instead, the existing tax system should be adapted, simplified, and clarified. Electronic trade in goods and services should continue to be treated as a service for VAT purposes. Services supplied over the Internet for consumption in the EU should be subject to VAT, notwithstanding their origin. If services are provided from within the EU for consumption outside the EU, no tax should be levied, and input VAT should be deductible. Compliance should be made easy, for example, by electronic filing of VAT returns, which will ensure control and enforcement.

In spite of these discussions, there is still no global consensus on characterizing revenue generated from online magazines, newspapers, database services, advertising, enhanced telecommunications services (online video conferencing, online long-distance services), online games, online movies, and other online goods. An online magazine, for example, may offer free access to much of the daily content or to only a portion of the daily content. A fee might be charged to obtain full access or to receive a customized version of the daily content. The *Wall Street Journal,* for example, offers online subscriptions with benefits of real-time reporting and a clipping service. The sale of a traditional newspaper is characterized as the sale of goods. What if only the mode of delivery changes? The same newspaper is delivered electronically. Is that considered a provision of services? A license of an intangible? New technology makes it possible to download books, music, and movies. How should the revenue from each of these be characterized—as services or tangible goods?

Database services charge based on time spent, number of searches made, number of files searched, or the number of users with access. Content is then downloaded or viewed. It could be argued that payments for an inquiry into a database of copyrighted material should be treated as a royalty. Does the answer change if the supplier provides the client with the data and data-extracting and report-writing tools that allow a custom report to be created?

A content provider will often want to establish servers in different time zones to prevent them from becoming overloaded with demands for downloading. Local servers also reduce international calls. How would each of these applications be characterized for purposes of taxation?

Compliance Issues

Online content providers that are not ISPs may find it impossible to identify the locations of buyers. In many cases, the provider has only a credit card and email address. In the future, the use if e-cash and smart cards will make this determination even more difficult. No one knows how such a vendor will determine the location of its customers for sales tax purposes.

In the future, pay-per-view will be available on the Internet. When the cable television company provides this service state sales tax accrues and is collected by the cable company. Content providers will obtain a real, but perhaps fleeting, competitive advantage by locating a server offshore and offering pay-per-view movies to customers worldwide who are not charged tax. Downloadable data, such as music and video, may be untaxable just on the Web. How do you tax something distributed on the Internet? Companies headquartered in Sri Lanka are going to sell goods produced by people in Russia to people in Wisconsin.

Taxation of Internet-based personal services should be similar to the taxation of those services provided in person or via the telephone. There are differences, however, stemming from the anonymous nature and worldwide reach of the Internet.

Online banks issue e-cash as currency that can be used to purchase goods and services over the Internet.[21] E-cash is downloadable onto a card-shaped disk, which is inserted into a device connected to a PC. Transactions completed with the card are as untraceable as cash.

A computer programmer can conceivably write a program, transmit it to the client, collect a fee, and never know the name or location of the client. It may be decided that the only way to tax such a transaction is to tax it based on the location of the programmer.

---

21. E-cash is the generic name given to the concept of currency that is digitally signed using the issuing institutions private encryption key.

The Internet and electronic commerce have created many unanswered questions regarding international taxation, global logistics, and export controls. In spite of these challenges, there remains a tremendous opportunity to profit through reaching out to our international neighbors.

Wendy Kennedy is an attorney and international tax expert and has been a Member on the Boards of Directors for 32 North American companies and 3 European companies. Wendy is an expert in devising global e-commerce business development strategies aligned with overall global structure and long-term business objectives. In addition to establishing and directing programs for the worldwide protection and maintenance of intellectual property, Wendy has directed internal/external auditing of all receipts, disbursements, assets, and liabilities of numerous technology companies. Wendy holds an LL.M., International Law (Honours), University of Cambridge, England, J.D. Cum Laude, University of Baltimore School of Law, and was the Executive Editor of the Law Review. She has also served as Provincial Prosecutor, Ontario Ministry of Labour, and Professor-at-Law, University of Liverpool at Cayman Islands Law School.

Resources

Educational

Michigan State IB Resources on the WWW
http://www.ciber.bus.msu.edu/busres.htm

UNC IB Resources
http://www.ibiblio.org/reference/moss/business/

CSU Fresno Global Business Center
http://www.lib.csufresno.edu

Governmental

The World Bank
http://www.worldbank.org

U.S. Business Advisor
http://www. fedworld.gov

U.S. Dept. of Commerce
http://www.doc.gov

U.S. International Trade Administration
http://www.ita.doc.gov

U.S. Trade Representative
http://www.ustr.gov

International Business Facilitation

Arab World
http://www.awo.net

Asian Markets
http://www.asiansources.com

Asia Inc.
http://www.asia-inc.com

Business Line (India)
http://www.indiaserver.com/businessline/

Canada (KPMG)
http://www.kpmg.ca

Europe
http://www.europages.com

Europe Financial Times
http://www.ft.com

Export Today
http://www.exporttoday.com

Exporter's Guide by the Canadian Dept. of Foreign Affairs and
International Trade
http://www.dfait-maeci.gc.ca/english/trade/

Far East Business Links
http://business-times.asia1.com.sg/

India
http://www.indiaserver.com

India IPAN
http://www.ipan.com

Industry Links
http://www.industrylink.com

International Business Forum
http://www.ibf.com

Israel
http://www.globes.co.il

Italy
http://www.tradenet.it

Japan
http://www.jetro.go.jp

Latin America
http://lanic.utexas.edu

Latin America—latinmarkets.com
http://www.latinmarkets.com

People's Republic of China
http://www.china-inc.com

Russia
http://www.spb.su/rulesreg/index.html

Singapore
http://www.sph.com.sg

Small Business Guide to Exporting
*http://www.sbaonline.sba.gov/gopher/Business-
Development/International-Trade/Guide-To-Exporting/*

Thailand
http://www.thaiindex.com

Trade Compass
http://tradecompass.com

The Economist
http://www.economist.com

The Exporter
http://www.exporter.com

WebIndia
http://www.webindia.com

Western Hemispheric Trade
http://lanic.utexas.edu/cswht

World Trade Magazine
http://www.worldtrademag.com

Electronic Commerce

Business Handbook
http://www.acq.osd.mil

Harbinger
http://www.harbinger.com

Premenos
http://www.premenos.com

Sterling
http://www.sterlingcommerce.com

U.S. Federal Government
http://snad.ncsl.nist.gov/dartg/edi/fededi.html

Letter of Credit

Quality Letters of Credit
http://www.qualitylc.com

Wells Fargo Bank
http://www.wellsfargo.com

International Logistics

American Association of Port Authorities
http://www.seaportsinfo.com

Cass Industry Links
http://www.cassinfo.com/industrylinks.html

Council of Logistics Management
http://www.clm1.org

Fedex Learning Lab
http://www.fedex.com

Freightworld
http://www.freightworld.com

MARAD
http://www.marad.dot.gov

Maritime Global Net
http://www.mglobal.com

LogisticsNetwork
http://www.logisticsnetwork.com

NSNet
http://www.nsnet.com

Port of Hong Kong
http://www.info.gov.hk/mardep/index.htm

Rigos Chartering
http://www.rigos.com

World Wide Shipping
http://www.wwship.com

Maritime-Related Sites

Electronic Shipping Guide
http://www.shipguide.com

Pacifier Maritime Home Pages
http://www.pacifier.com/~rboggs

Webcom Maritime Home Page
http://www.webcom.com/maritime/welcome.html

Other Helpful Links

Passport and Visa
http://travel.state.gov/

Airfare Tracker
http://www.expedia.com

Currency Converter (164 International Currencies)
http://www.oanda.com/convert/classic

To Speak in 32 Languages
http://www.travlang.com

Links to Other Useful Sites

I-Trade
http://www.i-trade.com

International Trade Administration
http://www.ita.doc.gov/

Bureau of Census, Foreign Trade
http://www.census.gov/foreign-trade/www/

CIA World Fact Book
http://www.odci.gov/cia/publications/factbook/

European Union
http://www.europa.eu.int/

U.S. Customs
http://www.customs.ustreas.gov/

Corporation for International Business
http://www.atacarnet.com

Export Import Bank
http://www.exim.gov/

The Bureau of Export Administration
http://www.bxa.doc.gov/

World Weather
http://www.intellicast.com

Foreign Language Dictionary
http://www.travlang.com/languages/

Travelocity
http://www.travelocity.com

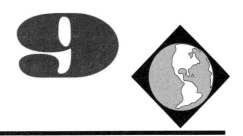

DATABASES AND EMERGING DATA EXCHANGE STANDARDS

Quite literally, the quality of the databases in an organization is the single greatest factor in determining the success or failure of the entire enterprise. It doesn't matter how great the application software is, how sexy the Web site is, or how wonderful the employees are—if the databases are poorly designed, ill-maintained, or corrupt, the business will degrade inexorably. And when you take the extremely data-rich, transaction-intense environment of electronic commerce and couple it with the urgent demands of inventory management, purchasing, procurement, logistics, and fulfillment, you have the ultimate challenge on your hands.

After databases, the quality of systems integration ranks next in importance. Without an overall integration strategy, you'll simply be trying to glue together a bunch of separate incompatible systems on an ad hoc basis—another recipe for disaster. In this chapter, we'll touch on the importance of databases and the latest on the newest standards and frameworks that promise to streamline the transfer of information within e-logistics and e-fulfillment processes. Because we'll be getting into a blizzard of acronyms, I've included an acronym translation table (ATT!) at the end of the chapter.

The Essential Ingredient

Databases are the essential ingredient of e-logistics systems, and they should be carefully designed and integrated with whatever systems a company has implemented. Database software must be scalable and robust enough to support the demands of a growing enterprise. The two most popular database systems out there are Oracle and Microsoft's Standard Query Language (SQL) Server. Oracle powers nine of the top ten largest Business-to-Business (B2B) e-commerce-enabled companies in the U.S., but the choice of which to use should be based on a careful analysis or your company's specific needs, including number of simultaneous users, future scalability plans, amount of transactions, and other factors. It's best to hire a database consultant up front before buying a database software package.

Whatever database system is chosen, it should utilize SQL and be ODBC (Open Database Connectivity) compliant. SQL enables queries to be written against a database without concern for vendor-specificity. ODBC is a standard that allows you to easily hook into any number of databases that are ODBC-compliant. Both SQL and ODBC make systems integration significantly easier.

Integration

In e-logistics, the movement of data is the precursor to moving funds and physical goods. If a company can't move data instantly and easily, without errors, it is doomed. How a company handles data should be such a high priority that it should determine everything from the software packages a company buys to the database systems it uses.

Systems integration must be made a priority from the beginning. Too often, a company will buy systems in a haphazard way, based upon isolated functions within a company. The accounting department will buy an accounting system without consulting the sales department, who has a different system for customer relationship management. Often, the same data is input multiple times into multiple systems, creating multiple chances for errors. In e-commerce, trying to glue together a bunch of "point solutions" won't work—the old way of operating in isolated information silos must be completely dismantled. This usually requires an outside expert to analyze the business processes in each department in an organization, and to start creating communications amongst the various functions.

Once a company has its database and integration issues settled, it needs to deal with another key issue of e-logistics: the movement of data and conveying of instructions between the many different entities involved in buying, selling, and shipping goods. This is why XML—Extensible Markup Language—was invented.

XML

Everyone familiar with the Web knows what HTML (Hypertext Markup Language) is. HTML does a fine job when it comes to presenting consumers with words, images, and graphics, but it is definitely not (nor was it designed to be) a high-powered business tool. HTML served to open our eyes to the uses of the Web browser as the universal client, and to demand the capability of integrating Web front-ends to complicated back-end database and legacy systems.

Other pressure has been coming from those companies who, for years, have been using electronic data interchange (EDI) as their means of exchanging messages with suppliers, manufacturers, and customers. The upside of EDI is that an EDI message can both notify a supplier that product levels at a remote location are low and trigger shipment levels of products from the supplier to the location. This has made EDI a widely used tool for large organizations, from automobile manufacturers to Wal-Mart. The downside is that EDI is rigid, complex, expensive to deploy and maintain, and is beyond the reach of most smaller companies. Somehow, the best of HTML—a universal open language that is available to anyone with a Web browser—had to be crossed with the functionality of EDI to be able create documents that function as both applications and carriers of data. In other words, XML had to be developed.

Although many technologies have been touted as true successors to EDI, e-logistics experts say that XML is the first one that truly fits the bill. Much work remains to be done on XML, but the language's fundamental capabilities make it a perfect fit for the world of e-logistics, where data and action are so intimately entwined, it's often almost impossible to separate them.

XML Infrastructure Exists Already

XML is derived from SGML (Standard Generalized Markup Language), and so was HTML. So in essence, the current infrastructure available today to develop HTML content can be reused to work with XML. This is a very big advantage towards delivering XML content using the software and networking infrastructure already in place today.

By taking the lowest common denominator approach—by being Web enabled, protocol-independent, network-independent, platform-independent, and extensible—XML makes it possible for heterogeneous new systems and old systems to communicate with each other. Regardless of the programming language used to process XML, it will enable the new, networked environment.

With XML, Web pages are generated dynamically from information available to the Web server. That information can come from databases on the Web server, from enterprise databases, or even from other Web sites. What's more, that dynamic information can be analyzed, extracted, sorted, styled, and customized to create a personalized Web experience for the end user. Finally, you don't have to decide whether the information is data or documents; in XML, it is always both at once. You can do data processing or document processing, or both at the same time.

Unlike HTML, with XML you create your own tags, so they describe exactly what you need to know. Because of that, your client-side applications can access data sources anywhere on the Web, in any format. New *middle-tier* servers sit between the data sources and the client, translating everything into your own task-specific XML.

The Well-Formed XML Document

When you create your data using an XML editor (that you can write), you can not only input the content of your data, but also define the structural relationships that exist inside your data. Because you can define your own tags and create the proper structural relationships in your information, you'll need to validate that the XML document is *well-formed*. You'll also need to validate the XML document against a document type definition (DTD).

First, you can verify that an XML document is well-formed by loading the file into Internet Explorer 5, which has built-in support for XML. If a problem arises, Internet Explorer will tell you where in the file the problem was found. Second, check the XML document by using a DTD, which describes what tags are required, how they are put together, what attributes are legal, which tags are optional, and other information. An XML document that conforms to a particular DTD is considered *validated.*

The advantages of being able to validate an XML document are innumerable. A common technique in mission-critical systems is to have two groups write code to solve the same problem, without ever talking to each other. If their solutions agree, they'll have a much higher probability of success. The ability to use a DTD provides similar checks and balances because you have a "second opinion" other than your own code to verify that your XML is being created properly.

Emerging Data Exchange Standards

As XML has been catching on, a flurry of domain-specific standards bodies and industry initiatives have started to adopt XML and XML-based schema languages to specify both their vocabularies and content models. These schemas are becoming widely published and implemented to facilitate communication between both applications and businesses. Wide support of XML has also resulted in independent solution providers developing solutions that enable the exchange of XML-based information with other third-party or custom-developed applications. Several solution-specific or middleware/platform-specific approaches have been taken to address the lack of middleware-neutral, application-level communication protocols. However, no single proprietary solution or middleware platform meets all the needs of a complex deployment environment.

One such standards body is the Data Interchange Standards Association (DISA), a nonprofit organization that offers a wide variety of outreach e-commerce initiatives and educational programs. Accredited by the American National Standards Institute (ANSI) in 1987 to coordinate development of e-business standards and EDI formats, DISA functions as a hub for large industry groups such as the XML/EDI Group—a group working to develop a standard framework to exchange different types of data.

Another group producing XML specifications is the XML Industry Portal, hosted by the Organization for the Advancement of Structured Information Standards (OASIS). The OASIS is another nonprofit international consortium dedicated to accelerating adoption of product-independent formats based on public standards such as SGML, XML, and HTML. Well in excess of 100 associations are listed on the *XML.org* site.

Open Buying on the Internet

A major problem facing purchasers is that the internal practices of placing purchase orders, requesting quotes, and planning forecasts vary from company to company. Information sent through the supply chain often must be input manually to meet the required criteria. Until 1996, this problem continued to compound, as no one had taken on the challenge of tackling actual purchasing practices and helping the purchasing community speak the same language.

In October 1996, several Fortune 500 buying and selling organizations formed the Open Buying on the Internet (OBI) Consortium to create an open, vendor-neutral, scalable, and secure interoperable standard for business-to-business electronic commerce. The first OBI members included industry leaders such as American Express, BASF Corporation, Ford Motor Company, General Electric, Hoffmann-La Roche, Inc., Lexmark International, National Semiconductor, Office Depot, Pratt & Whitney, United Technologies Research Center, VWR Scientific Products, and W.W. Grainger. In June 1998, CommerceNet assumed management of the OBI Consortium.

Working in conjunction with other standards organizations, OBI is developing a specification that is an easy to use, open, standards-based purchasing solution for the procurement of high-volume, low-dollar indirect products and services.

The OBI specification is comprised of a common set of business requirements, a supporting architecture, technical specifications, and guidelines. OBI's objectives are to provide:

- an open, vendor-neutral and platform-neutral architecture for Internet purchasing, to allow companies to fit these solutions into their information technology infrastructure;
- consumer choice, to allow the creation of buying and selling partnerships for high-volume, low-dollar commodity goods and services, independent of technology providers;
- interoperability among purchasing systems, to conduct business-to-business electronic purchasing, independent of technology providers;
- healthy competition, to allow buying organizations to select suppliers and technology providers based on their own criteria, not on proprietary technology;
- standard solutions meeting the common needs of organizations, to conduct business-to-business electronic commerce;
- public documents (requirements, architectures, specifications, and guidelines), to allow all interested parties to implement OBI-based solutions.

The Consortium touts that OBI-compliant applications increase efficiency, reduce costs, improve the overall buy/sell process, and improve service levels to customers as well as end users. In addition, companies that adopt OBI are assured a secure, common method for conducting business online.

The current OBI specification supports multi-vendor requirements, customer-specific catalogs, and secure processing on the Web. Purchase orders fed directly into the customer's local procurement or finance systems are returned to the seller via the Internet, eliminating the need for duplicate data entry by either the customer or the seller.

Other features include guidelines for using EDI-based applications with OBI-compliant trading-partner systems, as well as standard processes for catalog access, standard data formats for order-related information, standard methods for transmitting order-related data between organizations, and standard security mechanisms for authentication, secure communications, and nonrepudiation. The specification also supports multinational transactions and allows trading partners to manage procurement using various currencies.

While OBI's current specification is being applied to Maintenance, Repair and Operations (MRO) buying, direct-materials procurement can also benefit from the group's efforts because trends such as globalization affect all segments of purchasing.

BizTalk

Not to be outdone, Microsoft has entered the data exchange standards fray by developing its own specification, called BizTalk™ Framework. As with the other standards bodies, Microsoft has identified similar challenges in regards to achieving efficient, cost-effective, automated interactions between applications across business boundaries. According to Microsoft, these challenges include, but are not limited to, the following:

- lack of a sufficiently flexible and rich universal language to specify, package, publish, and exchange both structured and unstructured information across application or business boundaries;
- lack of a flexible and rich universal language to specify, package, publish, and execute transformation rules to convert information from one format to the other as application and business boundaries are crossed;
- lack of middleware-neutral, application-level communication protocols that enable automated interactions across application or business boundaries.

Microsoft also recognizes that XML is the language of choice to address these interoperability challenges in a platform-neutral and technology-neutral manner. Microsoft's BizTalk™ Framework, then, provides specifications for the design and development of XML-based messaging solutions for communication between applications and organizations. This specification builds upon standard and emerging Internet technologies such as Hypertext Transfer Protocol (HTTP), Multipurpose Internet Mail Extensions (MIME), Extensible Markup Language (XML), and Simple Object Access Protocol (SOAP). Subsequent versions of the BizTalk™ Framework will be enhanced to leverage additional XML and Internet-related, messaging-standards work, as appropriate.

Microsoft is also quick to point out that the BizTalk™ Framework does not attempt to address all aspects of business-to-business electronic commerce. For instance, it does not deal directly with legal issues, agreements regarding arbitration, and recovery from catastrophic failures, nor does it specify specific business processes, such as those for purchasing or securities trading. The BizTalk™ Framework provides a set of basic mechanisms required for most business-to-business electronic exchanges. Microsoft expects that other specifications and standards, consistent with the BizTalk™ Framework, will be developed for the application-specific and domain-specific aspects.

Information and Content Exchange

The Information and Content Exchange (ICE) specification is the culmination of work by Vignette Corporation, Adobe, Microsoft, Sun Microsystems and more than 70 other companies to define an XML syntax for automating the business rules and processes needed to seamlessly syndicate, or distribute, content between Web servers.

What exactly is ICE? It's neither a content format nor an XML syntax for tagging content. Rather, it is a mechanism for setting up and automating business rules that govern Web-content exchange.

The authoring group defined a number of design goals for ICE based on requirements analysis and much thought and discussion. Some of the most important design goals for ICE are

- ICE shall be straightforwardly usable over the Internet.
- ICE shall support a wide variety of applications and not constrain data formats.
- ICE shall conform to a specific XML syntax.

- The ICE requirements shall constrain the ICE process to practical and implementable mechanisms.
- ICE shall be open for future, unknown uses.

Syndicators and Subscribers

Two entities are involved in forming a business relationship where ICE is used. The Syndicator produces content that is consumed by Subscribers. The Syndicator produces a subscription offer from input from various departments in an organization. Decisions are made about how to make these goods available to prospects. The subscription offer includes terms such as delivery policy, usage reporting, presentation constraints, and so on. An organization's sales team engages prospects and reaches a business agreement typically involving legal or contract departments. Once the legal and contractual discussions are concluded, the technical team is provided with the subscription offer details and information regarding the Subscriber. The subscription offer is expressed in terms that a Web application can manage (this could be database records, an XML file, a plain text file, and so on). In addition, the technical team may have to set up an account for the subscriber entity, so that the Web site can identify who it is accessing the syndication application.

The Subscriber receives the information regarding their account (their subscriber identification and location to request their catalog) and how to obtain a catalog of subscription offers. At this point, actual ICE operation can begin, and the relationship then moves on to the steady state, where the primary message exchanges center on data delivery. ICE uses a package concept as a container mechanism for generic data items. ICE defines a sequenced package model allowing syndicators to support both incremental and full update models. ICE also defines push-and-pull data transfer models.

Managing exceptional conditions and being able to diagnose problems is an important part of syndication management; accordingly, ICE defines a mechanism by which event logs can be automatically exchanged between (consenting) Subscribers and Syndicators.

Finally, ICE provides a number of mechanisms for supporting miscellaneous operations, such as the ability to renegotiate protocol parameters in an established relationship, the ability to send unsolicited ad hoc notifications (i.e., textual messages) between systems (presumably ultimately targeted at administrators), and the ability to query and ascertain the state of the relationship.

RosettaNet

Founded in 1998, RosettaNet is an independent, nonprofit consortium dedicated to the development and deployment of supply-chain e-business standards. Originally organized to represent computer resellers and their suppliers, the group expanded its focus and created an electronic-components management board. Members of the RosettaNet EC Managing Board include Advanced Micro Devices, AMP, Arrow, Avnet, AVX, IBM, Intel, Molex, and Motorola.

So why is RosettaNet any different than the other standards bodies mentioned previously? What sets RosettaNet apart is that its model seeks to drive the value proposition of business-to-business commerce, which is in implementing *processes*, not just in data exchange.

The foundation of RosettaNet is the development of a master dictionary to define properties for products, partners, and business transactions, coupled with exchange protocols termed Partner Interface Processes (PIPs). RosettaNet is, in essence, creating a language that will allow two [parties from different] companies to have a dialog, *process-by-process*.

RosettaNet's master dictionary will eventually consist of 10,000 common terms and processes, as well as the "grammar" that describes how systems communicate. The dictionary, which currently includes about 6,000 words, will be far more detailed than any other standards dictionary, considering the entire EDI dictionary comprises only 1,000 words.

The PIP is a business process, not a technical standard. It defines, for example, how the design-win registration process will work. Defining a PIP is a truly complex task, because in order for a company to establish a PIP, they need to really understand how it affects their internal processes.

Connecting the PIP messages with internal systems will also be key to realizing the full benefit of RosettaNet. Current tools on the market will facilitate this portion of the process without requiring companies to change the logic of their back-end systems.

Most enterprise application-integration vendors have already made their tools RosettaNet-ready, which means that on one side, they understand RosettaNet PIPs and can take them and process them, and on the other side, they have connectors into any proprietary system a company may have, like SAP or PeopleSoft.

RosettaNet aims to develop 100 PIPs, also going significantly beyond anything that is possible with EDI. In most cases, companies can exchange 5 to 10 transactions via EDI. RosettaNet's target of 100 PIPs means that the level of collaboration in a RosettaNet environment will be much higher.

RosettaNet's first 10 PIPs support catalog updating and purchasing. They define common XML dialogs for managing product subscriptions, distributing new-product information, querying product and technical information, distributing stock-keeping units, querying price and availability, transferring shopping carts, managing purchase orders, and checking order status.

RosettaNet has received high marks because its organizers were able to encourage industry executives to set aside professional—sometimes personal—differences to successfully create a comprehensive, industry-wide standard for conducting Internet-based electronic commerce.

CommerceNet's eCo

CommerceNet believes that the key to developing a successful e-commerce standard is not even to try to standardize the products or the processes used by businesses, but to standardize instead the interface between the two processes. To that end, Commerce Net launched its eCo Framework in 1998. Its goal is "to provide a single common protocol through which e-commerce systems can describe themselves, their services, and their interoperability requirements." To achieve its goal, the eCo Framework group set out to understand both the nature of the transaction and flow of information that occurs between organizations in real-life business situations. The result of these efforts was the creation of a set of specifications and a framework that companies can use as a roadmap.

Members of the industry-neutral eCo Framework Working Group include experts from over 30 companies and organizations throughout the world, as well as American Express, American Power Conversion, ASC/X12, Cisco Systems, Commerce One, Compaq, GEIS, Harbinger, Hewlett-Packard, IBM, Intel, Microsoft, Netscape, and 3Com.

The project also benefited from the contributions of a number of experts who participated in developing important XML and electronic commerce specifications, including OBI, OFX, IOTP, XML/EDI, and RosettaNet.

The primary focus of CommerceNet's eCo Framework Project is to demonstrate the value of the integration of three core common component-based electronic commerce services:

- semantic integration of multiple database types with multiple data constructs and data libraries,
- trusted open registries, and
- agent-mediated buying.

Increasingly, these core services will be offered in market environments that look and feel like communities. The facilitator/organizer of the community will be the "market maker" for a particular market-space. Semantic integration of data types and agent-mediated open registries will serve as the basis for the development and operation of these community-focused markets. CommerceNet's goal is to be the facilitator for market making within global communities.

eCo's Seven Layered Architectural Specification

The eCo Architectural Specification presents information about an e-commerce system in seven essential categories, or layers. The eCo Semantic Specification provides a sample set of business documents that can be used inside the eCo framework. They can be used as-is, or extended and modified to meet specific needs. Their use is not mandatory.

Each layer of an eCo-compliant e-commerce system presents information about itself. By examining this information, others can

- locate the system,
- understand what it is for,
- recognize what market(s) it participates in,
- identify protocols the system uses to communicate,
- discover what documents the system uses to conduct business, and
- learn how to interoperate with the system.

The promise for those businesses choosing to implement the eCO Framework is one of streamlined transactions through a variety of processes, including intelligent agents. For example, if a business wants to buy new office furniture for its office staff, they can fill out a query form and launch an eCo-compliant intelligent agent to initiate the transaction.

The Real Competition

Although the efforts of OBI, BizTalk, ICE, CommerceNet, and RosettaNet are getting the most attention, there are countless other standards efforts under way. Just which, if any, of these becomes the de facto standard doesn't matter. The real beneficial byproduct of all of this industry competition is that it will allow for a vision of competing *supply chains,* not just horizontal competition. And the winners of the competing supply chains will be those implementing end-to-end e-logistics.

OTAs—Oh, Those Acronyms!

See Table 9-1 for a listing of the most commonly used acronyms in e-commerce and e-logistics.

TABLE 9-1 Common Acronyms in Electronic Commerce and E-Logistics

Acronym	Description
3PL	third-party logistics
4PL	fourth-party logistics
A/P	accounts payable
A/R	accounts receivable
ABC	activity-based costing
AEI	Automatic Equipment Identification
AIAG	Automobile Industry Action Group
AMR	Advanced Manufacturing Research
ANSI	American National Standards Institute
ANX	Automotive Network Exchange
APQC	American Productivity and Quality Center
APS	Advanced Planning and Scheduling
ASC	Accredited Standards Committee
B2B	business-to-business
B2C	business-to-consumer

TABLE 9-1 Common Acronyms in Electronic Commerce and E-Logistics (cont.)

Acronym	Description
BIC	Business Information Center
C2C	consumer-to-consumer
CAD	computer-aided design
CAM	computer-aided manufacturing
CAM-I	Consortium on Advanced Manufacturing-International
CDF	Channel Definition Format
CEC	Contractor Establishment Code
CIM	Corporate Information Management
CKD	Complete Knockdown
CLM	Council of Logistics Management
CML	Chemical Markup Language
CP	constraint programming
CPFR	Collaborative Planning, Forecasting, and Replenishment
CPG	consumer packaged goods
CRM	customer relationship management
CRP	Continuous Replenishment Programs
CTI	computer-telephony integration
DISA	Data Interchange Standards Association
DTD	document type definition

TABLE 9-1 Common Acronyms in Electronic Commerce and E-Logistics (cont.)

Acronym	Description
DUNS	Data Universal Numbering System
EAI	Enterprise Application Integration
EC	electronic commerce
ECIC	Electronic Commerce In Contracting
ECOs	Engineering Change Orders
ECR	Efficient Consumer Response
ECRC	Electronic Commerce Resource Center(s)
EDI	electronic data interchange
EDIFACT	EDI for Administration, Commerce, and Transportation
EFT	electronic funds transfer
EPS	earnings-per-share
ERP	Enterprise Resource Planning
EVA	Economic Value Added
FACNET	Federal Acquisition Network
FGA	Finished Goods Inventory
GLS	Global Logistics System
GMA	Grocery Manufacturers Association
GMROII	Gross Margin Return On Inventory Investment
GUIs	graphical user interface
HTML	Hypertext Markup Language

TABLE 9-1 Common Acronyms in Electronic Commerce and E-Logistics (cont.)

Acronym	Description
ICE	Information and Content Exchange
ICO	Inventory Chain Optimization
ICT	Information And Communications Technology
IFX	Interactive Financial eXchange
ISO	International Standards Organization
ISP	Internet service provider
ISVs	Independent Software Vendors
JIT	just–in-time Manufacturing and Distribution
LDI	Logistics Development Incentive
LP	linear programming
MAP	Manufacturers Assembly Pilot
MIME	Multipurpose Internet Mail Extensions
MIP	mixed integer programming
MOTO	Mail Order/Telephone Order
MRO	Maintenance, Repair, and Operations
MRP	Material Requirements Planning
NAP	network access point
NISCI	National Initiative for Supply Chain Integration, Ltd.
NEP	network entry point
NFF	Notes Flat File

TABLE 9-1 Common Acronyms in Electronic Commerce and E-Logistics (cont.)

Acronym	Description
NIST	National Institute of Standards and Technology
NPV	Net Present Values
OASIS	Organization for the Advancement of Structured Information Standards
ODBC	open database connectivity
OEM	original equipment manufacturer
OLAP	online analytical processing
ORB	Object Request Broker
OSB	Order, Shipping, and Billing
OSA	open software distribution
OTA	Open Travel Alliance
PCA	Printed Circuit Assemblies
PIP	Partner Interface Process
PKCS	public-key cryptography system
PKI	public-key infrastructure
PO	purchase order
POP	point of presence
POTS	Plain Old Telephone System
RFQ	request-for-quote
ROA	return on assets
ROIC	return on invested capital

TABLE 9-1 Common Acronyms in Electronic Commerce and E-Logistics (cont.)

Acronym	Description
RTF	Rich Text Format
SBDC	Small Business Development Center
SBT	Scan-Based Trading
SCCI	Supply Chain Council International
SCE	Supply Chain Execution
SCM	Supply Chain Management
SCOR	Supply Chain Operations Reference-Model
SCP	Supply Chain Planning
SET	Secure Electronic Transaction
SGML	Standard Generalized Markup Language
SIC	Standard Industrial Classification
SKU	Stock Keeping Unit
SMEs	Small and Medium Size Enterprises
SMTP	Simple Mail Transport Protocol
SOAP	Simple Object Access Protocol
SPA	Specialty Apparel Business
SSL	Secure Sockets Layer
TCO	total cost of ownership
TIN	taxpayer identifying number
TOC	Theory Of Constraints

TABLE 9-1 Common Acronyms in Electronic Commerce and E-Logistics (cont.)

Acronym	Description
TOFC/COFC	Trailer On Flatcar/Container On Flatcar
UCC	Uniform Code Council
VAN	Value-Added Network
VICS	Voluntary Inter-Industry Commerce Standards
VMI	Vendor Managed Inventory
VPN	virtual private network
WERC	Warehousing Education and Research Council
WIDL	Web Interface Definition Language
WMS	Warehouse Management System
XML	Extensible Markup Language
XSL	XML Style Language

Resources

Articles

Gaskin, James. "Trade groups make big XML push." *Internet Week,* April 3, 2000. *http://www.internetwk.com.*

Goldfarb, Charles F. "XML in an instant: A non-geeky introduction." *http://www.oasis-open.org/html/goldfarb.htm.*

Karpinski, Richard. "New spec breaks the e-commerce ICE." *InternetWeek,* October 20, 1998. *http://www.internetwk.com.*

Microsoft Corporation. "BizTalk Framework 2.0 draft: Document and message specification." June 2000.

Seideman, Tony. "Weapons for a new world." *Logistics Management and Distribution Report.* April 1, 2000.

Shah, Jennifer Baljko, "OBI seeks even path amid tangled Web—Strives to achieve standards for b2b Internet procurement." *Electronic Business,* May 29, 2000. *http://www.ebnonline.com.*

Trommer, Diane. "Building a common basis for communication." *Information Week,* January 31, 2000.

Links

BizTalk
http://www.microsoft.com

CommerceNet's eCO
http://www.commercenet.com

ICE (Information Content and Exchange Protocol)
http://www.w3.org/TR/NOTE-ice

OBI
http://www.openbuy.org

RosettaNet
http://www.rosettanet.org

XML
http://www.xml.com

10

SEND IT BACK! THE ROLE OF REVERSE LOGISTICS

For most people, the idea of returning a product they have purchased brings to mind images of waiting in long lines at a department store or post office, hours on the phone arguing with customer services reps, or worse yet, being stuck with something that doesn't work. The way a manufacturer or retailer handles product returns can be either a nightmare or an opportunity to increase customer satisfaction, achieve greater cost reductions, and preserve the environment. Enter reverse logistics—the process of pushing returns back through the pipeline in an effective and cost-efficient manner and, when possible, recovering some of the products' value.

What Is Reverse Logistics?

We've seen that logistics is defined by the Council of Logistics Management as:

> *The process of planning, implementing, and controlling the efficient, cost effective flow of raw materials, in-process inventory, finished goods, and related information from the point of origin to the point of consumption for the purpose of conforming to customer requirements.*

Reverse logistics is essentially all of the activities that are mentioned in the definition above, except operating in reverse. Therefore, reverse logistics, as defined by the Reverse Logistics Executive Council, is:

> *The process of planning, implementing, and controlling the efficient, cost effective flow of raw materials, in-process inventory, finished goods, and related information from the point of consumption to the point of origin for the purpose of recapturing value or of proper disposal.*

More precisely, reverse logistics is the process of moving goods from their typical final destination for the purpose of capturing value, or proper disposal. Reverse logistics also includes processing returned merchandise due to damage, seasonal inventory, restock, salvage, recalls, and excess inventory. It also includes recycling programs, hazardous material programs, obsolete equipment disposition, and asset recovery.

Reverse Logistics as a Competitive Weapon

Returns started spinning out of control back in the late 1980s, when many retailers began using returns as a competitive weapon in the battle to win market share. Consumers quickly took advantage of liberal, no-hassle return policies and retailers perpetuated them, often taking back items they knew were older than their return policy allowed. In some cases, retailers took back products that they didn't even sell—all in the name of keeping customers happy. In fact, there's an urban legend about Nordstrom's return policy being so gracious that someone actually returned an automobile tire to the clothing retailer and Nordstrom accepted it.

There can be a fine line between a fraudulent return and the return of a defective product. Customers who believe that an item does not meet their needs will return it, regardless of whether it functions properly or not. A humorous example is one retailer's report of the return of two Ouija boards. Ouija boards are children's toys that supposedly allow contact with the spirit world. On one Ouija board, there was a note describing that it did not work because "no matter how hard we tried, we could not get any good answers from the 'other side'." The other Ouija board returner said that the reason for return was, "too many spirits responded to the Ouija board session, and things became too scary." In both cases, the consumers were allowed to return these "defective" products (Rogers and Tibben-Lembke, 1998).

This philosophy of accepting product returns as a competitive weapon has resulted in huge reverse logistics challenges. Examples of the scale of the problem include

- At Federated Department Stores, 25 million units amounting to $820 million in merchandise goes back to the vendors.
- At Estee Lauder, which does $4 billion in sales worldwide, returns, excess, obsolescence, and destruction amounts to $190 million on an annual basis.
- In the consumer electronics industry, product returns cost more than $15 billion a year.

Table 10-1 shows that while the trend of liberal return policies has started to level off, U.S. firms still believe that a satisfied customer is the most important strategy for maintaining a competitive advantage.

This same attitude has fueled an increasing ramp-up in the sheer volume of total retail product returns. Figure 10-1 shows the rise of returns from around $40 billion per year in 1992 to well over $65 billion per year currently.

TABLE 10-1 *Strategic Role of Returns*
Source: Rogers and Tibben-Lembke

Role	Percentage
Competitive Reasons	65.2%
Clean Channel	33.4%
Legal Disposal Issues	28.9%
Recapture Value	27.5%
Recover Assets	26.5%
Protect Margin	18.4%

The story is different outside the U.S., however. In many other countries, returns are never allowed. Some international managers believe that if liberal returns were ever allowed in their countries, both businesses and consumers would abuse them. In other countries, return models are moving closer to North American models, indicating that they too will be pressured to improve their reverse logistics capabilities.

Table 10-2 shows the return percentages for several categories of products in the offline world. The online world is often faced with much higher return percentages, particularly for "high-touch" items such as clothing.

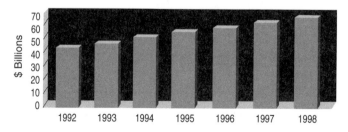

Total Retail Product Returns

FIGURE 10–1 Total Retail Product Returns
Source: BizRate

TABLE 10-2 Sample Return Percentages
Source: Rogers and Tibben-Lembke

Industry	Percent
Magazine Publishing	50%
Book Publishers	20–30%
Book Distributors	10–20%
Greeting Cards	20–30%
Catalog Retailers	18–35%
Electronic Distributors	10–12%
Computer Manufacturers	10–20%
CD-ROMs	18–25%
Printers	4–8%
Mail Order Computer Manufacturers	2–5%
Mass Merchandisers	4–15%
Auto Industry (Parts)	4–6%
Consumer Electronics	4–5%
Household Chemicals	2–3%

Barriers to Reverse Logistics

Reverse logistics is such an important area that the Reverse Logistics Executive Council was formed to research and analyze the many barriers to its success. In a survey of 311 logistics managers, the council found that the major barrier to reverse logistics was simply that many of the managers—40 percent of them in fact—considered the topic of "relative unimportance," as shown in Figure 10-2. Lack of company policies and lack of systems were cited next by a tie vote of 35

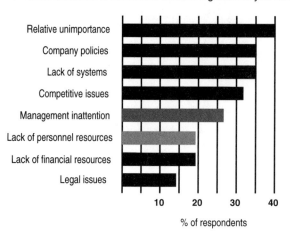

Barriers to Reverse Logistics

What obstacles to successful reverse logistics do you face?

% of respondents

FIGURE 10–2   *Barriers to Reverse Logistics*
Source: Reverse Logistics Executive Council

percent. Other barriers were also listed, but it is interesting to note that the top two barriers were *not* technology-related— they relate strictly to a refusal to give reverse logistics a business priority and to create policies to enforce that priority.

The Special Challenges of Electronic Commerce

While pure Internet retailers have preoccupied themselves with building attractive Web sites, launching huge offline marketing campaigns, and trying to create the coolest place to shop, they have neglected the very physical processes of product returns. Online product returns are skyrocketing, and as illustrated in Figure 10-3, the trend shows returns tripling between the years 2000 and 2004. Why have so many pure dot-com retailers overlooked this huge problem?

Some of the reasons these electronic commerce retailers have yet to fully develop returns policies and processes are

- Relative Unimportance. Sound familiar? Online retailers, like their offline counterparts, have their priorities elsewhere. Most online merchants are so busy setting up their

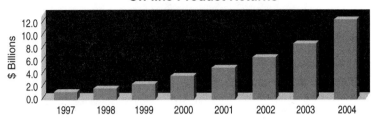

On-line Product Returns

FIGURE 10–3   Online Product Returns
Source: BizRate

sites and attracting customers that they have relegated product returns to the back burner.

- Unknowns. There are so many factors that most online retailers don't know when they start out. They don't how much volume they are going to have or how they are going to handle it, so they start out handling everything manually. Then, if the site is successful, they are inundated with orders and with returns, and they are caught in a real bind.

- Lack of Experience. Many online merchants have never sold anything before, or have very little retail experience. They don't know the importance of strong return policies and procedures, and they haven't had the years of hard-won experience that offline merchandisers have had.

- Multiple Product Sources. In addition, online retailing is often more complex, as many dot-coms sell products from multiple manufacturers who drop-ship their products directly to the customers. Each manufacturer may have its own return policies and its own procedures, creating some very complex return scenarios.

In contrast to the lack of interest in return policies and processes by online retailers, online customers are very interested in how their returns will be handled. In fact, in a survey of 9,800 e-shoppers, BizRate found that return policies were enough to turn some potential buyers away. These include the inability to receive credit on a credit or debit card (85 percent)

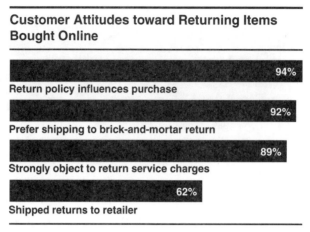

FIGURE 10–4   Customer Attitudes towards Returning Items Bought Online
Source: BizRate.com, 1999

followed by a time limit to return products that is "too short" (68 percent).

Figure 10-4 shows that fully 94 percent of those surveyed are influenced by an online merchant's return policies.

The three leading products returned were clothing (27 percent), computer software (20 percent), and books (15 percent). The majority wanted refunds, although exchanges were also favored, as shown in Figure 10-5.

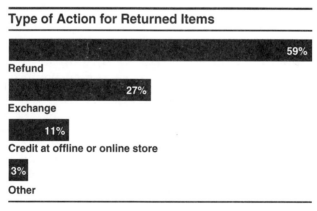

FIGURE 10–5   Type of Action for Returned Items
Source: BizRate.com, 1999

Tips for Internet Retailers

Although the rest of the chapter on reverse logistics is relevant to e-tailers, there are a few features that can be built into a Web site to help start the Internet retailer out on the right foot.

Start Out Backward. First, try to design your systems with forward and reverse logistics as a top priority. Design from the warehouse backward. Regardless of how attractive your site is, if you can't handle product returns, the customer won't come back.

Make the Presentation Accurate. You can't try on clothing on the Web, so some people are simply buying the small, medium, and large sizes of an item, seeing which one fits best, and sending the other two back. One of the biggest ways to keep returns down is to make sure that the quality of the images and the information that you get to the customer in terms of the fit, size, and so on is accurate. The same concept applies to other products—the more information you can give (specs, colors, scale, etc.) the better off the shopper is.

An Impulse Buy Can Mean an Impulse Return. One-click purchase technology has made it easier than ever to buy an item on impulse; however, buyer's remorse can set in immediately after clicking the Buy button. Build in a facility so that when an order is created online, a cancel option is created and remains online for an hour. Some retailers are finding that the cancel button is hit on average three times for every hundred "quick buys."

Tell the Customer Where to Go. It is amazing how many sites ship products without instructions enclosed on how to return the product. This forces the shopper to get back online to find out what to do. This is compounded by the fact that since many online retailers outsource fulfillment to other companies, the items might need to be returned to a different address than they were shipped from. Detailed return instructions and return policies should be included both online and offline with the product packaging.

Absence Does Not Make the Heart Grow Fonder. The chances of a return increase when the time between the purchase and the receipt of the product is prolonged. Along with providing online order tracking, you should proactively keep customers advised via e-mail if a product's shipment status is taking longer than it should.

Go Configure. Sites that offer online product configurators are noticing a dramatic drop in product returns. By giving customers the ability to configure products such as PCs online, the final product order is less prone to error because customers can choose specifications at their leisure and even take a break from the task and finish it later. Dell Computers found that their rate of product returns was actually lower from customers who had configured their own PCs online versus those calling Dell for help from live sales reps.

Include Online Tools. FedEx, UPS, and the U.S. Postal Service (USPS) have free online tools that merchants can integrate into electronic commerce sites that will make product returns a lot easier. To use USPS's Electronic Merchandise Return Service, online retailers must obtain a merchandise-return permit and set up an account at any local post office. When a customer alerts the online retailer of the need to return an item, the retailer provides the customer, via the Internet, with a merchandise return label, which the customer prints and applies to the package being returned. The package can then be tendered to a letter carrier, dropped in a collection box, or taken to the nearest post office. Federal Express's online returns-management system is called NetReturn. It captures customer information, schedules pickups, arranges transportation, and tracks the status of returned goods—all online. All the customer has to do is call the merchant and request a return authorization. Once the shipper transmits the shipment details, FedEx's information system takes over. It even prompts the merchant to follow up when items are not picked up as scheduled.

Capitalize on Click and Mortar. Companies that are hybrid online and offline retailers ("Click and Mortar" companies) can create a real competitive advantage by offering online shoppers the option to return products at their physical locations rather than using a package delivery service. This added convenience also creates an opportunity for an online shopper to come into the store and buy even more after their return has been processed.

Toughening Up Return Policies

Not only is it of utmost importance to have clear return policies, the key is to stick to the established policies and make sure the customer is aware of them. Consistent, universally enforced return policies are reducing some retailers' return rates by up to 20 percent. Offline retailers have found that simple measures, such as clearly posting return policies at cash registers and in all departments, are very effective. One consumer electronics chain places large signs displaying the return policy every 8 feet within stores and prints the policy on the back of customer receipts. Others have begun to set up on-site service centers to address customer education issues and prevent potential problems. In training, sales associates are being encouraged to be completely candid about the usefulness, as well as any shortcomings, of the items they're selling. Other solutions merchants are experimenting with in-store testing centers and electronic registration of product serial numbers.

Reverse Logistics and Environmental Impact

The conventional view of the flow of goods in a supply chain usually ends with the consumer. Waste disposal, probably the most basic post-consumer activity, is notably absent on most supply chain flowcharts. This lack of awareness is changing, however, in large part due to growing consumer awareness of recycling, coupled with more stringent federal, state, and local regulations on waste disposal—particularly disposal of environmentally hazardous materials such as motor oil, vehicle batteries, paint, and tires.

Many companies are realizing that a reverse logistics system combined with source-reduction processes can not only achieve cost savings and regulatory compliance, they can enable the companies to be perceived as good citizens that are committed to protecting the environment.

For example, one of the major cosmetics manufacturers used to dump about $60 million worth of its products into landfills each year, destroying more than a third of the name-brand cosmetics returned by retailers. The manufacturer tackled this monumental problem by developing processes and a proprietary IT system that reduces the volume of destroyed products by half.

Today, with the new IT system, boxes of returned merchandise are scanned as they come into the warehouse. The scanned data provides expiration dates for products, and the receiving system calculates whether items can be sold in other markets or at employee stores, or given away to charities instead of being discarded. Inventory levels of the returned items are kept according to their eventual disposition until sufficient goods have been returned to make it economically worthwhile to ship them out.

During the system's first year, the manufacturer was able to evaluate 24 percent more returned products, redistribute 150 percent more of its returns, and save $475,000 a year in labor costs. The company destroyed 27 percent of returned products because they were beyond their shelf life—down from 37 percent in 1998. The manufacturer expects to reduce that percentage by mid-2000 to just 15 percent as the new systems enable the company to process returns in a timelier manner. This is a cosmetics company with a goal of beautifying the environment as well as its customers.

Developing a Reverse Logistics Strategy

Whether you're a pure Internet-only retailer, a pure bricks-and-mortar, or a hybrid clicks-and-mortar company, developing a reverse logistics strategy is a significant effort and usually requires hiring outside consultants. Effective planning is based on a "walk-through" of the reverse logistics process you are designing. First on paper and then on-site, diagram a theoretical shipment, step by step from the origin of the returns process (the phone call from a customer) to the final disposition of the waste or product. Most importantly, try to foresee every problem that's likely to be encountered and to plan how the system you are designing would handle those situations. Several excellent books have been written on this incredibly complex topic. Here are some very basic questions and issues that should be addressed. These are compiled from a variety of reverse logistics experts.

What Are Your Priorities?

Analyze your reasons for starting a reverse-logistics program.

❏ Why is there a need to do reverse logistics at my company?

❏ Is it for the environment? If so, you will have to address how to manage waste disposal and develop recycling programs.

❏ Is it for better customer service? If so, product returns should be designed as an integral part of customer relationship management systems.

❏ Is it for economic reasons? If so, you must design programs to retrieve and refurbish salable products, and must incorporate a repair operation.

What Resources Are You Willing to Commit?

A reverse logistics program is not merely a side job for an employee—it must be made a top priority and allocated sufficient resources.

❒ How much time are you willing to commit to properly conduct a reverse logistics program?

❒ How much of the company's budget will you allocate?

❒ What are the personnel resources you will commit?

❒ Will reverse logistics be a tactical exercise or a true strategy for your company? The difference between a tactical program and a strategic one can be summed up in one phrase: a strategic initiative is one where the CEO is committed and involved.

❒ Realizing that the level of potential benefits will influence how much a company will invest in a reverse logistics program, how will you forecast potential cost savings? What is an acceptable level of return on investment?

❒ Who will proactively manage the process? Even if you decide to outsource the function to a third party or a transportation company, someone needs to manage their efforts; otherwise, it's bound to result in higher costs and missed opportunities for savings and profits.

❒ If you decide to utilize third parties, how much of the process should be outsourced to them?

Communicate Clearly with Customers

A key part of any reverse logistics program is deciding how and what to communicate with customers.

❒ When your customers call about returning an item, whom should they deal with? Will you set up an in-house call center, or outsource the function? Alternatively, will you send the customer directly to the manufacturer for a return authorization?

❒ Whether you outsource customer service or keep it in-house, you'll need very clear policies and procedures, as well as scripts for the service representatives to use when handling calls. Who will develop these tools?

❒ Will you include systematic, written return instructions in the original outbound shipment? When you leave it up to the customer to decide where and how a return shipment is supposed to go, it could return to the billing address rather than to the warehouse location. Once it gets there, if it's not properly marked the people who receive it won't know what to do with it.

❏ Some companies even include detailed packing instruction and preprinted labels. Will you? Product damage can be avoided if customers receive detailed packing instructions. Customer ignorance can result in returned goods' suffering more damage coming in than they did going out, making it difficult to reuse or resell the item.

❏ Some companies that want customers to call for a return authorization often fax instructions once the authorization has been issued. How will you handle this?

❏ What kind of email will be used to communicate with customers, and at what points in the process? Will any of the email be generated by autoresponders?

❏ What about updating stores and field offices on new policies and procedures? Will you issue a newsletter, set up an intranet, or use email?

❏ What kind of training will you offer? On-the-spot training may be necessary; for example, provide hazardous-materials training to a customer that recycles batteries.

❏ How will you handle and communicate return freight charges? Most often, the manufacturer pays the freight for returned goods, yet typically the customer estimates the weight, guesses at the bill-of-lading description, and routes the shipment via a carrier that has no pricing agreement in place with the manufacturer. As a result, incorrect weights and product classifications can lead to thousands of dollars in excess freight charges. One way around this is to have the customer-service representatives complete the bill of lading for the customer, showing the carrier routing, correct weight, description, and class to customers when they call for a return authorization.

Planning Key Reverse Logistics Management Elements

In their book, *Going Backwards: Reverse Logistics Trends and Practices*, Dr. Dale S. Rogers and Dr. Ronald S. Tibben-Lembke have identified ten key reverse logistics management elements:

- Gatekeeping
- Compacting Disposition Cycle Time
- Reverse Logistics Information Systems
- Centralized Return Centers
- Zero Returns
- Remanufacture and Refurbishment
- Asset Recovery
- Negotiation
- Financial Management
- Outsourcing

Here are some of the questions and issues surrounding each element that can also be used in developing a reverse logistics strategy.

Gatekeeping

Gatekeeping is the screening of defective and unwarranted returned merchandise at the entry point into the reverse logistics process.

- ❑ What resources will be set aside for the gatekeeping function?
- ❑ Who will do the screening of the returned merchandise?
- ❑ What criteria will be developed to determine what is defective and what constitutes an unwarranted return?
- ❑ How much authority will you give to the gatekeepers?
- ❑ How will you screen merchandise at the store level? Employees typically have no incentive or authority to screen merchandise. Without training, employees can unwittingly contribute to customer abuse of product returns.

Compacting Disposition Cycle Time

Returns are exception-driven processes, making it difficult to reduce cycle times related to return product decisions, movement, and processing. The mechanics of decision-making when determining product disposition need to be carefully defined.

❒ When a product comes back in to a distribution center, how will you determine whether the item is defective, can be reused or refurbished, or needs to be sent to a landfill? Often this is a very difficult decision that can impact profitability and slow down cycle time.

❒ How will you reward employees for taking responsibility and making a timely decision as to how a product should be dispositioned? Employees have difficulty making decisions when the decision rules are not clearly stated.

Reverse Logistics Information Systems

Software specifically designed for supporting the reverse logistics process doesn't exist, leaving businesses with the choice of developing proprietary systems or building reverse-logistics capabilities into existing systems. Most IT departments within companies are already stretched to their limits, so developing a system in-house is virtually impossible.

Even if a company did have the resources to build a system, it has to be flexible enough to handle the many exceptions in the reverse logistics process, and complex enough to work across boundaries between business units of the same company. A successful reverse logistics program depends heavily on gathering meaningful information that can help manage the returns process while tracking costs. It also allows a firm to obtain credit for a returned product, improving cash flow management.

An effective reverse logistics information system should also be able to track the reason for each return and to assign a code for final disposition. Rogers and Tibben-Lembke have developed some potential codes for each of these steps, shown in Tables 10-3 and 10-4.

TABLE 10-3 Return Reason Codes
Source: Roger and Tibben-Lembke

Return Reason Codes

Repair / Service Codes

- Factory Repair – Return to vendor for repair
- Service / Maintenance
- Agent Order Error – Sales agent ordering error
- Customer Order Error – Ordered wrong material
- Entry Error – System processing error
- Shipping Error – Shipped wrong material
- Incomplete Shipment – Ordered items missing
- Wrong Quantity
- Duplicate Shipment
- Duplicate Customer Order
- Not Ordered
- Missing Part

Damaged / Defective

- Damaged – Cosmetic
- Dead on Arrival – Did not work
- Defective – Not working correctly

Contractual Agreements

- Stock Excess – Too much stock on hand
- Stock Adjustment – Rotation of stock
- Obsolete – Outdated

Other

- Freight Claim – Damaged during shipment
- Miscellaneous

TABLE 10-4 Disposition Codes
Source: Roger and Tibben-Lembke

Disposition Codes
Disposal
• Scrap / Destroy
• Secure Disposal
• Secure Disposal (Videotaped)
• Donate to Charity
• Third Party Disposal
• Salvage
• Third Party Sale (Secondary Markets)
Repair / Modify
• Rework
• Remanufacture / Refurbish
• Modify (Configurable or Upgradeable Products)
• Repair
• Return to Vendor
Other
• Use as Is
• Resale
• Exchange
• Miscellaneous

Centralized Return Centers

Centralized return centers (CRCs) are processing facilities devoted to handling returns quickly and efficiently. In a centralized system, all products for the reverse logistics pipeline are brought to a central facility, where they are sorted, processed, and then shipped to their next destinations. CRCs have been utilized for many years, but in the last few years, they have become much more popular as more retailers and manufacturers have decided to devote specialized buildings and workforces to managing and processing returns. Reasons for this trend include

- increased salvage revenue,
- improved returns processing,
- focused and experienced teams,
- reduced inventory levels and improved inventory turns,
- increased consumer approval by reducing landfill use and promoting environmental awareness, and
- improved bottom-line performance.

There are many factors to consider in developing a centralized reverse logistics strategy. Some of the questions to address are:

❏ What reduction can you achieve in store labor processing costs?

❏ How much return goods inventory is being held in the stores? Most vendors require certain minimums (dollar volume, number of units, length of time, etc.) to be reached before they will authorize returns. These minimums are reached much earlier through use of a centralized facility, based on the consolidated volume from all of the stores.

❏ What opportunity costs are being incurred? Many stores do not place a priority on returns. This results in returns merchandise being thrown away since the stores do not want to handle it. A centralized facility makes it easy for stores to get rid of their returns and not spend a lot of time processing them. Instead of being thrown away, returned goods are either sent back to the vendor or become candidates for salvage, thus increasing revenues.

❏ What are the costs associated with operating a centralized facility?

❏ Do you have the resources and expertise to run a central facility?

❑ What volume of returns will be going through this facility?

❑ What credit terms have you obtained from your vendors? Typically, vendors will give retailers better terms based on the reduced costs associated with consolidating shipments.

❑ What transportation network will be used and how will transportation costs be impacted? Typically, shipment costs increase because merchandise is shipped to the central facility from the store and then shipped again to the vendor. However, consolidating these shipments will usually yield a much lower freight rate because the shipment sizes are larger.

❑ Who will develop the reporting and systems requirements to manage the information, track the returns, and ensure you meet the vendor minimums?

❑ How will the processes be integrated through the stores, returns facilities, MIS, and finance?

❑ Who will design the best practices for store processing and the returns facilities? Who will develop the policies you will follow with your vendors under a centralized returns operation?

❑ How will the information flow, and how will the processes in both the stores and returns facility be tested?

Zero Returns

In zero return programs, the manufacturer or distributor does not permit products to come back through the return channel. Instead, they give the retailer or other downstream entity a return allowance and develop rules and guidelines for acceptable disposition of the product. A typical return allowance in many industries is three-and-a-half to four percent of sales to the retailer. A zero returns policy, properly executed, can result in substantially lower costs, according to the research respondents. Firms using zero returns can reduce the variability of returns costs by presetting the maximum dollar amount of returned product. Stabilizing return rates using a zero returns program promotes planning and fiscal health.

Zero returns enables the firm to avoid physically accepting returns altogether, a strategy being adopted by some consumer product companies and several electronics companies. Interestingly, most retailers do not track the cost of returns. Instead, merchandise buyers factor the return allowance into their pricing, which ignores the cost of returns.

While zero returns release upstream channel participants from dealing with the physical portion of reverse logistics management, it does not reduce much of the physical burden placed on downstream channel participants.

In a typical zero returns program, a supplier tells its customers that no product will be accepted for return, once ordered. Instead, the supplier will give the customer a discount off the invoiced amount. Depending on the supplier, the retailer either destroys the product or disposes of it in some other manner. In another model being utilized in the computer industry, the retailer returns all products to a central point on open return material authorization (RMA). Usable product is paid for and shipped to a third party for refurbishment and disposition. Ineligible or unusable product is disposed of based on a predefined set of rules. In this model, the goal for the retailer is to enlist as many manufacturers as possible to participate, to enable centralized receiving, auditing, and payment processing. From the computer manufacturer's point of view, all product from the channel is returned to the refurbishing third party. The product is audited by an independent entity to determine its usability and the retailer's credit entitlement. All aspects of the RMA process and the disposition of the returned product are handled by the third party.

Remanufacture and Refurbishment

Thierry, et al. (1995) defined five categories of remanufacture and refurbishment. These five categories are repair, refurbishing, remanufacturing, cannibalization, and recycling. The first three categories, repair, refurbishing, and remanufacturing, involve product recondition and upgrade. These options differ with respect to the degree of improvement. Repair involves the least amount of effort to upgrade the product, and remanufacture involves the greatest. Cannibalization is simply the recovery of a restricted set of reusable parts from used products. Recycling is the reuse of materials that were part of another product or subassembly.

Remanufacturing and refurbishing of used product is on the rise. Even NASA spacecraft are being built with remanufactured and refurbished tools.

Asset Recovery

Asset recovery is the classification and disposition of returned goods; surplus, obsolete, scrap, waste, and excess material products; and other assets in a way that maximizes returns to the owner while minimizing costs and liabilities associated with the dispositions. This definition is similar to the one that the Investment Recovery Association uses to define investment recovery. The objective of asset recovery is to recover as much of the economic (and ecological) value as reasonably possible, thereby reducing the ultimate quantities of waste.

Asset recovery has become an important business activity for many companies. The importance of asset recovery to the profitability of the company depends on the ability of that company to recover as much economic value as possible from used products while minimizing negative impacts, such as environmental problems. The attitude of many firms towards used products has been to ignore them and avoid dealing with them after they are originally sold. Manufacturers in the United States typically are not responsible for products after customer use.

Reselling products overseas is just one of several possible ways to dispose of returned goods. Essentially, you can refurbish, resell, recycle, repackage, or destroy returned goods. Whichever a manufacturer chooses, it should maximize what used to be unproductive assets that are eating up valuable inventory dollars and space, or dispose of an item in the most economical and environmentally responsible way. That decision will determine the design of a processing facility, what kind of training workers need, and the specific procedures for handling products as they arrive. Kitchen appliances that can be repaired and sold in discount markets, contaminated food products or expired pharmaceuticals that must be destroyed, and packaging that needs to be cleaned and reconditioned before being refilled all require different handling procedures and physical layout of the processing facilities.

Negotiation

Deal-making is a key part of the reverse logistics process. In the forward flow of goods, prices are often set by brand managers and marketing specialists. Reverse logistics often includes a bargaining phase, where the value of returned material is negotiated without pricing guidelines. These negotiations may be handled loosely. In addition, one or more of the negotiation partners often does not fully understand the real value of the returned materials, creating opportunities for third parties to operate on the margin. These third parties often employ some of the sharpest logisticians. In other cases, the negotiations are handled by specialist third parties. These third parties act in an advisory capacity to the primary participants in the supply chain, who are working to transfer ownership of the material back to the original source.

Financial Management

Financial management issues are the primary determinants in the structure of a reverse logistics system and the manner in which product is dispositioned. Most firms need to improve internal accounting processes. Accounting problems drive the actions of managers. In a few firms included in the research, accounting issues drove store managers to sidestep normal return systems. In these cases, internal policies and controls moved them to inefficient, incorrect behaviors.

An example of a policy-created problem surfaced in the research. Merchandise designated to go back to the supplier due to overstocks, or because it is not selling, is earmarked for processing through a centralized return center. However, internal accounting takes a markdown on those items that move through the centralized return center, and stores expense those items. When the centralized return center processes the material, they get full credit, and the stores are punished. The stores do not want to be punished, so they slow the flow back to the vendor to postpone the negative financial impact for as long as possible. This delay causes a store-level backup of material that should be dispositioned. In addition, the loss of consolidation opportunities increases transportation costs. Often, the cost of returns is charged against the sales department. While this policy may generally be a reasonable one, it can complicate reverse logistics processes.

Know the tax, finance, and credit implications of the program. This is an area that may not be very visible to logistics managers, but it is one of the primary reasons upper management will support a reverse logistics program. The act of returning goods sets off a flurry of finance-related activities, including issuing refunds and credits, accounting for inventory costs, and tracking tax liabilities.

Reverse logistics programs can help make those activities easier and more accurate by collecting and providing the necessary information. For example, retailers and manufacturers traditionally have clashed over the issue of credits and refunds for returned products. Retailers sent back a product and deducted for what they sent back from their payments. For manufacturers, it was an annual nightmare trying to reconcile the physical product with the paperwork. Now, with the proper information gathering and dissemination, manufacturers can immediately reconcile their customers' claims. There are enormous financial benefits to managing returns this way. Before, manufacturers didn't know their profitability until they reconciled at the end of the year. Now, they don't have to carry unreconciled claims and they don't have to build cash reserves to cover those claims. The net effect is a reduction in the cost of doing business.

Outsourcing Reverse Logistics

Many companies are outsourcing most or all of their logistics activities. These firms are using their reverse logistics outsource supplier as a benchmark to help determine what and how reverse activities should be performed and how much those activities should cost. Often, these outsource suppliers perform reverse activities better, and their customers find that using these service firms reduces the administrative hassle of doing it themselves. These outsource suppliers have become specialists in managing the reverse flow and performing key value-added services, such as remanufacturing and refurbishing.

Out of this focus on reverse logistics, some third-party providers are offering a new type of warehousing service dedicated to the returns process. Here, returns are to be salvaged, disposed of, or returned to the manufacturer, depending on the customer's needs.

Turning the job of reverse logistics over to a third-party provider allows customers to concentrate on their core competency. Just because you use a third party, however, doesn't mean you abdicate responsibility. The level of success in a reverse logistics program is directly tied to your level of control. Very often, a virtual retailer will spend a lot of money in getting returns back just so they keep the customer happy, without really having a process or procedure that focuses on that particular piece of the business.

Another reason for outsourcing the reverse logistics process is that quality assurance also benefits. The outsourcer's software will usually provide retailers with computerized tracking of products, which merchants can use to alert vendors of problems. In addition, the merchants can use the information to make more-informed buying decisions, and so continue to bring the rate of returns down.

Handling International Returns

Whether goods and materials are being returned for repair, refurbishing, recycling, or resale, reverse logistics has its own unique considerations. In addition, when companies need to manage returns across international borders, reverse logistics becomes an even more complex process.

That complexity—not to mention the cost of freight, which often outweighs the benefits of taking the item back—discourages many companies from bothering with international returns.

Yet, sometimes there are compelling reasons to become involved in reverse logistics internationally. In some instances, a returned product can be sold to recover some of the costs incurred, says Dale Rogers, professor of supply chain management at the University of Nevada-Reno. "If you can recover some asset value out of the refurbished product above the cost of transportation, it may make sense to ship it outside the country," he says. "And if a company imports items into the United States and they are returned by the end customer unused," he adds, "it may be possible to resell them in a third country and claim a refund on the original import duties under duty-drawback regulations."

Tips from the Pros

Managing returned goods across international borders is a complex and specialized process. Here's some advice from experienced logistics professionals on what to watch out for.

Documentation

Be sure you know exactly which documents customs authorities in both the origin and destination countries will want. Customs will accept nothing less than what is required. Some governments require special documentation for returned goods—when they leave or enter a country on a temporary basis, for example. Be aware and ask all the questions about how your specific circumstance affects documentation.

Regulatory Controls

When highly regulated products, such as pharmaceuticals and foodstuffs, cross borders because of quality problems or because their expiration dates have passed, they inevitably raise red flags with customs and other authorities. There are laws in most countries about the quality of the products that can be brought across their borders. These laws can be in conflict—such as when salvaged pharmaceuticals are shipped to Europe but are rejected by customs authorities because national laws prohibit entry of pharmaceuticals within six months of their expiration date. It's vital, therefore, that shippers thoroughly research relevant laws in the destination country prior to making a commitment to ship regulated goods.

Valuation

When companies import returned goods, they usually prefer to declare a used item's resale value, which can be considerably lower than its value when new. However, customs laws in some countries may require shippers to use the item's original value. It's important to straighten that out before shipping.

Barriers to Immediate Replacements

Before promising immediate replacement of parts to customers overseas, shippers should be sure there are no regulatory barriers to providing that service. Some countries, such as Peru, Colombia, and Ecuador, require preshipment inspections of all commercial shipments—even replacement parts—prior to export. These inspections are carried out by agencies appointed by the importing nation's government. Inspections can delay emergency shipments, so shippers must consider that when establishing repair-and-replacement services for international customers.

Cultural Differences

Shippers in the United States have many options for handling returned goods, including resale in secondary (discount) markets, export to a third country, and destruction in landfills or by incineration. However, cultural differences may limit a U.S. manufacturer's options when dealing with a customer overseas. For example, U.S. manufacturers often include an allowance for damaged merchandise and expect the customer to dispose of those items. That's not acceptable in the food industry in Europe. Distributors and retail stores are encouraged to recycle in whatever way they can. Their reverse logistics process is built around recycling as the primary avenue for disposing of merchandise. It is very different from the typical bill-back or resell situation in the U.S.

Return Merchandise Authorization (RMA) Process

An RMA (return merchandise authorization) is a numbered authorization provided by a mail-order merchant to permit the return of a product. Most mail-order businesses have a policy concerning returns. Some companies allow only defective products to be returned; others allow any software to be returned if it is unopened. To return a defective product, a typical process is:

- First, the customer must call the technical support office and speak with a technician. The technician helps to determine whether the product is indeed defective. This usually involves the customer answering several questions and following the technician's directions for testing the product in question. If the technician feels that the product is defective, the technician issues an RMA. This process is especially important concerning software. Most merchants do not allow the return of software unless the packaging is unopened. This policy prevents software piracy. Some merchants allow the customer to send an email message requesting an RMA instead of having to call.

- Second, the customer must write the RMA number on the outside of the box that the product is being shipped in. It is important to mail all the original boxes, manuals, and any other items along with the product. If a return is sent without an RMA number, the merchant can return the product to the customer or charge a restocking fee.
- Finally, the customer mails the product. Most merchants recommend using a shipping company that can track packages.

RMA numbers are important to both the merchant and customer. An RMA number tells the merchant that a return is being made and offers protection against fraudulent returns. The customer can use the RMA number to inquire on the progress of a return. For example, if the customer hasn't received any information about the return, the customer can call the merchant and use the RMA number as a reference.

Sample Return Policy

General Terms

All products sold by ACME are brand new and are manufactured to meet the highest industry standards. All prices and specifications are subject to change without notice. Products are shipped F.O.B. (Freight On Board) and become the sole property of the purchaser upon delivery to the specified shipping agent. For shipping damage, customers should file claim to their carrier immediately. Any discrepancy, including wrong items or missing items, should be reported to ACME within 24 hours. All packages will be shipped the following business day. Because of the nature of the Internet, online ordering your purchase from ACME acknowledges that you have read and agree to these terms and conditions. All brands and product names mentioned are trademarks and/or registered trademarks of their respective holders.

ACME Return Merchandise Authorization (RMA) Policy

- All order changes or cancellations should be reported prior to shipping and by phone on 1-555-555-5555. Email is not accepted.

- Brand name items may be returned for a replacement or a complete refund.

- Generic items may be returned for replacement only.

- All returned parts may be subject to quality, operation, and/or performance tests by ACME testing facility or by a third party authorized by ACME. Upon the explained test(s) results, nondefective generic items may be subject to a 15% restocking fee.

- Defective return does not include returns for incompatibility.

- ACME reserves the right to replace defective parts or to issue a refund if ACME sees more fit.

- All refunds after one week from the time item is received will be of the original value or the current market price, whichever is less.

- There will be no refund for shipping under any circumstances.

- All products, unless otherwise stated, are covered by their respective manufacturer's warranties. Within thirty (30) days, we will repair or replace, at our sole discretion, any product that is deemed defective. After 30 days, the manufacturer's warranty process must be followed.

- All returns require prior authorization and must be returned in the original packing with all disks, cables, accessories, and documentation, including manuals, warranties, and a copy of original purchase invoice. To request a Return Merchandise Authorization, call (555-555-5555), obtain an RMA number, and clearly write the number on both the invoice copy enclosed with the returned merchandise and on the packing from outside. Please keep the RMA number and reference it when calling to check on the status of your return. All calls requesting RMA should be in the time designed for them (10:00 AM to 4:00 PM Monday through Friday, excluding the national and religious holidays). Incomplete or unauthorized returns will be refused and will be returned to you.

What This Warranty Does Not Cover

This warranty does not cover: installation or service of product; conditions resulting from consumer mishandling such as improper maintenance or misuse, abuse, accident, or alteration; all plastic surfaces and all other exposed parts that are scratched or damaged due to normal use; products which have had the serial number removed or made illegible; products rented to others.

Limits and Exclusions

There are no expressed or implied warranties except as listed above. ACME shall not be liable for special, incidental, consequential or punitive damages, including, without limitation, direct or indirect damages for personal injury, loss of goodwill, profits or revenue, loss of use from this product or any associated equipment, cost of substitute equipment, downtime cost, loss of data, programs or business information, or any other losses, or claims of any party dealing with buyers from such damages, resulting from the use of or inability to use this product or arising from breach of warranty or contract, negligence, or any other legal theory. All expressed and implied warranties, including the warranties of merchantability and fitness for a particular purpose, are limited to the applicable warranty period set forth above.

State and Provincial Law Rights

Some states and provincial laws do not allow the exclusion or limitation of incidental or consequential damages, or limitations on how long an implied warranty lasts, or the exclusion of warranty in certain situations, so the above limitations or exclusions may not apply to you. This warranty gives you specific legal rights, and you may have other rights, which vary, from state to state and from province to province.

Software RMA Policy

We can only accept unopened boxed software for return within 7 days of the purchase date. Defective merchandise may be exchanged for the same item.

- All returned products must be accompanied by a Return Merchandise Authorization (RMA) number. We do not accept returns without an RMA. To obtain an RMA, send us an email at *rma@acmeonline.com*.

- Please include the following information in your email.

  Full name of purchaser (i.e., name of buyer)

  Email address used to place order (i.e., *johndoe@acmeonline.com*)

  Your four- or five-digit order number

  If the product is opened or unopened

  Reason for return

  If the product is defective or damaged, please tell us if you want an exchange for the same product

- Once you have an RMA, ship the product back to us. Make sure you fill out the back of your yellow copy of your invoice (this is your receipt) and sign it. You'll need to cover the cost of shipping, unless given alternative instruction from an authorized Returns Representative. Please use a shipping company that can track packages. We are not responsible for lost or stolen merchandise.

- When your return has been received and processed, we will credit your account or ship you a new copy of your software. Any items marked "Back-ordered" are temporarily out of stock. We will ship them to you immediately when they are available.

Back-order Policy

If you order an out-of-stock software title from us, we will email you when we expect that product to be available. You will be among the first to receive the item. ACME will not charge your credit card for back-ordered items until we ship your order. No additional shipping and handling charges will be added when your order ships. Products on back-order will be shipped using the shipping method you chose. If you would like to change your shipping method, please send email to *support@acmeonline.com* and we will change it for you.

Reverse Logistics Glossary[1]

"A" channel–
The primary sales channel, carrying first quality goods that have not been available elsewhere.

Advance Ship Notice (ASN)
EDI transaction that informs users what, where, how, and when product is arriving.

Asset recovery
The classification and disposition of surplus, obsolete, scrap, waste, and excess material products, and other assets, in a way that maximizes returns to the owner, while minimizing costs and liabilities associated with the dispositions.

"B" channel
Secondary sales channel for goods that have been through a reverse flow. Can carry first quality goods.

Barter companies
Allow firms to get rid of unwanted inventories of first-quality and other goods by trading for other products or for commodities such as airline tickets or advertising time.

Brokers
In reverse logistics, brokers are firms specializing in products that are at the end of their sales life. Often, brokers are willing to pur-

---

1. *Source*: Dr. Dale S. Rogers, Ph.D., professor of supply chain management at the University of Nevada-Reno, and Dr. Ron Tibben-Lembke, Ph.D.

chase any product, in any condition, given a low enough price; often the customer of last resort for many returns.

Brown goods
Electronics goods (such as computers, televisions, fax machines, and audio equipment).

Buy-out
When one manufacturer buys out a retailer's inventory of another manufacturer's product. This allows the buying manufacturer to replace its competitor's product with its own.

Cannibalization of demand
In reverse logistics, cannibalization of demand is when secondary market sales reduce sales in the "A" channel.

Cannibalization of parts
When parts or components are taken off one item and used to repair or rebuild another unit of the same product.

Centralized return center (CRC)
A facility where a company's returns are processed.

Chargeback
A deduction from a vendor invoice for product return amount; sometimes occur without vendor permission.

Close-out liquidators
Firms specializing in buying all of a retailer's product in some particular area; it usually happens when a retailer decides to get out of a particular area of business.

Controlled tip
A sanitary landfill where refuse is sealed in cells formed from earth or clay.

Core
A valuable and reusable part or subassembly that can be remanufactured and sold as a replacement part; often found in the automotive industry.

Core charge
The amount charged by a supplier on a remanufacturable product to encourage the consumer to return the defective item being replaced.

Design for Disassembly (DFD)
Designing a product so it can be more easily disassembled at end-of-life.

Design for Logistics (DFL)
Designing a product to function better logistically. Taking into consideration how the product will be handled, shipped, stored, and so on.

Design for Manufacturing (DFM)
Taking manufacturing concerns into account when designing a product, to enable easy manufacturing, cost effectiveness, or a higher standard of quality.

Design for Reverse Logistics (DFRL)
Designing products so that their return flow functions better; designing reverse logistics requirements into product and packaging.

Disposition
How a product is disposed of, for example, sold at an outlet, sold to a broker, or sent to a landfill.

Disposition cycle time
The duration of time from an item's initial return to the item reaching its final disposition.

Duales System Deutschland (DSD)
The German organization responsible for collecting and recycling consumer packaging.

Electronic Data Interchange (EDI)
A system for business-to-business electronic communication.

Extended Producer Responsibility (EPR)
A requirement that the original producer of an item is responsible for ensuring its proper disposal.

Factory-renewed
A product that has been refurbished by the manufacturer; typically carries a full new-product warranty.

Footprint
Building size, in square feet. A large footprint store requires a large number of square feet.

Gatekeeping
The screening of products entering the reverse logistics pipeline.

Gray market
Products sold through unauthorized dealers or channels; generally do not carry a factory warranty.

Green Dot
A symbol on packaging sold in Germany that indicates that the product is eligible to be recycled through the Duales System Deutschland.

Green logistics
Attempts to measure and minimize the ecological impact of logistics activities.

High-learning products
Items that require education or instruction before being able to operate; a computer, for example.

Insurance liquidators
Secondary market companies specializing in buying products damaged in shipment and declared as losses by insurance companies.

Investment recovery
See asset recovery.

Irregular
Products that do not meet the standards for first-quality product, perhaps for cosmetic reasons, but which generally still satisfy most of the basic performance requirements.

Job-out liquidators
Secondary market companies specializing in buying end-of-season products from retailers.

Landfill
A controlled environment for burying municipal solid waste.

Leachate
Water that seeps through a landfill, picking up pollutants as it travels.

Lift
See buy-out.

Liquidator
A secondary market company that buys product that has reached the end of its sales life in the "A" channel.

Logistics
The process of planning, implementing, and controlling the efficient, cost-effective flow of raw materials, in-process inventory, finished goods, and related information from the point of origin to the point of consumption for the purpose of conforming to customer requirements.

Made-for-outlet
Products made especially to be sold at outlet stores; generally of slightly lower quality than "A" channel products.

Marketing returns
Unsold product a supplier has agreed to take back from the retail customer; usually overstocks; can be the result of product shipped to the retailer with the understanding that sales are guaranteed.

Municipal Solid Waste (MSW)
Garbage generated by residences and small businesses.

Nondefective defectives
When customers return a product claiming it to be defective, when in fact, the problem is not with the product, but often with the customer's ability to properly operate the product.

Nondefective returns
A nondefective defective returned by a customer.

Outlet sales
Products sold at an outlet store; typically irregular or off-season products.

Overstock
Excess inventory; may be from ordering too much, order cancellations, or product's failure to sell.

Partial returns credit
Giving a customer a partial refund for a product because not all components of the product are present.

Point of sale (POS)
The point where ownership of the product transfers to the customer.

Point-of-sale (POS) registration
Collecting customer registration information for warranty purposes at the time the product is sold.

Prebate
Providing a discounted purchase price on a product linked to the promise not sell the product to a remanufacturer at the end of its life; paying the customer at the time of purchase for returning the product at end-of-life.

Preselling
Contracting ahead of time (during the selling season) with a job-out company to purchase all remaining product at the end of the season.

Primary packaging
  The first level of product packaging; for example, the tube that toothpaste is packed in, or a bottle that contains beer.

Producer pays
  The principle that the manufacturer should pay for ensuring the recycling and proper disposal of product at end-of-life.

Radio Frequency Identification (RFID)
  A technology in which a tag that broadcasts a unique, low-frequency radio signal is attached to each item.

Reclaim materials
  See recycling.

Reclamation centers
  Centralized processing facilities for returns; term used widely in the grocery industry.

Reconditioning
  When a product is cleaned and repaired to return it to a "like new" state.

Recycling
  When a product is reduced to its basic elements, which are reused.

Refurbishing
  Similar to reconditioning, except with perhaps more work involved in repairing the product.

Remanufacturing
  Similar to refurbishing, but requiring more extensive work; often requires completely disassembling the product.

Re-returns
  When a customer tries to return for full price a product that was sold as a returned product.

Resell
  When a returned product may be sold again as new.

Restocking fee
  A charge to the consumer for accepting their returned product.

Returnable tote
  Transport packaging that can be used multiple times to move materials between or within facilities.

Return abuse
When a customer tries to return a product at a chain other than where they bought it, or for a price higher than what they paid for it, or after the warranty period has expired.

Return Authorization (RA)
Authorization to return a product to a supplier.

Return Material Allowance (RMA)
Authorization to return a product to a supplier. Also called a Return Merchandise Authorization.

Returns
Products for which a customer wants a refund because the products either fail to meet his needs or fail to perform.

Returns allowance
The quantity of product that a customer is allowed to return; usually calculated as a percentage of total purchases.

Returns center
Same as centralized return center.

Return to supplier
Returning damaged products or customer returns to the vendor from whom they were purchased.

Return to vendor (RTV)
Same as return to supplier.

Reusable tote
Same as returnable tote.

Reuse
Using a product again for a purpose similar to the one for which it was designed.

Reverse distribution
The process of bringing products or packaging from the retail level through the distributor back to the supplier or manufacturer.

Reverse logistics
The process of planning, implementing, and controlling the efficient, cost-effective flow of raw materials, in-process inventory, finished goods, and related information from the point of consumption to the point of origin for the purpose of recapturing value or for proper disposal.

Rotable parts
Using a closed loop of repairable products; when a customer sends in a broken product, a repaired product is sent, and the

customer's product is repaired and stored to be sent to another customer.

Salvage

When a product is sold to a broker or some other low-revenue customer.

Sanitary landfill

A landfill scientifically designed to prevent groundwater contamination from leachate.

Secondary market

A collection of companies that specialize in selling products that have reached the end of their selling season in the "A" channel.

Secondary packaging

The second level of product packaging; for example, the box that contains a tube of toothpaste, or the carton that holds six bottles of beer.

Secure disposal

Requiring a company to destroy the product under the supervision of a security guard to ensure the product is destroyed.

Secure returns

A reverse logistics process designed to minimize leakage of product; secure returns processes are designed to eliminate shrinkage and unwanted product disposition.

Source reduction

Reducing the usage of resources at the point of generation or production.

Supply chain position

The position in the channel that the firm occupies; this position could be manufacturer, wholesaler, distributor, retailer, or combinations of these.

Take-back

Requiring manufacturers to collect product at end-of-life to reclaim materials and dispose of properly.

Tipping fees

The cost of disposing of one ton of garbage in a landfill.

Transport packaging

Packaging used for transporting products from manufacturers to distributors or retailers.

Two-dimensional bar coding
A bar-coding technology that allows much more information to be stored in a given space; instead of a single row of line, the bar code label consists of a two-dimensional grid of dots.

White goods
Household appliances such as washers, dryers, refrigerators.

Zero returns
Manufacturer never takes possession of returns. Destroyed in the field by retailer or third party.

Resources

Articles

Bradley, Peter, Toby Gooley, and James Aaron Cooke. "U.S. Postal Service launches online return service." *Logistics Management and Distribution Report,* January 21, 2000.

Bunn, Jim. "Centralizing reverse logistics: How to understand if it will work for you." KPMG Peat Marwick LLP. Article on *http://www.us.kpmg.com,* August, 1999.

Caldwell, Bruce. "The Web can reduce returns." *Information Week,* April 12, 1999.

Caldwell, Bruce. "Untapped opportunities exist in returned products, a side of logistics few businesses have thought about—until now." *Information Week,* April 12, 1999.

"Five steps to success: Careful management of these five issues is the foundation of a cost-effective reverse-logistics program." *Logistics Management and Distribution Report,* June 1, 1998.

Gooley, Toby B, sr. ed. "There and back again." *Logistics Management and Distribution Report,* April 1, 1999.

Kane, Margaret, ZDNN. "E-tailers take on returns, offer discounts." *E-Business,* December 27, 1999. *http://www.zdnet.com//enterpirse/e-business.*

Koloszyc, Ginger, asst. ed. "Internet-only retailers struggle to improve product return process: One solution to returns headaches is to bring in third-party 'reverse logistics' provider." *Stores, July, 1999.*

Marien, Edward J. "Reverse logistics as competitive strategy." *Cahners Business Information,* Spring 1998.

Reda, Susan. "Getting a handle on returns: Stores counter growing losses by developing clear policies and improving the reverse logistics process." *Stores*, December, 1999.

Thierry, Martjin, et al. "Strategic issues in product recovery management." *California Management Review* 37, no.2, Winter 1995.

Books

Reuse and Recycling: Reverse Logistics Opportunities, published by the Council of Logistics Management. The book examines approaches to recycling system design, applications for inbound and outbound logistics, and the use of third-party providers. For information on ordering the book, contact the council at (630) 574-0985 or fax (630) 574-0989.

Rogers, Dr. Dale S., and Dr. Ronald S. Tibben-Lembke. *Going Backwards: Reverse Logistics Trends and Practices,* Reno, University of Nevada, Center of Logistics Management, 1998. Reverse Logistics Executive Council.

Stock, James, a professor at the University of South Florida and author of *Development and Implementation of Reverse Logistics Programs* (1998, Council of Logistics Management).

Reverse Logistics Vendors

BHP Logistics Services
http://www.bhplogistics.com

Burnham
http://www.burnhamcorp.com

CF Reverse Logistics
http://www.cflogistics.com

Federal Express Worldwide Logistics
http://www.fedex.com

GATX Logistics
http://www.gatx.cpm

Genco Distribution System
http://www.genco.com

UPS Worldwide Logistics
http://www.ups.com

USF Logistics
http://www.usf.com

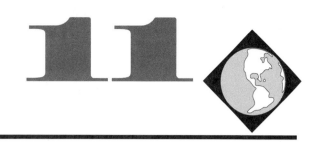

OUTSOURCING THE WHOLE THING

The Pros and Cons of Outsourcing

The previous chapters have discussed the various components involved in e-fulfillment and e-logistics, and by now you probably have a good idea of just how complex and far-reaching the challenge is. And, like most online businesses, you're probably wondering if it's not easier just to outsource the whole thing. There are some definite arguments in favor of outsourcing. For one thing, when distribution is not a core competency for your company and you do not have the resources to make it one, outsourcing the function can help your company grow by allowing you to focus on your mission-critical activities.

There are also some distinct disadvantages to outsourcing, chief among them being the loss of control. Regardless of whom you outsource to, you are still responsible for the quality of the customer relationship, and you are liable if anything goes awry.

In this chapter we'll discuss the pros and cons of outsourcing, the types of providers, how to evaluate potential outsourcing partners, how to prepare for outsourcing, and finally, a few of the major third-party e-fulfillment and e-logistics providers. The decision to outsource is not a trivial one, and proper research and preparation will lessen the chances of making a serious, possibly fatal, business mistake.

The Pros: Arguments for Outsourcing E-Logistics

Businesses outsource e-fulfillment and e-logistics for several reasons.

Speed to Market

Speed to market—being able to deploy quickly—is essential to capturing market share. Businesses who outsource e-fulfillment can deploy their sites quickly, with minimal capital investment, while maintaining the confidence that customers will receive the level of service they expect.

Scalability

If an e-business is successful, the ability to handle large volumes very quickly becomes of paramount importance. By outsourcing, an e-business is able to plug into the third party's infrastructure, which should be robust enough to handle the increased activity.

Focus

The reason cited most often for outsourcing is that the capabilities required are outside the core competencies of most e-businesses and would detract from the company's focus. By outsourcing key logistics, information technology processes, and customer response services, e-businesses can focus on their core business.

Lower Costs

Through a "shared tenancy" model, e-businesses share distribution and customer response services with other e-businesses. This minimizes costs and allows a business to easily adapt to growth or other changes. Outsourcing also alleviates the need to hire internal logistics and fulfillment staff, and to build and equip expensive warehouses. Performing e-logistics and e-fulfillment in-house is extremely expensive and time-consuming, and without third-party expertise, many companies can seriously jeopardize the customer relationships they have taken so long to develop.

Focus on the Customer

Outsourcing also allows an e-business to focus more on its customers and to provide greater overall customer satisfaction. In addition, through outsourcing, an e-business will be freed up to develop existing customer relationships.

Capitalize on Efficiencies

The e-commerce transaction has the potential to be an extremely efficient way to conduct business. One example is in data collection and utilization. Third-party providers have the advantage of capturing and processing the details of thousands of transactions. The sheer quantity of data can be very useful for trending and improving sales and customer service. The reports that can be generated from a third party will probably be much more valuable that those generated in-house.

Outsourcing the e-fulfillment and e-logistics functions can be the answer for many companies who do want to capitalize on its benefits and have done the research necessary to align themselves with the right outsource partner. For other companies, however, outsourcing can be simply too risky. The arguments against outsourcing are presented below.

Cons: Arguments Against Outsourcing E-Logistics

Logistics outsourcing, which has traditionally covered warehousing, transportation, and freight forwarding services, is undergoing a massive transformation. E-commerce, technologies such as EDI, the Internet, and supply-chain software are providing big opportunities and even bigger challenges for outsourcers. The truth is, few logistics outsourcers have figured out how to do e-commerce fulfillment well.

The field is full of traditional logistics outsourcers seeking upward services expansion. Most organizations posing as e-logistics providers spring from trucking or facilities management companies. These "new" e-logistics providers have operated for years on razor-thin profits, and many are unable to make the huge capital investments necessary to become world-class providers of IT services. So, while outsourcers tout a ton of logistics experience, many still lack vital IT skills and a basic understanding of how e-commerce works.

This means that average e-businesses have been trapped in a no-win situation. Most of them need to outsource logistics because they lack the resources to do it themselves. On the other hand, companies choosing to outsource risk providing a poor customer experience. The key is to evaluate how sophisticated the outsourcer's IT capabilities are.

"Real" e-logistics providers must depend on integrated IT systems and complex software to manage the dynamic flow of products. The quality of information must be much better than that of traditional outsourcers, so that companies can have visibility into their supply chains. Better information also reduces inventory throughout the supply chain, enabling companies to react quickly to market changes. But better supply-chain visibility changes the face of physical distribution. Since companies don't need to stock up on as much inventory, e-logistics providers must store and transport unit-sized shipments rather than traditional pallet-sized shipments. This requires a complete overhaul of business processes.

Do It Yourself?

Well then, why not overhaul your own business and do the logistics and fulfillment yourself? If you have an existing infrastructure, warehouses, and customer service center, you can probably retool your business for in-house e-logistics, but you should definitely hire an outside expert to evaluate your current logistics platform. If you don't have an existing fulfillment and logistics capability, be prepared to spend a huge amount of time and money—in other words, consider outsourcing.

If you do have the infrastructure, and you've hired an expert to assist in converting to e-logistics, the first thing to do is to determine how robust the existing logistics platform is and what revisions need to be made. Although orders may be initiated via a Web site, unless you've done an extensive amount of systems integration, much of that data must be manually input into other supply-chain management, planning, warehouse-management, and logistics systems. The logistics platform will also have to address content management, application development, cross-function integration, business intelligence, and mobile Internet access. The platform must also enable suppliers and customers to retrieve information about the demand picture, forecasts, delivery dates, shipment tracking, and other necessary data. Once those systems are in place, however, accessing the information strictly through a PC in the office doesn't cut it any more.

Customers, internal supply-chain managers, shippers, suppliers, and other parties will want that information to be fed into pagers, cell phones, PDAs, and other wireless devices in real time. This level of logistics will likely involve even more software integration (read: more time and more money).

Inventory

E-logistics has also brought back a burden many companies have worked hard to reduce in recent years: inventory. In an amazingly short time, e-logistics has begun to reverse the trend toward tighter, smaller inventories that has helped drive costs down for American businesses in recent years. Companies need to accept the fact that they're going to be in this environment and put in the distribution network they need to do the job.

Consumer demands for next-day or even same-day delivery mean that e-commerce merchants need to stock product not only on hand, but also in distribution centers across the country. It's possible to get around this by using service providers, but in the end, someone has to have product ready to move, and someone has to pay for that capability. You need to get product to consumers much more efficiently and cost-effectively. This again requires much more infrastructure, and the ability to forecast demand and plan to manufacture accordingly.

Back to outsourcing—assuming you don't have the time, money, and expertise or desire to do it yourself. Let's look at the types of outsourcing amongst what are called third-party logistics (3PL) providers.

Nonasset-based and Asset-based Providers

Customers seeking 3PLs may choose from two different types of service providers: nonasset-based and asset-based. There are significant differences between the two. The nonasset-based providers perform only the engineering services directly. In addition to designing the system, they coordinate the hiring of appropriate transportation and distribution service providers. One advantage of dealing with a nonasset-based 3PL is that the 3PL is independent of the carriers and warehouses bidding to perform the services. The 3PL is free to develop the most efficient and effective system under the circumstances and then to manage the selection of the service providers best suited to implement the system. The approach relies on analysis, computer systems, and metrics.

The asset-based providers, many of whom are owned and operated by the largest and best carriers and warehouses, also perform the engineering services. However, the system design assumes that the system will rely principally on vehicles, employees, and facilities owned and operated by the service provider. A proposal for logistics services may include much detail about the facilities and assets to be acquired by the 3PL specifically to serve the customer. The approach will be more practical, with emphasis on operating expertise.

The pricing strategies used in logistics service arrangements also serve to demonstrate the differences between the asset-based and nonasset-based 3PLs. Contracts with nonasset-based providers often pass the costs of the transportation services directly to the customer. The 3PL is compensated through a management fee. In this way, the costs of the pieces and parts of the total service package can be identified and analyzed separately.

In arrangements with asset-based service providers, the pricing structure may focus on compensating the 3PL for the cost of providing and operating each asset. In contracts requiring dedicated equipment, the customer may be required to purchase the assets at the end of the contract term. Given the attention paid to filling specific trucks and warehouses, some industry analysts have suggested that an asset-based 3PL has an inherent conflict of interest in the development of service proposals and in the selection of service providers.

The needs and capabilities of its operating divisions will heavily influence the 3PL's logistics engineers. Some logistics purists question whether asset-based 3PLs provide logistics services at all or whether the logistics function is more accurately characterized as marketing support. Recognizing the problem, some asset-based 3PLs have established a separate corporate shell to house their logistics business. The separate corporation makes the logistics business look more like a nonasset-based 3PL. However, true independence among this group of 3PLs may be hard to find. Many of these carrier-affiliated 3PLs look first toward their sister corporations when they need a service provider.

In what may be the next logical step in the development of the asset-based 3PL, a group of large truckload carriers has formed a joint-venture logistics company. These carriers intend to transfer their in-house logistics functions to the new 3PL and to own and operate the 3PL as an independent business. Many of the legal and operating questions related to the new joint venture have yet to be addressed. Will the services offered by the new 3PL look more like logistics or more like marketing support for the trucking services offered by the member carriers?

What About Drop Shipping?

The idea of drop shipping packages directly to the end user is also appealing to companies looking to streamline the delivery process. And, as more companies post inventory, shipment tracking, and product-availability information on the Web, the drop ship process gets easier because the necessary data is easy to find and access. This has made the choice for drop ship fulfillment (DSF) a seemingly easy decision.

With DSF, a company sells a product, charges the customer, generates a purchase order, and sends the purchase order to the manufacturer or supplier, who then fulfills the order by shipping the product directly to the customer. Since the company never took possession of the product, the company does not incur any of the costs associated with storing or purchasing the product. Many Internet start-ups have adopted this business model.

But, as you would suspect, there are a number of risks when you use drop shipping as your sole means of fulfillment. First, what about returns? Do you really want to give the customer a slip inside their package telling them to call a different manufacturer, depending on which product they want to return? Often these manufacturers aren't equipped to handle customer service calls, so the customer will invariably call you to complain. If you haven't set up the capability for 7/24 customer service inquiries, you'll have a real mess on your hands.

Remember the rules and regulations the Federal Trade Commission (FTC) has about delivery times, warranties, and other gotchas? You are held liable, regardless of the manufacturer's delivery problems. Also, unless you have an extremely robust IS system that can tie into all of the manufacturers' systems, you'll be caught with out-of-stock and back order problems, as well as other surprises.

Then there's the issue of partial shipments. Do you want your customers receiving a bunch of packages from your various suppliers at different times? The shipping costs will be exorbitant for all of these multiple packages, unless you can consolidate them somehow. You can also imagine the tracking and tracing headaches—particularly if a product requires assembly and the pieces come from various locations.

Evaluating Potential Outsourcing Partners

Unfortunately, companies need to be careful when choosing an outsourcing partner. Outsourcing is not a panacea—if your third-party distributor's procedures and performance are not carefully monitored, you risk permanently alienating the customers you have worked so hard to attract.

The key to a successful outsourcing relationship includes understanding the process, specifying objectives, establishing internal procedures for evaluating performance against objectives, and deploying systems that help to manage the function effectively.

Logistics service providers must be able to demonstrate the following:

- the ability to provide real-time logistics information in an integrated environment and across all modes of transportation;

- an evolution toward real consultancy by offering logistics strategy formulation, business process redesign, and organizational change;
- global reach and resources coupled with localized knowledge of regulations, taxes, and culture.

If the manufacturer or distributor, which may be the same company, fulfills the customer's order correctly, all parties are satisfied. However, in most cases, there are problems in one or more of the key areas discussed next.

Customer Service

Another company may be distributing your products, but ultimately you are responsible for the customer relationship. While it's true your company does not have direct control over the distribution process, the customer only cares about receiving the product—not about who sent it or how it got there. If something goes wrong, you are responsible and must do what is necessary to correct the situation.

Shipping Costs

Most manufacturers are set up to ship truckloads or pallets of products, not multiple orders of a single product. There are also manufacturers that require you to purchase more products than you need, others set ridiculously high prices for the service, and some simply will not ship the orders. In some cases, start-ups are "kitting" a number of products, not because it adds value for the customer, but because it pushes the dollar value of their order above a threshold where the manufacturer will agree to drop ship fulfillment of the products.

Profitability

Shipping costs directly affect your bottom line. Many start-ups are passing along the manufacturer's shipping costs to their customers, raising the price of their products and putting themselves at a disadvantage in a competitive market. If the start-up does not pass along the entire cost, the shipping expense cuts into the profitability of every transaction.

Getting Automated Help

Successfully managing a third-party distributor requires establishing internal monitoring processes and ensuring that specific employees are responsible for this function. These employees should also be responsible for developing and deploying computer systems to help automate the management function. Here are five critical requirements for your outsourcing relationship with your distributor.

- Establish measurable standards for distributor performance.
- Conduct periodic performance reviews.
- Visit distributor sites to check security procedures (only if the start-up owns the inventory).
- Monitor customer feedback and satisfaction levels.
- As sales volume grows, periodically revisit the decision to outsource the distribution function.

The right computer system can improve your ability to manage the distribution function in three areas.

Communication

To allow you to automate communication with your suppliers and manufacturers, you must establish a back-end system. This means that you should not rely just on basic email, generated by an employee, to track orders. For example, you send the supplier an email to check on a backlogged product, someone then emails you back with a response, and finally you rekey the information into your system—imagine a handful of employees checking 1,000 products. To be more efficient, you need a system that will scale this function as your volume expands and will use automated email, fax, Web portals, and/or EDI to communicate order information.

Visibility

You must know if a product is available before it is sold, and you cannot know this until you view your supplier's inventory to find out how much product you have been allocated and what is available. To do this, you need an application that provides you with visibility into your supplier's inventory tracking system.

Track and Trace

Customers want to know the status of their order: When was it shipped, where is it now, and when will I get it? If you want to retain customers, you need to be sure your computer system helps you manage returns, exchanges, and refunds efficiently.

Price Structuring

Third-party providers should integrate back-end pricing structures based upon your specific warehousing and distribution needs. Shipping rates are based on freight classification, weight, origin, destination, prepaid/collect, and any added services. Usually freight charges are determined by multiplying the tariff class rate by the hundredweight of each commodity. Some charges are based on rates per cubic foot, such as on shipments to Hawaii or Puerto Rico.

Product Availability/Out-of-Stock Notice

It is your responsibility to maintain adequate inventory levels required to meet demand. The outsourced provider should work with you to assist in managing inventory levels. Good 3PLs should have real-time inventory management systems that will allow immediate access to inventory on hand prior to the order being placed. In the case where items are not available for distribution, your customer should have the option to place the order and have it filled when stock arrives, or to wait to place the order until inventory is available.

Processing Orders

The 3PL should work with you to develop specific "rules of engagement." Order processing times should vary depending upon your specific needs, the type of product being shipped, and method of shipment. The 3PL should also offer personalized recommendations, product reviews, free gift-wrapping, and handwritten gift cards.

Customer Response Center

The 3PL should offer a multimedia approach to order processing that ensures your customers receive the highest level of service. The customer response services should support customer inquiries by email, phone, fax, or mail.

IT Management

The 3PL's IT capabilities should assure successful and timely communication of real-time data, as well as ensure that the data architecture between your site and their back-end operations is functional 7 days a week, 24 hours a day.

Managing Customer Expectations

Every product should have an associated Order Processing Time (OPT). This is the estimated amount of time it typically takes to process an order for that particular item and prepare it for shipping.

Once processed, the Product Shipping Time (PST) is the estimated time it takes for an order to get from the warehouse to the ship-to address. This time varies based on the selected shipping method.

You should be able to calculate the expected delivery date of an order by calculating the Product Delivery Time (PDT).

PDT = OPT + PST

PDT is the total time it is expected to take to process and deliver the product to the ship-to address indicated when an order is placed. A good rule of thumb is that the product is usually delivered within 48 hours of the calculated PST.

Fourth-Party Logistics Providers

We just discussed the role of a third-party logistics provider (3PL), a broadly used term in which a forwarder, trucker, or warehouse company takes over specific portions of a company's logistics or transport operations. A new term has now entered the scene—fourth-party logistics providers—4PLs. There's some debate over whether a "true" 4PL even exists today, but here's a brief description for your information.

A 4PL refers to an integrator that manages a company's supply chain from end to end, often hiring subcontractors. It is a term that is gaining popularity as manufacturers and retailers show increased willingness to outsource logistics services.

But, as in the case of 3PLs, predictions of widespread use of fourth-party logistics providers—defined as true strategic partners with full, online access to the client's manufacturing, marketing, and distribution data—may prove optimistic for the foreseeable future.

A partnership 4PL—a term invented and trademarked by Andersen Consulting—is the embodiment of the dream of many outside service providers: to become a long-term partner with the client.

The prototypical 4PL not only locates and manages specialized service providers, but advises on the design of the entire process. Electronic business enables this to be done in an integrated way.

4PLs have several other distinguishing characteristics: reliance on sophisticated information technology systems to link up closely with the shipper's organization, and creation of a separate organization—perhaps a joint venture between the

314

shipper and the 4PL—dedicated to managing that shipper's supply chain. However, not all logisticians are convinced that 4PL providers are a significant presence or even a truly different player from those in the business already.

Preparing for Outsourcing

Before you embark on the process of selecting the best third-party logistics provider (or even fourth-party logistics provider), you need to clearly define your requirements up front. You may have been carrying out your own fulfillment and distribution in-house for a while, or you may be starting with no inventory or previous experience.

The following checklist is compiled from various 3PLs. It should be helpful, even if you haven't been handling any significant fulfillment and shipping on your own. Try to predict what your growth rate will be. At least, list all your SKUs with their associated requirements so that you can provide potential outsource partners with a SKU profile.

Outsource Preparation Checklist

Operational Description

❑ How many distribution centers do you currently operate?

❑ How many square feet are currently used for each facility?

  ❑ Receiving _____

  ❑ Staging _____

  ❑ Storage _____

  ❑ Picking _____

  ❑ Shipping _____

  ❑ Offices/miscellaneous _____

❑ What do you anticipate the order volume growth rate (% by year) to be over the next five years?

SKU Profile

In the chart below, please define all the SKUs that will be handled. If it is not possible to provide a complete profile, please provide the information for the top 20 percent SKUs in terms of unit volume. Product class is defined as a client descriptor used to designate certain SKUs belonging to different SKU families.

Order #	SKU #	Units Shipped	Ship from Location	Order Date	Requested Ship Date	Actual Ship date	Cust #	Ship-to Cust Address	Mode	Service Level	Any Special shipping instructions

❏ What is the average dollar (U.S.) value per SKU?

❏ Are there any SKUs that have unique characteristics that the outsource partner needs to be aware of?

❏ Are any materials considered hazardous? If so, please include requirements for proper disposal/treatment.

Inventory Requirements

❏ Are there any peaking factors that should be applied to the average inventory numbers?

❏ Will there be a requirement for serial number or lot tracking?

❏ What kind of storage do you use today?

❏ In aggregate, what is the average value of the specified inventory in U.S. dollars?

❏ What are your inventory accuracy requirements? Include past history ratings with explanation of what was included in the history.

❐ What are your cycle counting and physical inventory requirements? (frequency performed/ frequency reported)

❐ What are your pallet stack height limitations (if any)?

Warehouse Labor

❐ What are the typical warehouse activities performed by direct labor? Define functions within your distribution center (DC).

❐ Is the direct labor temporary staff or full-time employees?

❐ Are they unionized?

❐ How many shifts do you operate? (list shift and shift time, start to finish)

❐ As far as workweek and shifts, what would you require of a third party (keeping in mind there are premiums associated with OT, weekends, holidays, and third shifts)?

❐ Are you looking for a 24 by 7 by 365 operation?

❐ What are your overall labor costs annually?

❐ What are your typical productivity rates (receiving, picking/processing/sorting, shipping)? Please define function and associated rate.

Order Profiles

Please provide a 12-month order history as detailed below:

SKU Characteristics						Case DIM (in)					
SKU #	SKU Description	Product Class	Retail Unit Cost $$	Pieces per case	Cases per pallet	L	W	H	Case Weight (lbs)	Avg On-hand inventory	Vendor name and Shipping Location

❐ What is the typical order profile (number of lines per order, number of pieces per line)?

❐ What is the typical number of orders per day?

❏ What is the average weight (lbs) per order?

❏ Do you have any seasonal trends as they relate to out-bound order volume?

❏ What are your estimated volume trends by month?

❏ What are the differences, if any, between an international order vs. domestic order?

❏ What percentage of the business does domestic orders and international orders represent?

Inbound Characteristics

❏ Define inbound shipment methods for each supplier (i.e., Truckload, LTL, UPS, 2nd Day Air, Next Day Air, etc.) and the associated volumes per each type. Also, please define port-of-entry into U.S., if international.

❏ What are the annual inbound shipment weights by supplier?

❏ Do your suppliers have EDI capabilities? If so, which VAN do they operate from?

❏ Will suppliers be providing an ASN (advance shipment notification) to the third-party provider, or will an ASN come from you? Please define where from, who from, how (EDI, fax, etc.).

❏ What are the exact inbound packaging and labeling char-acteristics for each SKU? Please specify whether receipts are by cartons, pallets, etc.

❏ What is the average number of inbound cases per pallet?

❏ What is the average number of inbound pieces per case?

Order Processing

❏ What are the order fulfillment cycle time commitments within the DC, once orders are received (24 hr, 48 hr. etc.)?

❏ What is the cut-off time(s) for orders to be filled the same day, if any? What percent of orders will require this cycle time requirement?

❏ Will there be a requirement for back order processing?

❏ Will there be an allowance for partial order fulfillment?

❏ What is your current back order percentage?

❏ How often will the 3PL receive orders from you (hourly, online real-time, etc.)?

❏ What are your picking accuracy requirements? List past history ratings with explanation of what was included in the history.

❏ Are there any special order labeling requirements, other than being able to produce an industry standard bar coded label? Please provide samples, if possible.

❏ Are there any special order consolidation or packaging requirements?

❏ What is your typical monthly cost of supplies for current operational levels?

Outbound Characteristics

❏ What is your typical outbound shipment profile?

❏ What are all the addresses for all finished goods destination points, including zip codes?

❏ How many ship-to points are there?

❏ What is the percentage of outbound orders that will go international? Domestic?

❏ What are your information requirements of outbound orders (bar codes, labeling, special logos, special packaging requirements, etc.)?

❏ Can you identify and provide examples of all literature (if any) to be included in outbound orders?

❏ Do your customers control carrier selection for outbound shipments?

❏ How many carriers are required for customer selection? Who are they?

❏ What are your carton specifications for outbound product and customization specs (if necessary)?

❏ Are there any pre-alert (notification) requirements that the outsource partner will need to send to you? To your customers? To any other party? Please define.

❏ What is the percentage volume that would qualify for small parcel and percentage volume that moves Less Than Truckload (LTL) for retail shipments?

Major E-Logistics and E-Fulfillment Players

There are a number of e-logistics and e-fulfillment organizations jumping into the outsourcing fray. Some of them have the weaknesses mentioned earlier and are best avoided. Others are frantically retooling themselves in order to capitalize on the tremendous amount of experience they've had in the physical world. UPS e-Logistics is a case in point. Realizing that e-commerce involves more than brown trucks, they have partnered with top technology partners and have launched a service offering, targeted specifically to start-up e-businesses. Look for FedEx and others to do the same in the very near future. Below is a very select list of e-logistics providers that should be considered if you decide to outsource the whole thing. I've included a brief description and the URL for the firm's Web site so that you can obtain the latest information.

Airborne Logistics Services

Airborne Express *(http://www.airborne.com)* made a decision a decade ago to develop a former military base in Wilmington, Ohio, into a 2,200-acre commerce park and private airport. A subsidiary, Airborne Logistics Services, was formed to supply outsourced warehousing and distribution services in the United States and abroad. Airborne Logistics operates critical parts warehouses, centralized print services, a U.S. Foreign Trade Zone, and more on behalf of its customers. Three warehouses, totaling 3 million square feet of space, are connected to Airborne's primary hub in Ohio, and nine regional hubs are located throughout the United States.

Escalate

Escalate *(http://www.escalate.com)* uses an Application Service Provider (ASP) model. It offers such standard functions as front-end personalization, online shopping carts, transaction processing, and fulfillment management. It also addresses back-end functions, from product procurement to supply-chain and distribution management, employing a combination of home-grown applications, third-party relationships, and in-house consulting services.

Escalate offers a flexible payment model. Customers must pay a setup fee for the core offering of e-commerce applications, ranging from $25,000 to $500,000, depending on the level of complexity and customization. Customers then pay monthly subscription fees as part of their one-year contracts. Escalate also takes a fee that can range from 6 percent to 12 percent of the value on every transaction, sometimes based on gross sales, sometimes on margins.

FedEx

FedEx Corporation *(http://www.fedex.com),* an $18 billion global enterprise, has the following divisions:

- FedEx Express, the world's largest express transportation company
- FedEx Ground, North America's second-largest provider of ground small-package delivery offering a new service, FedEx Home Delivery
- FedEx Logistics, a global logistics and transportation management company offering services via Caribbean Transportation Services and regional carrier Viking Freight
- FedEx Custom Critical, the world's largest surface expedited carrier
- FedEx Trade Networks, a high-tech customs broker and trade facilitator

FedEx and UPS announced new e-commerce fulfillment strategies within weeks of one another. Both services are called eLogistics. As FedEx has been aggressively acquiring companies and adding to their current e-commerce offerings, it is probably safe to assume that FedEx's e-logistics offerings will be very comprehensive.

Fingerhut Business Services, Inc.

Fingerhut Business Services, Inc. (FBS) *(http://www.finger-hut.com)* provides outsourced direct marketing, fulfillment, merchandising, customer service, and data mining solutions to businesses that want to go direct. They also provide equity investment capital to e-commerce ventures.

FBS has over 50 years of experience in direct-to-the-consumer marketing to over 75 million American homes. FBS processes over 80,000,000 orders per year.

Hanover Direct's Keystone Fulfillment

Hanover Direct's Keystone Fulfillment division *(http://www.hanoverdirect.com)* offers integrated services to support all areas of an operation, from purchasing to customer services, credit card processing, warehousing, and distribution, to data management and accounting.

Keystone's environmentally-controlled distribution centers house sophisticated handling, conveyor, and storage methods, with the space and the capacity to process over 11 million packages each year.

NewRoads (Formerly CyberGistics)

NewRoads *(http://www.newroads.com)* is an Application Service Provider (ASP) that offers a full range of services, including sales and marketing support, commerce fulfillment, customer care, eStore hosting, supply chain optimization, forecasting and replenishment, data mining, and other logistics and distribution services.

OrderTrust

The OrderTrust network *(http://www.ordertrust.com)* was custom-built to address e-commerce fulfillment. Their network provides a secure link between merchants, their trading partners, and their customers. OrderTrust manages information through all back-end e-commerce activities, from the moment a consumer hits the Buy button until the moment an order leaves the docks.

SubmitOrder.com

SubmitOrder.com™ *(http://www.submitorder.com)* is a dedicated e-fulfillment company that has integrated IT, distribution, customer service, and marketing. SubmitOrder.com boasts distribution centers designed for e-fulfillment—flexible, high-velocity pick, pack, and ship facilities that allow individual products to be pulled quickly from inventory, packed, personalized, and shipped.

TNT Post Group (TPG)

TNT Post Group *(http://www.tnt.com)* has set an ambitious goal of capturing 25 percent of Europe's outsourced business-to-business e-commerce fulfillment with a service called @TNT Demand Chain Management. TPG formed a strategic alliance with U.S. order processing firm OrderTrust, Inc. and Canada's Descartes Systems Group, which provides the e-fulfillment software. The service will be offered first in Germany, France, the United Kingdom, Italy, in TPG's home market, the Netherlands, and eventually on a global basis.

@TNT will offer order management, payment processing, warehousing, transportation, and delivery, and post transaction management for returns, repairs, and customer service. TPG claims that by leveraging its global distribution and logistics assets with the IT and order processing skills of its partners, @TNT will offer a real-time, integrated service for domestic, pan-European, and global e-fulfillment orders.

UPS E-Logistics

UPS e-Logistics *(http://www.ups.com)*, a wholly owned UPS subsidiary, has combined leading solutions from Pricewater-houseCoopers, Oracle, and EXE Technologies with UPS's global fulfillment and distribution network, IT infrastructure, and the logistics expertise of the UPS Logistics Group. The result is a complete range of services available to manage the back end of the e-business supply chain, starting when an order is placed on a client's Web site.

The UPS e-Logistics service offering includes warehousing and inventory management, order fulfillment (pick, pack, and ship), inbound and outbound transportation, returns management, customer call center, and management reporting. The standardized, prebuilt services can be bundled and configured, and are scalable for future growth.

From the client perspective, it will be agnostic with standard interfaces. Pricing for the service will be based on three-year contracts with a storage component and a transactional component. Actual costs will be specific to each client and the client's characteristics.

UPS e-Logistics will serve both business-to-business and business-to-consumer e-commerce clients, ranging from e-business start-ups to the dot-com divisions of established corporations.

UPS Logistics Group

While UPS' e-Logistics is rolling out their e-Logistics service offering, the UPS Logistics Group *(http://www.ups.com)* has been providing their services to the e-commerce community for quite a while. Their services include:

- supply chain consulting
- warehousing around the world
- inventory management
- supplier coordination
- transportation management (inbound and outbound)
- order management and fulfillment
- online track and trace
- returns management

- value-added services, including product inspections, labeling, gift wrapping, tagging, and packaging in branded boxes
- international customs clearance
- call center operations
- front-end and back-end IT systems integration
- post-sales services, such as spare parts management, warranty repair and refurbishment, and software upgrades
- MobileCast™, a technology system using handheld computers to provide delivery confirmation and credit processing at the customer's premises

USCO Shared Logistics Division

USCO's Shared Logistics Division *(http://www.usco.com)* provides an in-place nationwide network of public warehousing and distribution centers for companies with a need for a high-performance, yet flexible distribution infrastructure.

Through USCO's shared logistics capabilities, customers gain the benefits of

- nationwide facilities with networked communications capabilities
- standardized operating procedures in all locations
- value added expertise in kitting, returns, light assembly, labeling, and much more
- the ability to contract and expand with their business cycle, in terms of space and labor requirements
- economies of scale due to sharing of overhead costs

Locations throughout the U.S. allow clients to locate inventory closer to their customers and to expand into new markets without a large capital investment. Shared warehousing is also cost-effective, as the client pays only for the space and services they need.

Resources

Articles

Girishankar, Saroja. "Making it all work—Customers want robust, interoperable software suites for end-to-end e-commerce—but no single vendor can do it all." InternetWeek, June 12, 2000. *http://www.techweb.com.*

Kaneshige, Tom. "Choosing your allies." *Upside Today,* May 24, 2000. *http://www.upside.com.*

Koller, Mike. "UPS and Tech Companies join to help e-businesses." *InternetWeek,* Aug 2, 2000. *http://www.techweb.com.*

Shaw, Jennifer Balko. "To succeed, B-to-B players need logistics savvy." *Electronic Buyers' News*, July 31, 2000. *http://www.techweb.com.*

Staff. "Clicks vs. mortar: E-tail shipping strategies diverge." *Logistics Management and Distribution Report,* July 1, 2000.

Staff. "e-Fulfillment will breed new distribution services." *Logistics Management and Distribution Report,* June 1, 2000.

Technologic Partners, Private Profiles. "Escalate: Testing the limits of outsourcing e-commerce functions." Volume 16 Number 4, January 31, 2000, Copyright ©2000.

USER PERSPECTIVES

In Their Own Words: Two User Perspectives

There is nothing like a "war story" to illustrate the challenges and victories of a real-life endeavor. As the final chapter in this book, I've been fortunate to obtain two such war stories from two vastly different enterprises. The first, Lucky Brand Jeans, describes the challenges of starting up an online channel of distribution from scratch, including selecting a third-party fulfillment provider. The second, Ingram Micro, illustrates the challenges of the provider side. Ingram Micro started out solely as a computer products distributor, and eventually built an e-logistics and fulfillment powerhouse that is now in demand as a third-party logistics provider.

I believe the best way to present these two e-logistics solutions is in the words of the experts who implemented them. I asked them to take some time from their extremely busy schedules to answer a few questions about their operations.

Although confidentiality agreements prevented them from divulging the details of their facilities and resources, the details of their other answers prove fascinating. Perhaps you'll find some of their experiences helpful as you set up your own e-logistics and fulfillment capabilities.

Lucky Brand Jeans, a Division of Liz Claiborne
Starting Up an Online Channel

Bridget Belden
Director of E-Commerce

Bridget Belden has extensive experience in the retail and garment industries, and was assigned to plan and build the Lucky Brand Jeans site and e-commerce strategy as Liz Claiborne's first entry into the dot-com world. Bridget is a frequent speaker at industry and professional events.

Q: *How did Lucky Brand Jeans conduct logistics and fulfillment before the advent of the Internet and e-commerce?*

A: Lucky Brand Jeans primarily distributes products through third party accounts such as Nordstrom, The Brass Buckle, and a host of regionally based specialty stores. In addition to these distribution channels, we had several of our own stores as well. Our primary means of logistics and fulfillment was done in-house and handled out of our own warehouse.

Thus far, our current use of the Internet has not drastically changed that, except in regards to adding yet another distribution channel. We are investigating putting our business-to-business processes online in order to streamline them and maximize our business opportunities.

Q: *What were the challenges in e-logistics and e-fulfillment that you encountered?*

A: When Lucky Brand launched our first Web site in early 1998, fulfillment was handled out of the same warehouse as all other distribution. Our back-end systems were not integrated, and all Web site orders were handled manually. Because the systems were not integrated, there was a tremendous amount of time spent on "simple" things, such as identifying out of stock merchandise, managing returns, addressing customer service issues, and implementing new product online. There was one person who literally pulled the orders, conducted credit checks, forwarded them for fulfillment, billed the credit cards, answered email and the phones, and processed returns. Needless to say, it was a monumental task to do the business that we did.

Once we decided to proactively pursue developing our online business, we clearly understood that in order to be successful in this endeavor, we would need to ensure that flawless fulfillment and superior customer service were a priority. Because our expertise did not reside within the e-logistics and fulfillment arena, outsourcing seemed the best option.

Q: *What resources did you bring to bear to create the necessary functionality?*

A: Because Lucky Brand Jeans is an apparel manufacturer and not an expert in the e-commerce business, we decided to outsource all fulfillment, programming, hosting, and back-end technical support. We worked closely with our outsource partner to bring our brand vision to reality online. We supplied the art direction and graphics, and led the design of the navigation and architecture, and they applied the technical functionality to make it all work.

Q: *How would you describe your e-logistics and e-fulfillment framework?*

A: Our framework is currently based on a batch inventory system, although that will be changing towards the end of the year to a real-time exchange. Orders are placed and shipped within 24 hours and the majority of the product is in the customer's hands within three working days, no matter where they are in the country. We initially utilized FedEx as our primary shipper, but have recently changed to the

USPS, as their rates are better and their performance is comparable.

Q: *What have been the results achieved to date? What are the plans for the future?*

A: Our method of operation to date has been to build the business in a methodical, planned way in order to maximize our business and to ensure that we are addressing the critical priorities first. Our approach has been to focus first on fulfillment and customer service, and then broaden the scope to include marketing and content/community enhancement. As we approach the close of our ninth month of business since the re-launch in November 1999, we are beginning to see the results of our carefully planned marketing efforts to date. Not only are our core metrics building momentum in terms of sales and traffic, but also the feedback we have received from our customers regarding the service they receive on our site has been very encouraging.

The plans for the future are to continue to build the business and eventually develop it into the largest Lucky Brand Jeans retail store.

Q: *What advice would you give to an organization that needs to implement e-logistics and e-fulfillment?*

A: Be very clear on the business goals and objectives before pursuing the best options to meet those objectives. Whether you outsource or utilize your resources in-house, make sure that your partners fully understand what your objectives are, and what their deliverables are. This is an area where you can't spend too much time ensuring that you have identified the best possible resources to get the job done. Your business and your brand depend on it.

Ingram Micro, World-Class Computer Products Distributor and E-Commerce Provider

Guy P. Abramo
Senior Vice President and Chief Information Officer (CIO)

Guy P. Abramo is senior vice president and chief information officer (CIO) for Ingram Micro. He leads Ingram Micro's worldwide IT organization, including the company's IT infrastructure and systems development. He is in charge of defining and further enhancing the company's business applications and electronic-commerce solutions. He also will be responsible for the development and deployment of all IT programs and software designs.

Abramo joined Ingram Micro from Norwalk, Connecticut-based Yankelovich Partners, the world's premier market and consumer research firm. Yankelovich specializes in conducting market sizing and segmentation studies, brand identity and preference analysis, and customer behavior research. Prior to Yankelovich, he was managing director, marketing intelligence, for KPMG Peat Marwick, LLP, responsible for practice management, partner alliances, and business development.

He is a 12-year veteran of Mobil Oil Corp., where he held several positions of increasing responsibility: manager, planning and business analysis; regional manager, administration and controls; assistant gasoline business manager - U.S. Division; manager, marketing services and business automation - Americas Division.

Abramo holds a bachelor's degree in chemical engineering from the New Jersey Institute of Technology and a master's degree in business administration from Georgetown University.

Q: *How did Ingram Micro conduct logistics and fulfillment before the advent of the Internet and e-commerce?*

A: Logistics and fulfillment services have always been the core of Ingram Micro's business. Our internal logistics engine, a highly customized and extremely powerful mainframe system, has served as the backbone for our delivery of these services.

Before the advent of the Net, we relied heavily on a very knowledgeable and powerful sales force to interface with our customers, to do everything from managing orders to anticipating customers' preferences, needs, and likely purchases. The same is true for the post-order and account management processes—our sales force provided the information our customers needed to accurately track and manage their order histories and incoming product.

However, Ingram did engineer electronic connectivity with its customers, mostly through EDI and flat file exchange, to make order data available to customers in an aggregate form that could be readily manipulated. The business has always benefited from the rapid exchange of highly accurate data in a small amount of time. It was our experience and comfort with electronic exchange that allowed us to lead the distribution industry into the e-commerce arena.

Q: How did you tackle putting your back-end systems on the Net? What business processes did you define?

A: There were two main issues with creating a new "electronic" interface for our customers.

Appearance and New Information Needs

As we began to accept the challenge to meet e-commerce customers' needs, we needed to familiarize ourselves with the demands of this new population. Customers needed accurate content in user-friendly and readable form, and they wanted to be able to use and manipulate it. The interface to the customer, whether it be Web page or application interface, had to be logical and readily understood. It had to be simple and attractive.

Customers also needed a different way of doing business. The order process itself had to evolve from a rigid set of requirements to a flexible set of options. We had to alter our entire concept of "end-customer," and to change the e-commerce ordering experience accordingly. This was true not only of process, but also of information.

Historically, the data and processes housed within IMpulse (Ingram's custom order management system) needed only to be accessible to and understood by internal Ingram associates. However, we had embarked on a process of turning our business inside out—turning our internal data and processes external, and making them accessible and safe enough to survive the external customers' demands. The information we had used to run our business had become something extremely valuable externally, something that conferred considerable competitive advantage, and most importantly, something worth paying for.

How

Creating the bridge between extensive mainframe logic and e-commerce-ready functionality was a hurdle. Web-savvy customers needed to see and be able to use the data and functionality we provided, but it was unacceptable in its existing form. Making the processes and data structures within IMpulse "Web-ready" was our largest challenge.

We had to define one core type of business process: how customers of *all* types would use our information, and how and when they would use our services. We had to determine what each type of customer would use the information for, and what type of ordering experience they would need to be offered.

Q: *What were the challenges in e-logistics and e-fulfillment that you encountered?*

Accuracy and Customer Expectation

A: Our historic customers, resellers and manufacturers, understood the enormity of the channel process and all the possible and likely delays and problems. However, entering into a situation where we were serving consumers directly (albeit, often on behalf of another entity) required us to adjust to the demands of this different type of customer.

Consumers expected a simple order process, immediate order verification, continual access to order information, and timely and near-flawless delivery. Although they didn't require the same breadth of services, their concept of adequate information involved a lot more than what had been historically provided to our long-time reseller and vendor customers. We had to take a very time-tested logistics and fulfillment business, and add a host of new functions and enhanced information to it.

Expanding Our Concept of a *Customer*

Not only did we have to create an interface to customers that would provide them with all the types and depth of information listed above, we need to internally adjust to who those customers were. Where we had served mostly resellers and vendors, we now served millions of corporate end users and e-commerce consumers, as well. We had to take great pains to adjust our internal point of view to ensure that we accommodated the new needs and perspectives of this new customer base.

Making Our Information More Accessible

One of our most labor-intensive challenges was pulling the enormous amount of mainframe data into decision support systems and databases that were easily accessible by Web and other e-commerce applications. The information needed to be accessible instantly and consistently. Creating an environment where our mainframe-knowledgeable personnel could work effectively and quickly with Web designers and programmers was key. As old-world data arrived on the new-world scene, a good deal could be lost in the translation. We relied on a very talented and diverse set of professionals to drive this effort.

Making the Data Eye-Friendly

Because internal data (i.e., product specifications, descriptions, and orders) was always viewed by a trained eye, there was never a need for it to be eye-friendly or easily interpretable. However, as we turned this data external, it needed considerable scrubbing and manipulation. Because of the vast amount of data we deal with on a daily basis, this was no small effort.

Integrating Disparate Systems

In order to make our worldwide logistics system e-commerce ready, there was much more that needed to be performed beyond the mainframe-to-e-commerce-app integration. The standalone systems in our warehouses that make personalized delivery and label-printing possible needed to accept new types and amounts of data, and needed to process them correctly. Also, as our agency model and outsourcing support began in earnest, we needed to take steps to ensure the separation and security of customers' data in accordance with the unique contracts and business models we created with each.

Q: *What resources (outside expertise, hardware, software) did you bring to bear to create the necessary functionality?*

A: The majority of the resources brought to bear on architecting this new way of doing business were internal. These resources needed extensive fundamental knowledge about Ingram's business and about the systems and processes we used to accomplish our every day objectives.

We did bring on some external resources, especially those versed in the most current Web technologies and programming methods, to enhance the speed at which we pursued our vision. Our deadlines had to be extremely aggressive, and we needed to add resources to meet them.

Much of our projects were between Ingram and our customers directly, and we achieved a great deal in creating cross-corporation teams to innovate and to challenge each other.

Q: How would you describe your e-logistics and e-fulfillment framework?

A: Our e-logistics and e-fulfillment framework is essentially a virtual, mainframe-based fulfillment powerhouse with several different external faces and connectivity options.

We communicate via real-time exchange (proprietary, EDI, XML, RosettaNet) with several companies' Web sites, ERP systems, order management systems, and e-commerce engines. We host a selection of consumer and B2B storefronts that target specific customers. We engage in joint development efforts with select strategic reseller and vendor partners, allowing them to complete their business models by "plugging in" to our logistics engine.

The framework itself, the internal expertise, and the information generated around our core logistics make up our basic, but significant, value proposition.

Q: What have been the results achieved to date? What are the plans for the future?

A: Our results to date have been staggering. We serve millions of customers in our historic capacity, meeting their needs directly, while this new model allows us to service millions more indirectly and transparently. The resultant knowledge from touching these several different types of customers, and of pioneering their experiences, is enormously valuable.

Our reach into the market, because of electronic commerce, has expanded tremendously, and our command of our own information allows us to perform our operations with much more exacting intent.

Q: What advice would you give to an organization that needs to implement e-logistics and e-fulfillment?

A: Get assistance from the best, whether that be through consulting or outsourcing. Although the concept behind an e-logistics strategy is simple, its execution is extremely and unpredictably complex. It is an entire new venture in and of itself, not a simple complement to another strategy.

Know your customers, know your limits, and know your customers' limits. Thoroughly identify critical success factors, both from your company's point of view and from your customers' points of view.

Q: *Ingram Micro's fulfillment infrastructure is so comprehensive that other firms utilize it to conduct their e-business. Do you have plans to offer your e-logistics and e-fulfillment services on a plug-and-play basis to a wider audience?*

A: Ingram's logistics and fulfillment capabilities are truly without peer. Customers who recognize and choose to focus on their own core competencies have a lot to gain by asking Ingram to provide them with access to these capabilities. They realize that diluting focus on their own strategies can be disastrous. We will continue to offer our services, with several different types of connectivity, to customers who can use them.

However, as with anything else, our approach to distributing these services is evolving. With the many new ways of providing connectivity and of charging for provided services, we will likely have several new strategies to more accurately reflect and recoup the immense value, reach, and reliability of the services we provide.

Resources

Ingram Micro
www.ingrammicro.com

Lucky Brand Jeans
www.luckybrandjeans.com

INDEX

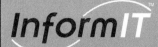